D1196248

THE THEORY OF
ECONOMIC DEVELOPMENT

THE THEORY OF ECONOMIC DEVELOPMENT

An Inquiry into Profits, Capital, Credit, Interest, and the Business Cycle

JOSEPH A. SCHUMPETER

Translated from the German by Redvers Opie

With a New Introduction by
JOHN E. ELLIOTT

Transaction Publishers
New Brunswick (U.S.A.) and London (U.K.)

Fourteenth printing 2008

New material this edition copyright © 1983 by Transaction Publishers, New Brunswick, New Jersey. Original material copyright © 1934 by the President and Fellows of Harvard College.

All rights reserved under International and Pan-American Copyright Conventions. No part of this book may be reproduced or transmitted in any form or by any means, electronic or mechanical, including photocopy, recording, or any information storage and retrieval system, without prior permission in writing from the publisher. All inquiries should be addressed to Transaction Publishers, Rutgers—The State University of New Jersey, 35 Berrue Circle, Piscataway, New Jersey 08854-8042. www.transactionpub.com

This book is printed on acid-free paper that meets the American National Standard for Permanence of Paper for Printed Library Materials.

Library of Congress Catalog Number: 79-67059
ISBN: 978-0-87855-698-4
Printed in the United States of America

Library of Congress Cataloging-in-Publication Data

Schumpeter, Joseph Alois, 1883-1950.
    The theory of economic development.

    (Social science classis series)
    Translation of: Theorie der wirtschaftlichen Entwicklung.
    Reprint. Originally published: Cambridge, Mass.: Harvard University, 1934. (Harvard economics studies v. 46) with new introd.
        "Transaction ed."—Introd.
    Includes bibliographical references.
        1. Economics. 2. Economic development. 3. Capitalism. I. Title.
II. Series. III. Series: Harvard economic srudies: v. 46.

HB175.S462   1983   330
ISBN 0-87855-698-2   79-67059

CONTENTS

TRANSLATOR'S NOTE

MY CHIEF aim has been to convey the meaning as accurately as possible, and to this end I have not hesitated to use a clumsy phrase in cases where there was no current English equivalent of the German word. After considerable reflection I decided upon "circular flow" for "Kreislauf," for reasons which it would take too long to relate. There are inelegancies which have nothing to do with the technical side of translating. To eradicate these would have meant rewriting the whole, and it did not seem expedient to do so. Professor Schumpeter is so much at home in the English language that he would inevitably have left his mark on the translation even if he had not given his time as freely as he did to the more difficult points involved. For this reason, as well as for those mentioned in the preface, the book is more than a translation.

The title of the German original is Theorie der wirtschaftlichen Entwicklung.

REDVERS OPIE

INTRODUCTION TO THE TRANSACTION EDITION

JOHN E. ELLIOTT

I

Joseph Alois Schumpeter, like his illustrious contemporary, British economist John Maynard Keynes, was born in 1883, the year of death of Karl Marx. He died in 1950, four years after Keynes. Thus, his adult life—and published works—roughly span the first half of the twentieth century, as Marx's did the middle decades of the nineteenth. Schumpeter's teacher, Eugene von Böhm-Bawerk, has sometimes been called the "bourgeois Marx," because of his focus upon the phenomenon of capital, the title of Marx's central lifework. The title better fits Schumpeter himself, who, many scholars believe, provided the most comprehensive and provocative analysis since Marx of the economic development and social transformation of industrializing capitalism. If Marx was Schumpeter's worthy opponent, Keynes was his contemporary rival and antagonist. Schumpeter describes Marx as the greatest social scientist of the nineteenth century, because of the passion and breadth of his vision of capitalist society and its future and his uncanny ability to connect the economic, social, and political dimensions of his analysis. The same kind of comment can be made about Schumpeter, whose analysis of capitalist development and change similarly blends historical, economic, and sociological elements, and whose studies of the capitalist order and its prospects provide, with the notable exception of the writings of Thorstein Veblen, the only truly comprehensive rival intellectual "system" to that of Keynes in the first half of the twentieth century.

The Theory of Economic Development,[1] the work which comprises this book, vividly illustrates one of Schumpeter's cherished interpretations concerning intellectual creativity. In Schumpeter's view, the foundations of significant creative achievements, notably theoretical ones, are almost always laid in the third decade of a scholar's life, "that decade of sacred fertility."[2] Subsequent scholarly work, he believed, typically builds on these foundations and fleshes out the details and applications of one's early creative insight. As Schumpeter put it in his review essay on Keynes, every comprehensive theory of society "consists of two complementary but essentially distinct elements. There is, first, the theorist's view about the basic features of that state of society, about what is and what is not important in order to understand its life at a given time. Let us call this his vision. And there is, second, the theorist's technique, an apparatus by which he conceptualizes his vision and which turns the latter into concrete propositions or 'theories.'"[3]

Whatever the general merits of this view, it fits closely the circumstances of Schumpeter's life and scholarly work. In the third decade of his life, Schumpeter vividly illustrated his hypothesis by a remarkable burst of creative energy, the establishment of an international reputation, and the laying of the foundations for his life's work. Schumpeter "was never a beginner but, a precocious genius; he entered the scientific arena a full-fledged master."[4] By the age of 31, he had published 20 papers, 50 book reviews, and three major works. His first, *The Essence and Principal Contents of Economic Theory* (1908),[5] outlined the basic elements of an exchange economy, at least from the perspective of pure economics, with precision and clarity. The second, *The Theory of Economic Development* (1911), was the now-classic work which made Schumpeter world-famous. It provided both his "vision" of the capitalist process and the central theoretical structure which underpinned his subsequent analysis of socioeconomic change. The last, *Epochs in the History of Doctrine and Method* (1914),[6] gave a brief but brilliant exposition of the history and methodology of economics. Arthur Spiethoff aptly summarizes the unusual character of Schumpeter's early work by asking, "What is more unheard of, a 25 year-old and a 27 year-old who stirs at the foundations of the discipline, or a 30 year-old who writes its history?"[7]

Schumpeter's colorful personality, eventful life, and early recognition complemented his creativity. From the age of 10, when his mother, widowed several years earlier, married a lieutenant-general in the Austro-Hungarian army, Schumpeter grew up in the aristocratic atmosphere of pre-World War I Vienna. Between 1893 and 1901, he was provided by his stepfather with a thorough and classical education at the Theresianum, an exclusive school for scions of the Viennese aristocracy. After leaving the Theresianum, he attended the University of Vienna as a student in the Faculty of Law, specializing in law and economics, and received the doctor of law degree in 1906, at 23. Three years later, after practicing law in Cairo and managing the finances of an Egyptian princess, Schumpeter was appointed full professor at the University of Czernowitz, located in an eastern province of the Austro-Hungarian Empire. At 26, the youngest full professor in the university, Schumpeter was a bit of an *enfant terrible* as well as a *Wunderkind*. Disdainful of what he perceived as the provinciality of most of his colleagues, he liked to shock them by wearing his riding boots at faculty meetings and formal dress even when dining alone with his wife.[8] In 1911, with the help of his teacher and benefactor Böhm-Bawerk, Schumpeter was appointed to the faculty at the University of Graz. At 28, he was, as at Czernowitz, the youngest full professor in the university. This, combined with the solid negative vote of the faculty (who had recommended, Gottfried Haberler comments, some "local nonentity")[9] against his appointment, and his practice of spending much of his time in the national capital, did little to endear Schumpeter to his academic colleagues. At 30, he accepted a visiting professorship at Columbia University, where he was awarded an honorary degree in 1914.

Between 1914 and 1925, there was a nonacademic interlude which included a short, and unsuccessful, stint as Austrian finance minister, followed by a presidency of a private bank in Vienna. Schumpeter returned to academic life in 1926 with a professorship at the University of Bonn. In the early 1930s, after a triumphal tour of Japan—where reception of his writings on capitalist development had created a minor sensation—he accepted a professorship at Harvard University and remained there until his death, in 1950. One of the more charming stories about Schumpeter during his Harvard period concerns his often-cited comment, in classes, that as a young man in Vienna he had three burning ambitions. One was to be the greatest lover of women in Vienna. A second was to be the greatest horseman in all Europe. The third was to be the greatest economist of his age. Alas, Schumpeter then would say, he had achieved only two of his three youthful ambitions.

II

Understanding Schumpeter's central work, *The Theory of Economic Development,* is enhanced by placing it in a broader intellectual and historical context and relating it to his other writings. There have been three great periods of creativity in the development of economic thought. The first, ranging from roughly the late eighteenth century to the middle decades of the nineteenth, was the era of classical political economy. This period was associated with such "classic names as Adam Smith, Thomas Malthus, David Ricardo, and John Stuart Mill. To this list, we should add Karl Marx, who both extended and critically evaluated classical economic thought. These men established economics as a systematic, social scientific discipline. Although their methods and some of their ideas seemed crude, even misdirected, to later generations of economists, theirs was a kind of golden age in the early development of economics. Most of them were concerned with the grand themes of economic growth and development, the relation of socioeconomic change to the distribution of income and power among social classes, and to the principles of production and value underlying market exchange, as well as to the more mundane issues of how a competitive, private enterprise economy goes about allocating its resources and marketing its products. Several were philosophers as well as social scientists, and most perceived the discipline in sufficiently broad terms as to connect economic behavior to its social and political context.

The second great creative period in economic thought occurred in the latter decades of the nineteenth century. Although this period, like the classical era before it, had its predecessors, its generally acknowledged founding figures were an Englishman, a Frenchman, and an Austrian—Stanley Jevons, Leon Walras, and Carl Menger. Each of these three independently published a major treatise embodying a significant shift in the scope, content, and methodology of economics during the early 1870s.[10] Under the essentially separate, though with time reinforcing, leadership of this trio, the focus of economics shifted from the broad themes of economic development and distribution of income among social classes to the narrower and more manageable issues of the allocation of resources and the associated distribution of income among individuals. The time frame changed from the dynamic to the explicitly static, and the discipline became self-consciously positive rather than normative, symbolized by the shift from the broader phrase "political economy" to the narrower term "economics." Although Menger and his "Austrian school" colleagues, Böhm-Bawerk and Friedrich A. von Wieser, eschewed mathematics, on the perceived

ground that it was inappropriate for piercing the basic qualitative factors underlying economic quantities, Jevons, Walras, and their successors emphasized the need for a quantitative approach to their subject and to the contributions of
mathematics to development of a more exact formulation of
economic theories.

The new economics of the 1870s was sometimes called the
"marginal utility" school. During the first generation of the
new approach, emphasis was placed on the noun "utility"
rather than the adjective "marginal," to contrast the new
focus upon subjective factors of utility and demand in determination of market exchange values with the earlier classical stress upon cost of production and supply. By the late
nineteenth century, focus had shifted to the adjective, as the
"marginalist way of thinking" in terms of incremental bene-
fits and costs of alternative individual decisions spread to the
interpretation of various aspects of economic life, illustrated,
for example, by the marginal productivity theory of income
distribution developed by the American marginalist John
Bates Clark. According to Clark's analysis, in static, competitive equilibrium, the price of any agent or factor of production such as "labor" or "land" would equal its marginal contribution to the total product produced, and the total product would be exhausted by payments to all individuals contributing to production in accord with their marginal productivities.

Focus upon either component in the phrase "marginal
utility," however, probably exaggerates the extent of differentiation from classical political economy. Important elements of continuity included essential similarities concerning
underlying assumptions, notably concerning motivations, institutions, and technology. Economic orthodoxy of the late
nineteenth century, like that of its classical predecessors,
tended to suppose rational, calculating "economic men," interested in promoting individual economic gain through
market exchange. Markets were presumed to be essentially

competitive, dominated by large numbers of small-scale enterprises. Technologies were assumed to permit atomistic competition. Indeed, the main constraint upon the size of enterprises was perceived to be "diminishing returns" to existing production units and "diseconomies of scale" to expansion in overall enterprise size, rather than problems in profitably marketing larger output. Another important element of continuity was the general acceptance of "Say's law," named in honor of early–nineteenth-century French economist Jean Baptiste Say. This theorem postulated a tendency toward stable equilibrium at full employment and utilization of resources in the economy as a whole resulting spontaneously from the generally beneficial functioning of the competitive market exchange processes of supply and demand.

Continuity with the classical political economy was substantially greater in the writings of the "neoclassical" Cambridge economist Alfred Marshall than was true for Jevons, Walras, and Menger. Marshall's *Principles of Economics,* which went through eight editions, dominated economics teaching in the English-speaking world for several decades after its initial publication in 1890. Marshall was as thoroughgoing a marginalist as were the founders of the marginal utility school. Like them, he also independently incorporated a strategic role for utility and demand considerations in his analysis of exchange value, notably in relatively shorter periods of time. He also shared with them the view that "equilibrium" would involve not only the most satisfactory position for each individual in the economic system, but the elimination of any above-normal profits, that is, any profits above those necessary to reward the owner of an enterprise for the contributions of his own productive resources. Unlike them, however, he maintained an explicit linkage with classical political economy by incorporating a co-strategic role for supply and cost considerations in the analysis of exchange value, especially in relatively longer periods of time. He anticipated briefly two major post-Marshallian developments in economic analysis by observing, first, that sellers often have a degree of local monopoly based on customer loyalty, but that attempts to extend sales beyond that market would require enhanced marketing expenses or lower prices, and second, that, in contrast to a smooth working of Say's law, though people may have the power to spend (based on income from production), they may choose not to exercise it.

What may be called the "central tradition" in economic thought, whether in its classical or neoclassical form, was never free from critique. Throughout the nineteenth century, socialist writers criticized capitalist market economy for its proclivities toward inequality, working class poverty, depression and unemployment, and monopoly and other forms of power by capitalist employers. Marx and his successors analyzed economic contradictions and social conflicts in capitalist development and transformation. Historically-oriented economists dissented from the deductivist and ahistorical methodology of orthodox economics. In the early decades of the twentieth century, American institutionalists such as Veblen and John Rogers Commons called for and partially provided analyses of the economic process that were more explicitly cognizant of the technological, cultural, and psychological framework of economic life, and of the impact of economic behavior upon the changing institutional structure of society. By the early twentieth century, neoclassicists themselves were beginning to challenge selected aspects of their intellectual heritage. A prominent example was expanding interest in analysis of business cycles, largely by continental economists, including some mainstream writers, an enterprise which by its very nature challenges the hoary proposition of Say's law. Contributors included, among others, the Russian revisionist Marxist Tugan-Baranowsky, Arthur Spiethoff (Schumpeter's later colleague at Bonn), the Swedish theorist Knut Wicksell, and the French economist Albert Aftalion.

By the mid-1920s, dissatisfaction with the current state of

economics by its practitioners, changing technological and institutional structure, and the shocks of world war, revolution, and postwar economic dislocations combined to create an atmosphere receptive to intellectual innovation. The decade and a half ending in 1940 may be characterized as the third great creative period in the development of economic thought. These years of "hard times" were also ones of "high theory."[11] They commenced with a seminal article calling for the reconstruction of economic analysis around the concept of monopoly instead of competition, by Piero Sraffa in 1926,[12] and continued with the publication of major works on market structure by Joan Robinson and Edward Chamberlin,[13] on value and capital by John R. Hicks,[14] on legal and institutional foundations of capitalism by John R. Commons,[15] and, most impellingly, on money and employment by John Maynard Keynes.[16] This period coincided with a second great outpouring of writings from Schumpeter, who extended, refined, and developed the implications of his early German work of 1908–14. The second German edition of *The Theory of Economic Development* appeared in 1926. Its English translation was published in 1934. This was followed by the publication, in 1939, of Schumpeter's monumental two-volume study , *Business Cycles*,[17] and, in 1942, of his provocative and widely-read *Capitalism, Socialism, and Democracy*.[18] The steady stream of articles and reviews written during this period focused on the dynamic properties of capitalist development and transformation.[19]

III

If we now ask, What are the salient ideas expressed in *Economic Development* and how do they reflect the perspectives emanating from these three great creative periods in economic thought? our answer commences with the observation that Schumpeter was a special blend of eclectic and innovator. This is illustrated pointedly by the very structure of

Schumpeter's seminal work, that is, by his division of economic processes "into three different classes: into the processes of the circular flow, into those of development, and into those which impede the latter's undisturbed course" [218].[20]

(1.) The "circular flow of economic life as conditioned by given circumstances" [3], described in the early chapters of virtually every contemporary textbook on basic economics, was Schumpeter's expression for a general equilibrium system of mutual interrelations among economic variables and phenomena under stationary conditions.[21]

In the absence of economic development, the competitive capitalist economy, Schumpeter held, would tend to settle into the routine of the circular flow in stationary general equilibrium. Demands would match supplies on product and resource markets, and individuals, given market prices, would adjust their quantities demanded and supplied until they had maximized their economic gain in positions of individual equilibrium. Resources would be allocated according to the market-revealed preferences of sovereign consumers. Income would be distributed according to the market value of the marginal product of the two basic resources, land and labor, in the form of rents and wages (capital being resolved into land and labor). Competition and equal credit availability would eliminate all "surplus values" and, thereby, both pure economic profits and the interest income derived from productive, profitable investment.[22] Equilibrium, in markets for money, goods, labor, and financial assets, would assure full employment and economic stability. Because of stability and the certainty associated with a stationary economy (except for marginal changes in tastes and resource supplies, and resulting adjustments), the "store of value" function of money would atrophy and new money through credit creation by commercial banks would disappear. The economy would move along a stable equilibrium path of economic growth, determined by small and gradual increases in the labor force, savings, and capital accumulation. Such marginal and mere quantitative economic expansion would entail "no qualitatively new phenomena, but only processes of adaptation . . ." [63] similar to those of adjusting to changes in consumer tastes and other external data.

In such a general equilibrium system, there would be no leaders, directors, or initiators, except insofar as consumers could be termed "leaders." Businessmen would react passively to market demand and cost conditions, combining land and labor in a routinized fashion, making no special contributions other than that of superintendence, and receiving no special income beyond wages and rents for their own labor services and use of land.

In presenting this argument, Schumpeter drew upon the *content* of his Austrian and marginalist forebears, including the "American Austrian," John Bates Clark,[23] and the *form* of his (and that of his teacher, Böhm-Bawerk) intellectual hero, Leon Walras.[24] References to Carl Menger, the founder of the Austrian school, and to Böhm-Bawerk, Philippovich, and Wieser, three of his teachers at the University of Vienna, are interspersed throughout the first chapter of *Economic Development*. Such basic concepts as classification of goods into those of "lower order" (consumption) and "higher order" (produced means of production and, ultimately, labor and land), imputation, opportunity costs, and equality of costs and revenues all have clear Austrian antecedents. The notion that the economic process is "automatically synchronized" [38], in the sense that "waiting" for a future flow of revenues to offset current costs is unnecessary, is a variant of Clark's earlier analysis, as is the concept that owners of labor and land receive incomes according to their "marginal productivity." Debts to Walras also abound, notably in the concept of the entrepreneur in stationary equilibrium,[25] the mutual interdependence between households and business firms and the flows of expenditures between them for products and resources, and the tendency toward equilibrium.

Although Schumpeter drew freely from the writings of his

predecessors and contemporaries in constructing his conception of the circular flow, his analysis of even this most basic economic process showed both methodological independence and creative insight. For Schumpeter's contemporaries, analysis of resource allocation and income distribution under static and stationary conditions had a logically analytic, a descriptive, and/or a prescriptive purpose. Such "neo-Austrians" as Ludwig von Mises (a contemporary of Schumpeter's in Böhm-Bawerk's seminars at Vienna in 1905–06) and Friedrich von Hayek perceived the circular flow in terms of what Hayek later called the "pure logic of choice," as coordinated by competitive market processes.[26] British neoclassicist Alfred Marshall intended his analyses of basic economic processes to be at least roughly descriptive of real-world phenomena. J.B. Clark believed that distribution of income in accordance with marginal productivity was morally just as well as empirically relevent. Vilfredo Pareto, successor to Walras's chair in economics at the University of Lausanne, perceived general equilibrium as a state of maximum satisfaction, in the sense that no economic agent could be made better off without another being made worse off.[27]

Schumpeter did not deny the analytical usefulness of the general equilibrium concept under stationary conditions. He also believed it had some empirical significance. As he later put it, it is possible "to distinguish definite periods in which the system embarks upon an excursion away from equilibrium and equally definite periods in which it draws toward equilibrium." There are thus "neighborhoods" in which equilibrium conditions are approximately fulfilled.[28] The "essential point to grasp about capitalism," however, is that it is an "evolutionary process," as "was long ago emphasized by Karl Marx." Capitalism is "by nature a form or method of economic change and not only never is but never can be stationary."[29] Consequently, Schumpeter's analysis of the circular flow in a deeper sense is not intended to be either descriptive or prescriptive; that is, it neither accurately describes actual capitalist economies nor provides normative benchmarks for evaluation of capitalist economic performance.[30] Instead, it constitutes a useful mental experiment by asking what a capitalist market economy *would* be like *if* the dynamic, revolutionary changes of economic development were absent. The very austerity of the circular flow model is justified by Schumpeter on the suggestive ground of its corollary implication that the pulsating processes of real-world economic life are better explained from an explicitly dynamic and evolutionary perspective.[31]

2. In contrast to the stationary processes of the circular flow, Schumpeter's concept of economic *development* (chapter 2) has three salient characteristics: it comes from within the economic system and is not merely an adaptation to changes in external data; it occurs discontinuously, rather than smoothly; it brings qualitative changes or "revolutions," which fundamentally displace old equilibria and create radically new conditions. Economic development is accompanied by growth, that is, by a sustained upward movement in national income, saving, and population. But mere quantitative growth does not constitute development: "Add successively as many mail coaches as you please," said Schumpeter, "you will never get a railway thereby" [64n].

The strategic stimulus to economic development in Schumpeter's analysis is innovation, defined as the commercial or industrial application of something new—a new product, process, or method of production; a new market or source of supply; a new form of commercial, business, or financial organization.[32] The great innovations in the history of capitalist industrialization, for example, those associated with railroadization in the nineteenth century and the development of the automobile in the twentieth, typically have emerged from the commercial and industrial sectors of the economy, not from the "sovereign consumer" of classical and neoclassical economic theory. The innovational process,

Schumpeter subsequently observed, "incessantly revolutionizes the economic structure *from within*, incessantly destroying the old one, incessantly creating a new one. This process of Creative Destruction is the essential fact about capitalism."[33]

The commercial application of a new idea, often involving the acquisition and redirection of the employment of existing means of production, must be financed. It cannot be financed from the revenues received in the stationary circular flow, because these are just sufficient to cover existing costs and depreciation. They are not sufficient and not generally available for the daring experiments involved in shifting to new ways of doing things, especially when these new ideas involve (as they customarily do) new net investment beyond replacement requirements. Innovations, both logically and historically, must be financed by turning to a source of credit above and beyond the circular flow, namely, the commercial bank, the only private financial institution in the capitalist economy with the unique power to create new money, new purchasing power above current saving out of current income.

Innovation thus is distinguishable from the financing of the innovation, and the innovator or "entrepreneur" is distinguishable from the capitalist "owners of money, claims to money, or material goods" [75], even when, coincidentally, they are the same person. The innovator–entrepreneur must convince the capitalist that the higher revenues and/or lower costs stemming from his innovation will enable him to pay both principal and interest on the loan. The innovator must convince himself that the profits expected from the innovation will be sufficient to do this and leave a net profit for him. Thus, credit creation is a necessary but not, by itself, sufficient condition for economic development in a capitalist economy.

The provision of credit by capitalists to entrepreneurs to finance innovations is a vital function in a capitalist economy, indeed, "important enough to serve as its *differentia specifica*" [69]. But the linchpin of economic development, according to Schumpeter, is the "carrying out of new combinations," the putting into practice of the new ideas by entrepreneurs. Entrepreneurs are distinguishable not only from inventors and capitalists, but from businessmen–managers as well. Entrepreneurship is broader than business management because not all entrepreneurs operate established businesses. It is narrower than business management because not all managers, immersed as they are in the routine calculations of the circular flow, engage in entrepreneurial activities, that is, innovations.

Innovation faces immense difficulties, Schumpeter contends. First, the knowledge necessary for entrepreneurial decisions lies outside the known and accurate data of the circular flow and thus is shrouded in uncertainty. Second, objective uncertainty is compounded by subjective reluctance of individuals to strike out into the unknown. Third is the antagonism of noninnovators to the pioneer—in the form of legal and political obstacles, social mores, customs, and the like.

It takes a special kind of person to overcome these difficulties. In contrast to the "economic man," who carefully calculates marginal costs and revenues of alternative courses of action on the basis of known data, the entrepreneur must be a man of "vision," of daring, willing to take chances, to strike out, largely on the basis of intuition, on courses of action in direct opposition to the established, settled patterns of the circular flow. The entrepreneur is more of a "heroic" than an "economic" figure: he must have "the drive and the will to found a private kingdom" as a "captain of industry"; the "will to conquer," to fight for the sake of the fight rather than simply the financial gains of the combat; the desire to create new things—even at the expense of destroying old patterns of thought and action.[34] In any society, including capitalism, said Schumpeter, such people are in the minority.

Schumpeter's sharp distinction between the stationary circular flow and the developmental process may inadvertently obfuscate his recognized intellectual debts to more conventional predecessors and contemporaries. Böhm-Bawerk's famous argument that "roundabout methods" of production (that is, methods involving longer "gestation" periods between initial investment of productive resources and final appearance of outputs) "lead to greater results than direct methods" [35] has its counterpart in Schumpeter's observation that *"adoption* of roundabout methods of production . . . would be an entrepreneurial act—one of the many subordinate cases of my concept of carrying out new combinations" [159]. Schumpeter's distinction between mere economic growth and genuine economic development parallels Walras's earlier one between "economic progress" and "technical progress." [36] Schumpeter expressly commended the earlier work of J.B. Clark, notably in *The Essentials of Economic Theory* (1907), "whose merit is in having consciously separated 'statics' and 'dynamics'" and who, like Schumpeter, "saw in the dynamic elements a disturbance of the static equilibrium" [60n].

In contrast to Böhm-Bawerk and Walras, "Schumpeter's great contribution lies in dynamising the system by putting the role of [the] entrepreneur in the forefront and clearly indicating the fundamental differences between this system and the system of equilibrium." [37] Schumpeter's analysis is differentiated from and an improvement upon Clark's in three major ways. First, Clark places in one overall category five sources of economic change: increases in capital, increases in population, changes in the direction of consumers' tastes, improvements in technique, and changes in productive organization. In Schumpeter's more exacting formulation, the first two are perceived to evoke mere quantitative expansion or economic growth. The third pertains to a change in the *composition* of the circular flow, and in itself requires no special dynamic theoretical framework. The last two, however, are prominent examples of the qualitative phenomenon of economic development, which goes substantially beyond mere disturbance of equilibrium. Second, according to Schumpeter, essential economic phenomena depend upon and are profoundly affected by the process of economic development, notably, credit and capital, profit, and interest. Thus, for Schumpeter, the theory of economic development is not a mere adjunct or appendix to the central body of economic analysis, but the foundation for a reinterpretation of most of the economic processes which, in conventional mainstream economics, are considered within the constraining framework of static and stationary general equilibrium. These topics are examined in great detail in chapters 3, 4, and 5 of *Economic Development.*

There is a third difference between Clark's and Schumpeter's conception of economic development which may be highlighted by reference to Karl Marx. Clark regarded his five sources of economic change as "external data" that impinge upon economic processes. In Schumpeter's view, this fails to recognize that changes in technique and productive organization "require special analysis and evoke something different again from [mere] disturbances in the theoretical sense. The nonrecognition of this is the most important single reason for what appears unsatisfactory to us in economic theory. From this insignificant-looking source flows . . . . a new conception of the economic process" [60n].

This new conception, Schumpeter continues, "is more nearly parallel to that of Marx. For according to him there is an *internal* economic development and no mere adaption of economic life to changing data" [60n]. Schumpeter elaborated on this point in the preface to the Japanese edition of *Economic Development.* The aim of his work, he there observes, was to "construct a theoretic model of the process of economic change in time, or perhaps more clearly, to answer the question how the economic system generates the force which incessantly transforms it."[38] In contrast to economists like

Walras and Clark, Schumpeter believed there was "a source of energy within the economic system which would of itself disrupt any equilibrium that might be attained. If this is so, then there must be a purely economic theory of economic change which does not merely rely on external factors propelling the economic system from one equilibrium to another." Now, "this idea and aim are exactly the same as the idea and the aim which underlay the economic teaching of Karl Marx. In fact, what distinguished him from the economists of his own time and those who preceded him, was precisely a vision of economic evolution as a distinct process generated by the economic system itself."[39]

Of course, the analyses of the character of this internally-generated dynamic of capitalist development and transformation found in the works of Marx and Schumpeter show both similarities and differences. One difference is that whereas Schumpeter's conception of the stationary economic process abstracts from both the capitalist and the entrepreneur, Marx's conception (which he called "simple reproduction") abstracts from capital accumulation. Consequently, Marx's analysis of stationary capitalism includes an express identification of social power and class relations based upon property and wealth that is missing from Schumpeter's argument. As a corollary, entrepreneurial innovation is, for Schumpeter, the central autonomous cause of economic development, and capital accumulation is a major result. For Marx, by contrast, capital accumulation is itself the primary force in the development process.

This difference, however, should not be exaggerated. First entrepreneurship and innovation are key elements in Marx's analysis of the capital accumulation process. Second, successful entrepreneurs *become* capitalists in Schumpeter's analysis. Moreover, in the later stages of capitalism, innovation increasingly becomes the business, as in Marx's argument, of wealthy established enterprises rather than new industrial soldiers of fortune.[40] Third, Schumpeter emphasizes that his theoretical "structure covers only a small part of [Marx's] ground" [60n]. Specifically, in his second edition of *Economic Development*, Schumpeter responded to critics of his first edition who had alleged that he had neglected all "historical factors of change" [61n] except individual entrepreneurship.[41] To the contrary, insisted Schumpeter, *Economic Development* "is not at all concerned with the concrete factors of change, but with the method by which these work, with the *mechanism of change*. The 'entrepreneur' is merely the bearer of the mechanism. And I have taken account not of one factor of historical change, but of none" [61n].

3. The concluding chapter of *Economic Development*, on business cycles, can be better appreciated by placing it in the context of his later, magisterial two-volume study on this subject in 1939. The importance which Schumpeter attached to business cycles can be better appreciated by noting the subtitle of this later work: *Business Cycles: A Theoretical, Historical and Statistical Analysis of the Capitalist Process.*[42] In this book, Schumpeter distinguishes among three "approximations" or stages in the study of cyclical fluctuations. The first approximation is essentially that found in the concluding chapter of *Economic Development*, which was substantially rewritten for the second edition. Although this basic model abstracts from many particular features of cyclical change, Schumpeter considered it useful because, as he put it in 1939, it isolates the most essential cyclical elements in the absence of the "innumerable layers of secondary, incidental, accidental and 'external' facts and reactions" that "cover the skeleton of economic life, sometimes so as to hide it entirely."[43] The second approximation, described very briefly in *Economic Development*, and presented more fully in his later writings, incorporated supplementary, complicating features of business cycles, causing "secondary waves" on top of the underlying "primary wave." The third approximation, alluded to in the preface to the English translation of *Economic Development*, in 1934, and developed in his 1939 study, distinguishes cycles of different lengths and amplitudes.

One of the ironies of the intellectual history of economics

in the twentieth century is that Schumpeter is often remembered more for his analysis of business cycles than for his theory of economic development. In part, this is a testimony to the high quality and creativity of his cycle analysis. As Alvin H. Hansen aptly put it, "Schumpeter was one of the most brilliant and original of the five Continental writers who originated nearly all of the really basic ideas in modern business-cycle theory" in the early twentieth century.[44] Indeed, Hansen observes that it was the belated effort of English-speaking economists to catch up with Continental literature on money, business cycles, and allied matters which led to the English translation of *Economic Development* in 1934.[45] The publication, in 1939, of Schumpeter's monumental two-volume study on cycles reinforced his image as essentially a cycle theorist, albeit a highly gifted one. No doubt, the emphasis of the economics profession upon short-run issues of depression and unemployment, stimulated by a combination of the Great Depression of the 1930s and the publication and dissemination of Keynes's *General Theory of Employment, Interest, and Money,*[46] further reinforced this process, as did the expositions of Schumpeter's cycle theory in the prominent texts of his Harvard colleagues Alvin Hansen[47] and Gottfried Haberler.[48]

What differentiates Schumpeter's cycle analysis, however, from that of his continental contemporaries—especially in *Economic Development*—is precisely his explicit and careful linkages between economic development and cyclical fluctuations. For Schumpeter, development occurs *through* a cyclical process, while cyclical disturbances bring development. Consequently, cyclical fluctuations are no barrier to economic growth, and depressions are not necessarily indicators of capitalist failure or breakdown. Indeed, cycles are the normal means by which capitalism develops and thereby grows.

This perspective is reflected in Schumpeter's fundamental question: why does economic development proceed cyclically rather than evenly? Schumpeter's answer—that innovations are not *"evenly distributed through time,"* but *"appear, if at all, discontinuously in groups or swarms"*—places his core interwoven ideas on both development and cyclical flunctuations in one sentence [223]. Entrepreneurs, financed by bank credit, make innovative investments embodying new technologies, resource discoveries, and so on. *If* these innovative investments are successful, imitators follow, in the original industry and elsewhere (for example, successful innovations in the automobile industry encourage secondary innovation and investment in petroleum, rubber tires, glass, and so on) and the economy embarks upon a dramatic upward surge: prosperity. Eventually, innovations are completed and investment subsides; an avalanche of consumer goods pours onto the market with dampening effects on prices; rising costs and interest rates squeeze profit margins: and the economy contracts: recession.

In this perspective, economic growth emerges from and as a consequence of cyclical development. Discontinuous bursts of innovative investment are the basic, underlying cause of cyclical fluctuations. The qualitative changes arising from within the system which comprise innovations are associated with innovative investment and are the fundamental source of economic development. Economic development embodies technological, organizational, and resource changes which, by raising productivity and reducing costs, lay the foundations for economic growth despite, indeed because of, the interruptions of the business cycle and its associated economic contractions.

From this perspective, also, depressions (or, in current language, moderate recessions) are, largely, a normal and healthy process of adaptation to the bunching of innovations during the preceding prosperity. Thus, the fundamental cause of depression is prosperity itself. If we want prosperity, we must accept the depression which necessarily succeeds it. Moreover, economic contractions yield higher real incomes through innovation; force reorganizations of production, greater efficiency, and lower costs; and eliminate inefficient, noninnovating businesses, as new products and methods replace the old in what Schumpeter later called a "perennial gale of creative destruction."[49]

In practice, of course, cycles and economic contractions come in different lengths and amplitudes. First, business expansion, though rooted in innovation, may be amplified by such factors as rising incomes, speculative ventures, excess optimism, and excess credit creation. In the succeeding contraction, which occurs once the force of the primary wave of innovational investment has been spent, the unproductive, unprofitable, and overextended ventures crumble. Contraction will then involve more than a normal recessionary adjustment to and absorption of the innovations of the prosperity and will drop into a major, severe depression. Liquidation and adjustment to a superboom may descend into a "vicious spiral" of decreased credit, decreased prices, and increased liquidation, heightened by speculative contractions in spending and errors of pessimism, perhaps even financial "panic" or "crisis." These deep, protracted depressions "are pathological in the sense that they play no indispensable role in the capitalist process, which would be logically complete without them."[50]

Because they are abnormal deviations from the logic of the capitalist process and depend on reactions to specific maladjustments, "no theoretical expectation can be formed about the occurrence and severity of depressions."[51]

Indeed, the vicious spiral in deep depressions conceivably may be so powerful that the system may not recover by itself and may require assistance from some external agent, like government action or a random favorable event.

Second, in his 1939 analysis, Schumpeter distinguished among short, medium, and long cycles, or, in honor of their "discoverers," the 3–4-year "Kitchen," the 9–10-year "Juglar," and the 54–60-year "Kondratieff." Schumpeter dated the first long-wave Kondratieff from the 1780s to 1842, the second from 1842 to 1897, and the third from 1898 to the end of the 1930s. The first of these long waves he associated with the "industrial revolution," the second, with railroadization, the third, with a broader set of innovations in the chemical, electric power, and automobile industries. The key to the Kondratieff is not a cyclical movement in the absolute level of aggregate real output, but instead a large-scale clustering or sequence of innovations, the appearance and absorption of which require a half-century or more.

Long-wave Kondratieffs are interconnected with the shorter cycles, notably the major Juglars. It is "clear that the coincidence at any time of corresponding phases of all three cycles will always produce phenomena of unusual intensity, especially if the phases that coincide are those of prosperity or depression."[52] The coincidence of the depressionary phases of a Kondratieff and a Juglar cycle as, for example, in the 1870s and the 1930s, can produce exceptionally long, severe depressions, whereas Juglar depressions during a long-wave Kondratieff upswing as, for example, between 1898 and the 1920s, are apt to be relatively short and mild.

4. Although *Economic Development* in its first edition contained a concluding sociological chapter, and in all editions incorporated insightful sociological commentary, there is a narrow though important sense in which Schumpeter's sociological thought is "incidental and subordinate to the economic argument."[53] After all, the focus of *Economic Development* is on the functioning of an internally-generated process of economic development. In a broader sense, however, this view is misleading. First, mainstream economics, in Schumpeter's time as in our own, focused upon the derivation of theorems from given technological, institutional, and motivational assumptions. By contrast, Schumpeter made the specification of a mechanism of change in these kinds of data the core of his analysis. Second, Schumpeter was much more explicit than his contemporaries in specifying institu-

tional aspects of his argument. Indeed, one is tempted to say that Schumpeter was more successful, in a limited way, in synthesizing an analysis of institutional change with economic theory than "institutionalist" critics of mainstream economics in the early twentieth century. At the very least, Schumpeter's analysis provides an interesting Continental quasi analogue to the writings of such American institutionalists as Thorstein Veblen and John R. Commons.[54]

In any event, Schumpeter provided considerable sociological and political commentary in his subsequent writings, notably in his papers on "The Sociology of Imperialisms" and "Social Classes in an Ethnically Homogeneous Environment,"[55] and in his widely read work *Capitalism, Socialism, and Democracy*. In addition, Schumpeter's posthumously published, though somewhat eccentric, masterpiece *History of Economic Analysis* contains lengthy and learned discussion of the sociocultural setting and *Zeitgeist* of economic theories in their historical development.[56]

In the interest of reasonable brevity, we shall not review systematically the content of these works, and the reader is referred elsewhere for details.[57] Two broad points, however, one methodological and the other substantive, should be mentioned here, the second in some depth. First, these writings are not mere forays into adjacent, but distinguishable, fields. Instead, they are strategically complementary to the analysis in *Economic Development*. If Schumpeter's early work of 1911 may be said to focus on the functioning and development of capitalism, his subsequent "sociological" studies may be described as both elaborating and illustrating these early ideas and supplementing them by considering the origins and transformation of, the future prospects for, and the prospective successor(s) to capitalism. Together, Schumpeter's lifeworks constitute a more or less integrated study of the birth, development, and historical transcience of industrializing capitalism in Western societies.

Moreover, in his centennial essay on the *Communist Manifesto*, Schumpeter distinguishes between "economics" and

"economic sociology" (from the German *Wirtschaftssoziologie*).
By economics, Schumpeter means "the interpretive description of the economic mechanisms that play within any given
state of . . . institutions, such as market mechanisms." By economic sociology, Schumpeter denotes the interpretive description of "economically relevant institutions, including
habits and all forms of behavior in general, such as government, property, private enterprise, customary or 'rational'
behavior."[58] In his *History of Economic Analysis*, Schumpeter
observes that any economic inquiry which goes beyond mere
"technique in the most restricted sense of the word has such
an institutional introduction that belongs to sociology rather
than to economic history as such" and that, consequently, economic sociology must be introduced as a "fourth fundamental field to complement" economic history, statistics, and
theory, even though this necessitates going beyond the "mere
economic analysis" embodied in these three.[59] Schumpeter
greatly admired Marx's ability to blend economic analysis
and economic sociology, defined in these two senses. Marx's
economic theory, he suggests, attempted to show how social
class relations "work out through the medium of economic
values, profits, wages, investment . . . and how they will
eventually break its own institutional framework and at the
same time create the conditions for the emergence of
another social world." Marx's economic sociology, on the
other hand, especially his theory of social classes, provided
"the analytic tool which, by linking the economic interpretation of history with the concepts of the profit economy,
marshals all social facts, makes all phenomena confocal." It
had the "organic function" of synthesizing the Marxian theory of capitalist development and transforming it into a uni-
fied whole.[60] Much the same sort of thing might be said
about Schumpeter's imaginative attempt to complement his
more strictly economic analysis of capitalist development
with a broader sociological and historical perspective on the
origins, transformation, and future of capitalist civilization.

   Turning to the second, substantive point, Schumpeter's

"sociological" writings, notably *Capitalism, Socialism, and Democracy*, elaborate and complement *Economic Development* by providing a conservative, antisocialist alternative to both Marx and Keynes.

In simplified terms, we may characterize the relations among Marx, Keynes, and Schumpeter as follows: Marx (1) identified some major properties of captalist behavior (for example, depressions, inequality in income distribution), (2) designated these properties as flaws or contradictions of the system, and (3) predicted the death of capitalism significantly because of its economic contradictions. Keynes also (1) identified leading properties of capitalism (notably its proclivity toward unemployment because of the absence of a viable self-regulatory mechanism), and (2) designated them as failures of the system, but (3) proposed (limited) reforms of the system to eradicate or control them. Schumpeter agreed with both Marx and Keynes on (1), disagreed with both on (2), and agreed with Marx on (3), partly because of undesirable side effects of liberal-labor reforms of the Keynesian variety.

Focusing first on Schumpeter's reaction to Marx, it may be observed that, although he differed from Marx on details (for example, concerning such long-run tendencies as increasing cyclical intensity and increasing "immiserization" of labor), Schumpeter never denied the existence of any of Marx's *major* contradictory features of capitalism. Class struggles, surplus values, cyclical crises, depressions, unemployment, inequality in wealth, power, and income, and monopoly and centralization of capital are all woven into Schumpeter's analysis. The character of Schumpeter's critical assessment of Marx is radically different from that of Böhm-Bawerk and other contemporaries of Schumpeter who bothered to consider Marx's ideas.[61] The conventional view rejected Marx's theories *from the perspective of stationary equilibrium*, albeit typically without express recognition of the confining nature of the critique. For Schumpeter, by contrast, stationary equilibrium is defined in such an exacting and rarefied manner that the exclusion of such phenomena as capital-labor relations, surplus values in the form of interest and pure economic profits, depressions, and unemployment follow as a virtual tautology. On the other hand, Schumpeter is perfectly prepared to recognize the existence of these aspects of capitalist behavior, *from the dynamic perspective of capitalist industrialization and development.*

Schumpeter's response to Keynes was both similar to and different from that of his reaction to Marx. It was similar in that Schumpeter expressly recognized and provided a theoretical framework for analyzing Keynes's major themes of depression and unemployment (as well as his minor theme of inequality in wealth and income). As already observed, Schumpeter also perceived a quality in the creative life-process of both Keynes and Marx similar to that of his own, that is, each presented an early "vision" subsequently worked out in greater theoretical depth. For Marx, this was represented by the movement from the *Communist Manifesto* to *Capital*. Schumpeter perceived a somewhat similar process in his own work from *Economic Development* to *Business Cycles*. For Keynes, the "social vision first revealed in the *Economic Consequences of the Peace* [Keynes's brilliant early study of 1917], the vision of an economic process in which investment opportunity flags and saving habits nevertheless persist, is theoretically implemented in the *General Theory of Employment, Interest and Money*" of 1936.[62] Lastly, Schumpeter's dissent from Keynes's interpretation of capitalism's malaise, like his critique of Marx's analysis, and his corollary alternative interpretative defense of capitalism is based on an explicitly dynamic theoretical framework.

Although Keynes's analysis contained "several dynamic elements, expectations in particular," the "exact skeleton" of his analytical system, Schumpeter held, lay in the realm of short-run, static equilibrium. According to Schumpeter, the lack of a primarily dynamic theoretical framework is precisely the leading defect of Keynes's analysis.[63] "*All the phe-*

nomena incident to . . . creation and change . . . that is to say, the phenomena that dominate the capitalist processes, are thus excluded from consideration."[64] By contrast, Schumpeter's alternative to both Keynes and Marx is explicitly dynamic and evolutionary.

Thus, Schumpeter confronts Marx and Keynes directly. First, whatever its contradictory proclivities, capitalism has been an immense success. Second, contradictory propensities actually perform a creative function in industrialization. Third, capitalism shows no likelihood of imminent breakdown under the weight of "economic failure." To illustrate, consider Schumpeter's dynamic interpretation of cyclical depressions, inequality and surplus values, and monopoly.

In Schumpeter's original analysis, an explained earlier, cyclical fluctuations are no barrier to economic growth, and depressions are not necessarily an indicator of capitalist failure or breakdown. Schumpeter's "Economica" article of 1927, published about the time of the second edition of *Economic Development*, supplements the revised final chapter in that work and should be read in conjunction with it. In this article, Schumpeter reproduces one of his favorite propositions attributed to Clement Juglar, the French physician-turned-economist who initiated the study of business cycles in the mid-nineteenth century: "La cause unique de la dépression c'est la prospérité." Alternatively put, "the phenomena which we have got in the habit of calling 'depression' are no irregular heap of disturbances, but can be understood as the reaction of business life to the situation created by the boom. . . ."[65] Subsequently, in *Capitalism, Socialism, and Democracy*, Schumpeter returns to this theme in the context of the three-cycle model presented in his "third approximation." The expansionary phase of the Juglar cycle from 1932 to 1937 in the United States, Schumpeter argued, exhibited roughly the kind and amount of innovations and technological change to be expected in such industries as automobiles, rubber, steel, and chemicals during a Kondratieff downswing. The subnormal performance of the 1930s also can be attributed in part "to the difficulties incident to the adaptation to a new fiscal policy, new labor legislation and a general change in the attitude of government to private enterprise. . . ." Thus, even severe depressions like those of the thirties do "not prove that a secular break has occurred in the propelling mechanism of capitalist production. . . ."[66] Further, in contrast to Marx's prognosis, unemployment as a percent of the labor force has shown no upward secular trend. If capitalism's future economic promise, based on its past experience, were to be fulfilled, the burden of providing ample compensation for the unemployed would decrease, thereby eliminating the major "terror" of unemployment in terms of "the private life of the unemployed. . . ."[67]

Similarly, economic inequality is not a flaw or failure of capitalism. In a stationary world, without innovation and economic development, competition eventually would reduce profits to "normal" levels. But in a dynamic, developing economy, above-normal profits are often the reward for innovation. Because of the tremendous uncertainties surrounding innovations—that is, the possibility of failure and the likelihood of competitive encroachment in the event of success—the lure and occasional realization of extraordinary profits may well be the price society pays for the revolutionary contributions of its business leaders (chapter 4). Marx's concept of surplus values, Schumpeter also observes, must be understood in a dynamic context. By incorporating new technologies and other sources of qualitative change, entrepreneurial innovations create surpluses of revenues above costs (and thereby also the capacity to pay interest). Competition tends to eliminate these surplus values, but innovation recreates them. Thus, Schumpeter defends Marx's conclusion (and his own) under dynamic conditions: "Surplus values may be impossible in perfect equilibrium but can be ever present because that equilibrium is never allowed to establish itself. They may always tend to vanish and yet be always there because they are constantly recreated."[68]

Furthermore, Schumpeter contended in his later writings,

capitalism in practice reduces inequality in several ways: first, by increasing equality of opportunity relative to earlier, more class-bound societies; second, by the creation of mass-produced products that benefit working masses more than they do any other sector of the economy; third, by philanthropy and social legislation underwritten by the process of capitalist economic growth; and fourth, because although "relative proverty" or inequality is necessary for the sustenance of capitalism, "absolute poverty" falls as capitalist development proceeds.

Schumpeter's assessment of monopoly parallels his commentary on cyclical depressions and inequality. He clearly recognizes the emergence of big business and the associated market power of oligopoly and monopoly enterprise in the late nineteenth and early twentieth centuries. He also agrees with both Marxian and non-Marxian critics of monopoly that comparisons of static equilibrium positions reveal lower outputs and inputs, higher prices, and lower wages for monopoly-monopsony enterprises than for competitive ones. Still, he denies that monopoly is a flaw, contradiction, or failure in capitalism's "economic engine."

In part, Schumpeter's evaluation of monopoly reflects his conception of competition as a *dynamic process* rather than as a set of structural conditions or a static, equilibrium end-state. In this, he is closer to Marx than to such contemporary individualist-conservative economists as Friedrich Hayek and Milton Friedman. The neoliberalism of the contemporary individualist-conservatives, like the classical liberalism of Adam Smith and John Stuart Mill, rests on the principle of atomistically competitive markets as social processes for economic coordination and control of business enterprise. By contrast, Schumpeter's analysis of the role of "big business" bears a striking resemblance to certain features of the laissez-faire conservatism and "Social Darwinism" of the late nineteenth century. Schumpeter's hero is not the competitive market, but the creative, daring entrepreneur, the "captain of industry," who makes the innovations that introduce new products, embody resource discoveries and technological improvements, and open new markets, and, in the process, build new industrial empires.

To Schumpeter, the dynamic innovations of the entrepreneurial class constitute a powerful competitive force in economic development. The "perennial gale of creative destruction," whereby new products and processes displace old ones, is vastly more important than price competition among existing firms and products. Because capitalism is a dynamic, evolutionary economic system, it, and short-run market strategies of business firms, must be appraised in terms of "the perennial gale of creative destruction," that is, in terms of long-run developmental dynamism. The really "relevant problem" is not "how capitalism administers existing structures," but "how it creates and destroys them."[69]

Stated differently, it is quite possible that short-run semimonopolistic positions, agreements, and strategies, with accompanying short-run inefficiencies in resource allocation and inequalities in income distribution, are necessary to provide a basis for the innovational investment that brings greater long-run performance and more vigorous long-run competition. Entrepreneurship may be, in large measure, a function of an institutional sociopolitical structure which permits protection (through, for example, patents and secret processes) to the innovator and the generation of pure economic profits through the manipulation of price, quantity, and quality variables via techniques which in the short run appear restrictive and monopolistic. Thus, the possibility of retention, at least temporarily, of above-normal profits from innovations may well stimulate a higher rate of innovation and technological improvement. Short-run strategies and practices that protect the monopoly position of the innovator thus may be the price society pays for technological progress and thereby a higher growth rate over the long run. Moreover, because of the tendency for innovations to spread, by

imitation and extension to allied fields, the monopoly position—and associated monopoly profits—of the industrial
pioneer is only temporary [152].

IV

The reception and impact of *Economic Development* pro-
ceeded through three main stages, roughly paralleling the
work's three editions, the third phase becoming mingled with
reaction to his mature analysis, in *Business Cycles*. Responses
to the first edition were generally favorable. Indeed, in the
words of Erich Schneider, Schumpeter's prominent student
at the University of Bonn in the late 1920s, Schumpeter's
work "created a sensation in international professional circles." [70] One enthusiastic early reviewer, for example, com-
menting on both *The Essence and Principal Contents of Economic
Theory* and *Economic Development*, declared: "Seldom has clear
and consecutive reasoning had more definite expression in
economics than in Schumpeter's two volumes. . . . He shows
rare knowledge . . . keenness of observation, . . . coherence in
reasoning, and . . . fearlessness and discrimination in sifting
and combining old notions with new. . . . Beyond question he
has blazed paths [and] yielded results unusually stimulating
and suggestive." [71] Another reviewer of the first edition
wrote: "The reviewer . . . knows no book that would be more
stimulating to a class in economic theory, and he feels that
the constructive doctrine of the book contains much that is
destined to become a permanent part of economic theory." [72]
Even critical reviewers, such as R.S. Howey, a strong advo-
cate of the Austrian and marginal utility traditions in economics, acknowledged the "unorthodox and audacious ideas
which the book contains. . . ." The English translation of
Schumpeter's seminal work, Howey continued, "certainly
will add to the list of his critics and possibly to the list of his
followers. . . . It is apparent that the fundamentals of the theory are those which have not met, and are not likely to meet,

with ready acceptance. . . ." Still, he concludes, the book gives "a brilliant and unconventional picture of the economic process."[73]

Most reviewers recognized Schumpeter's dynamic methodology and developmental framework as the core of his original contribution. According to R.C. McCrea, for example, "Schumpeter's thought has advanced beyond the mechanistic interpretation of the physicist–economist. He has made a significant contribution in carrying us over to the newer evolutionary method and evolutionary viewpoint."[74] J.B. Clark, in another early review, declared that *Economic Development* connects such phenomena as capital, interest, and profit with "economic evolution, and it studies them as they appear in a world of change and progress. It thus makes an important addition to the limited amount of scientific literature which deals consciously and systematically with what is commonly termed 'economic dynamics.'"[75] L.B. Naymier, an English reviewer of the first edition of *Economic Development*, similarly identifies "spontaneous, economic development, development due to new combinations in economic life, to constructive economic leadership,"[76] as Schumpeter's central theme. Oscar Morgenstern, in his review of the second edition, states that it is, "since it gives the first elaborate dynamic economics in the proper sense, very revolutionary. . . ."[77] Hans Neisser, in his review of the English translation, describes Schumpeter's book as providing "the first realistic theory of economic development."[78] "Nowhere else," Hansen observed in his highly favorable review of the English translation, "does one find so penetrating a treatment as here of the significant characteristics of the process of development, of economic dynamics, in contrast with the 'circular flow' of an essentially static society."[79] Simon Kuznets, in his extensive review of *Business Cycles*, emphasized the close connection between Schumpeter's cycle analysis and his "thought-provoking judgments concerning the general course of capitalist evolution."[80] Three years later, Paul M.

Sweezy observes that, although the most important part of Schumpeter's theory of economic development "which falls within the traditional scope of Anglo-American economics is that which is concerned with business cycles," his basic objective "is nothing less than to lay bare the anatomy of economic change in capitalist society." This contrasts, Sweezy continues, with conventional English and American economics which "has traditionally been content to confine its attention to what may be called the normal functioning of the capitalist economy."[81]

Economic Development justly established Schumpeter's international reputation. Although his later work amplified, illustrated, supplemented, and to some degree amended ;his early ideas, the central core of his theoretical system was presented in 1911 "with a directness of exposition and a cogency of argument that he was never again to attain."[82] The book has certainly become a "classic." Moreover, Schumpeter's dynamic methodology and vision of the evolutionary process have had significant and salutary effects on later writers. Hansen's work on business cycles, for example, reflects the influence of Schumpeter (and other early twentieth-century Continental scholars) perhaps as much as it does that of Keynes, normally perceived as Hansen's mentor.[83] Writings of John Maurice Clark (the son of J.B. Clark) on "competition as a dynamic process" and of Edward Mason on competition in the form of new products and product design display a strong Schumpeterian influence.[84] Although Sweezy objects to Schumpeter's notion of the entrepreneur (rather than capital accumulation) as the *primum mobile* of change, he strongly agrees with Schumpeter's "conception of innovation as a central feature of economic development,"[85] and incorporates innovation as an important component of a Marxian analysis. Indeed, the analysis of monopoly capitalism, by Sweezy and Paul Baran, rests upon the perceived innovational pressures of large firms under a kind of Schumpeterian "trustified capitalism," pushing down production costs, thereby substituting a "law of rising surplus" for Marx's original notion of a "law of the falling rate of profit" under competitive capitalism.[86] The field of the economics of development, which has mushroomed since Schumpeter's death in 1950, exhibits both direct and indirect influence of his ideas. Drawing upon Schumpeter's basic perspective, Everett E. Hagen and others have challenged the traditional view of technology as simply an external force impinging on the economic system, and have broadened the scope of their inquiry to encompass institutional and sociocultural bases of technological change in the process of transition from traditional to developing societies.[87] Richard Nelson and others have extended the analysis of the diffusion of innovations and the process of cross-country technological transfer.[88]

Yet, despite the brilliance and originality demonstrated in *Economic Development*, its critical acclaim, and its direct and indirect influence, Schumpeter's bold objective of conquering the world of economics like an intellectual samurai, and reconstructing and redirecting the discipline along radically new paths, was never achieved. Schumpeter's reach exceeded his grasp; the intellectual transformative effect for which he yearned eluded him. Part of the explanation for this, no doubt, lies in unfortunate circumstances of timing. The first edition of his classic work was published, in German, shortly before World War I. English-speaking economists, for example, Keynes, largely ignored the book, and the outbreak of war shifted economists' attentions to more immediate, practical issues. By the time the English-speaking world of economics began to catch up with Continental literature and an English translation of *Economic Development* was arranged, in 1934, the Western capitalist countries were in the depths of the greatest depression in modern history. Economists, no less than politicians, were in no mood for glowing descriptive analyses of the activities of heroic captains of industry and the effects of their innovative ventures on economic development. The publication, in 1936, of Keynes's *General Theory*, profoundly reinforced this mood. By the time *Business Cycles* was published, in the very late 1930s, depression had begun to abate. But, the exigencies of war and the absorption of the Keynesian analysis demanded the attention of many members of the economics profession.

In addition to these external circumstances were factors of Schumpeter's own life and temperament. After World War I, as noted earlier, Schumpeter spent several years in government and business, largely withdrawn from academic pursuits. His brief period at the University of Bonn in the late 1920s, on the eve of the Nazi revolution, although highly productive and influential, did not give him time to establish deep intellectual roots, and his years at Harvard were disrupted by depression and war.

Perhaps even more important, Schumpeter was temperamentally at odds with his own ambitions. Despite his "many ardent admirers and scores of devoted students," he actively discouraged establishment of a Schumpeterian "school" of thought.[89] In a farewell address to his students at Bonn, for example, he declared: "I have never tried to bring about a Schumpeter school. There is none and it ought not to exist. . . . Economics is not a philosophy but a science. Hence there should be no 'schools' in our field."[90] At Harvard, his teaching program—economic theory, history of economic thought, business cycles, and socialism—paralleled his fundamental intellectual interests and provided ample opportunity and an effective platform for propagation of his views. But, as many of his students and colleagues complain, "there was an unforgivable omission; his students never heard one word of Schumpeterian economics."[91] Even in his written works, Schumpeter tried to minimize controversy, an important ingredient one suspects, in attracting epigones. In the preface to the English translation of *Economic Development*

Schumpeter observes that he did not follow the example of

"my great teacher Böhm-Bawerk, who with infinite care took notice of every objection or critique and embodied his own comments in his later edition" [x]. Moreover, in contrast to Keynes, Schumpeter consistently refused to simplify his argument by stating it (or permitting others to state it) in skeletal form to facilitate quick exposition and analysis. Nor, as we have already observed (again, in contrast to Keynes) did he construct or adapt his analysis so as to facilitate drawing policy conclusions for short-run problems. In short, Schumpeter was temperamentally indisposed toward any of the kinds of things an intellectual innovator normally does to gather a following and propagate his views.

This combination of a powerful drive for intellectual achievement and influence and principled opposition against actions likely to promote these aspirations is discernible in Schumpeter's writings on other economists. On Böhm-Bawerk, for example, he observes that success was slow in coming. Böhm achieved recognition "solely through the force of his written argument, without pursuing literary success, without appeal to public opinion, without a journalistic campaign, without academic politics—that is, without any of those means which, granting that they may occasionally be necessary or justifiable, fall short of the highest ideals of scholarly enterprise—and without causing bitterness or engaging in personal squabbles."[92] Schumpeter describes Pareto as a person of "independence and pugnacity . . . in the habit of dealing vigorous blows right in the midst of arguments that might in themselves be agreeable to some party or another" and thus as one who "has little chance of being popular."[93] Considering that Walras's "vision" was "as far removed from the current interests of the profession as was the case" and that his novelty consisted essentially "in the manner of looking at things and not in discoveries and inventions which appeal to the interest and understanding of wide circles, . . . it is readily understood that external success could come neither easily nor quickly."[94] Menger, to give another example, was innocent of the tactics of "scientific advertising" as means to gain acceptance of his ideas, and in any event "lacked the means of conducting his own campaigns. But his powerful strength penetrated through all the jungles and triumphed over all the hostile armies."[95] These commentaries by Schumpeter on his intellectual heroes might just as easily have been written about Schumpeter himself. By contrast, Schumpeter's assessment of the easier or more rapid achievement of practical success by such economists as Marshall and Keynes combine admiration with reproof and, on occasion, a trace of condescension. Marshall's desire to present a text which would be read and understood by businessmen is described as a "strange ambition." His "analytic schema" is described as being "embedded in a luxuriant frame that conciliates and comforts the layman." In exact opposition to Schumpeter, Marshall "cheerfully sympathized, from a warm heart, with the ideals of socialism and patronizingly talked down to socialists from a cool head." Marshall's "preaching of mid-Victorian morality, seasoned by Benthamism, the preaching from a schema of middle-class values that knows no glamour and no passion" was personally "irritating" to Schumpeter and of questionable propriety in a scientific treatise.[96] Keynes's achievements are described more in terms of the creation of a "Keynesian school" and an ideological program than analytical prowess.[97]

Schumpeter's eschewal of "schools" of thought combines intellectual integrity with a basic naiveté. In fact, there are schools of thought within social scientific disciplines, and with good cause. To some extent, of course, rival theories contend for influence in the same domains. For example, monetarist, Keynesian, and supply-side economists in the early 1980s debated the prospective effects of the Reagan administration's economic policies. In most instances, however, contending perspectives in the historical development of economic thought may be distinguished by the different questions they have asked or insights they have brought rather than primarily by the different answers they have given to the same questions. Because different theoretical perspectives are often complementary rather than competitive, they may validly coexist and enrich understanding of social phenomena. Moreover, "testing" economic theories is fraught with major difficulties, not the least of which is that such alternative theoretical structures as classical, neoclassical, Marxian, Keynesian, and institutionalist economic thought constitute intricate congeries of ideas rather than simple, single hypotheses.

Because of the coexistence of contending perspectives in social theory, a major alternative strategy to building a "Schumpeterian school" would have been to infiltrate other approaches to the discipline. To some degree, Schumpeter did this. But there were important barriers to this approach. Marxists found much to admire in Schumpeter's vision and grand design of capitalist development and transformation. But his conservative ideological antipathy toward socialism, his exclusion of consideration of property and power relations *except* under dynamic conditions, and his (from the Marxist perspective) overemphasis on entrepreneurship relative to capital accumulation kept even such friendly Marxists as Schumpeter's student, Paul Sweezy, at an intellectual distance. Schumpeter typically fared no better at the hands of institutionalists. Some institutionalist writers have praised Schumpeter for taking "the entire story of capitalist evolution and possible decline" as his province, in contrast to economists such as Veblen and Commons, whose analyses have been framed "within a limited time perspective and with reference chiefly to American conditions."[98] Generally, though, Schumpeter's influence on the course of institutionalism has been mild. His positivist approach to economic science and his disinterest in, indeed distrust of, social reform no doubt help explain this. His name appears only once, for example, in Allan G. Gruchy's comprehensive volumes on the subject, in a footnote reference to Mitchell's cycle theory.[99] Schumpeter's hostility toward Keynes, described earlier, combined with his lack of interest in blending his analysis with Keynesian ideas where the relationship between the two was complementary and where some sort of synthesis might have been feasible, diminished his chances for influencing the direction and development of post-Keynesian thought.[100]

Schumpeter's greatest disappointment must have been the cool reception *Economic Development* received from some of his prominent Austrian and neoclassicist colleagues, notably concerning his theory of interest. In the strictly stationary conditions of the circular flow, Schumpeter argued, interest rates would be zero, because of the assumed absence of systematic time preference for the present over the future (based, in turn, on synchronization of production and consumption) and because opportunities for additional profits through investment in more roundabout methods of production become exhausted when those methods are a matter of routine. In an economy characterized by stable economic growth (but not development), a variant of Schumpeter's argument would permit some investment opportunities yielding a positive rate of profit (and an accompanying, though low, rate of interest) to be adopted as saving increased, even in the absence of innovations. Consequently, the "web of controversy"[101] surrounding criticism of Schumpeter's theory of interest in a stationary economy is often regarded as merely an unfortunate digression from the central themes of his theory of economic development. "Anyone who holds a theory of interest according to which some positive rate would exist in the circular flow is perfectly free to insert this correction into the Schumpeterian System at whatever point he feels it appropriate to do so."[102]

Certainly Schumpeter took special pains to ease the desired transition of his more orthodox colleagues into a new perspective of economic life. The economic theory of the stationary circular flow, he asserted innocently early in *Eco-*

nomic Development, "will simply be improved for its own purposes, by building onto it" [61] in constructing a theory of economic development. Moreover, he continued, his theory of development would not ask such broad, historical questions as "what changes of this [developmental] sort have actually made the modern economic system what it is? nor: what are the conditions of such changes? We only ask, and indeed in the same sense as theory always asks: how do such changes take place, and to what economic phenomena do they give rise" [62]? Later, in his discussion of "interest on capital," he insists, "I am concerned with the truth and not with the originality of my theory. In particular I willingly base it upon that of Böhm-Bawerk as much as possible, however decidedly the latter has declined all communion" [158].

These pains were in vain, however, as is acknowledged by the final phrase in the last sentence of the preceding paragraph. The barbs of Schumpeter's more conventional critics were often exaggerated, misdirected, or based on misunderstanding of his argument. Böhm-Bawerk's long critique of Schumpeter's interest theory,[103] for example, returned to Böhm-Bawerk's familiar contention that a systematic time preference for the present over the future and the greater productivity of roundabout methods of production would ensure a positive rate of interest, even under stationary conditions,[104] thus suggesting that Schumpeter's analysis lacked logical cohesion or at least empirical realism. Schumpeter replied amiably that he actually accepted most of Böhm-Bawerk's analysis of interest. First, the only one of Böhm-Bawerk's famous reasons for expecting a premium upon the present over the future which he rejects, Schumpeter tells us, is the argument that future enjoyments are systematically underestimated, "so far as Böhm-Bawerk asks us to accept it as a cause not itself requiring any explanation" [158]. Second, if Böhm-Bawerk "had kept strictly to his expression *'adoption* of roundabout methods of production' and if he had followed the indication which it contains, this would be an entrepreneurial act—one of the many subordinate cases of my concept of carrying out new combinations. He did not do this; and I believe it can be shown with the help of his own analysis that no net income would flow from the mere repetition of roundabout methods of production which have already been carried out and incorporated in the circular flow" [159].

A second example of critical reception to Schumpeter's interest theory by mainstream economics is that given by Lionel Robbins, a prominent British economist strongly influenced by Austrian perspectives, a few years after publication of the second edition of *Economic Development.* Robbins argued that interest must exist, even in a stationary economy, as a return for the use of capital (produced means of production). If there were no yield on the use of capital, Robbins contended, there would be no reason to refrain from consuming it. Depreciation would be neglected; produced means of production would wear out; and the circular flow could not be maintained. According to Robbins, Schumpeter based his static analysis upon J.B. Clark's formulation in which the supply of capital is "*held* rigid. Then when he comes to argue that there is no interest unless there is dynamic change, ignoring the fact that a wider conception of stationary equilibrium is possible, he is blind to the consideration that if things are free to move, stationariness depends *inter alia* upon the interest payment being at a certain level."[105] A more sympathetic interpretation of Schumpeter's analysis, however, would reverse the argument. That is, Schumpeter does not begin (as J.B. Clark did) by *assuming* constancy of capital. Instead, he *deduces* it from the conditions of his conception of the stationary economy. "When the special assumptions of the static state are held in mind," Doreen Warriner observed in a remarkably perceptive review article, "Professor Robbins's criticism, that if there is no yield to the use of capital, there is no reason to refrain from consuming it, does not affect the argument."[106] These "special assumptions," as noted earlier, include routinization of investment and absence of any systematic time preference for the present over the future. Under these conditions, the same income would yield the same utility at different moments in time. Consequently, an attempt to increase consumption today, by failing to provide for depreciation in one's business, for example, would gain less increase in satisfaction than the marginal loss in utility from reducing consumption tomorrow. Thus, the most economical solution would be to provide for depreciation and maintain capital at the same level.[107]

There is an important element of practical wisdom in the interpretation which regards Schumpeter's debates with Böhm-Bawerk and other critics over the rate of interest in the stationary economy as digressionary from the main argument. Whether interest rates, in a stationary circular flow, are zero or positive but quite low, is a petty issue which today hardly seems worth the ink that was spilled on it.[108] However, Schumpeter's Austrian and neoclassicist contemporaries had good cause to be wary of his argument, though on grounds which they did not clearly articulate. The core of Schumpeter's challenge to economic orthodoxy was quite fundamental. Once Schumpeter had provided his new and very austere conception of a stationary economy as one involving merely processes of *adaptation* to given conditions, his view that interest, profits, money, and business cycles required an expressly dynamic and evolutionary analytical framework followed as an essential corollary. Because capitalism is a dynamic system, as Schumpeter later put it, it cannot be understood with the same theoretical apparatus used for examining the stationary economy. There are, in short, two domains—the stationary and the evolutionary—requiring two different organizing principles. Because the phenomena of the developmental realm "link up so as to form a coherent and self-contained logical whole," Schumpeter argued in 1928, "it is obviously conducive to clearness to bring them out boldly; to relegate to one distinct body of doctrine the concept of equilibrium, the continuous curves and small marginal variations, all of which, in their turn, link up with the circuit flow of economic routine under constant data; and to build alongside of this, and *before* taking account of the full complexity of the 'real' phenomenon—secondary waves, chance occurrences, 'growth' and so on—a theory of capitalist change, assuming in so doing, that noneconomic conditions or data are constant and automatic and gradual change in economic conditions is absent."[109] As Warriner aptly stated, the weakness of orthodox neoclassical economics exposed by Schumpeter's analysis lay, not in its incompleteness, "but in its attempt to force dynamic elements into the static mould."[110] This methodological gauntlet thrown down by Schumpeter—however blunted in *Economic Development* by a "soft sell" evidently designed to encourage the more timid of his contemporaries to follow his lead—was unacceptable to his more orthodox colleagues. In any event, the gauntlet was not picked up. To this day, mainstream economics remains essentially a static analysis of stationary conditions. "Dynamic models" which have supplemented the core static apparatus of economic theory have been mainly "mechanistic" rather than developmental-evolutionary. This appears to be true even in the field of the economics of development, which, like that of the economics of industrial organization, has received special stimulus from Schumpeter's ideas. According to Jeffrey B. Nugent and Pan A. Yotopoulos, the "ruling paradigm of the economics of development rests on the classical-neoclassical view of a world in which change is gradual, marginalist, non-disruptive, equilibrating, and largely painless."[111] One suspects that Schumpeter, with his vision of rapid, large scale, disruptive, disequilibrating, and at times heroic but painful socioeconomic change, would agree.

It is precisely this developmental-evolutionary methodology and perspective which constitutes the primary legacy of *Economic Development* and the major reason for reading the book today. Perceived narrowly, Schumpeter's work gives a creative and imaginative analysis of strategic aspects of innovation and entrepreneurship in the process of transition from competitive capitalism to big-business capitalism. This accomplishment alone should ensure Schumpeter's niche in the intellectual history of the twentieth century. Interpreted more broadly, *Economic Development* challenges contemporary social theory to construct a genuine, historically dynamic, analytical structure for more realistically and fruitfully examining processes of development in various socio-institutional settings, including advanced capitalism, the Communist societies, and the Third World. Schumpeter's conceptualizations of economic leadership and internally-generated processes of revolutionary, qualitative change are pregnant with implications transcending his own particular historical setting and social perspective.

Notes

1. The book appeared in its first German edition in the fall of 1911, with a 1912 publisher's copyright, under the title *Theorie der wirtschaftlichen Entwicklung*. A second German edition, incorporating expository alternations but no significant substantive changes, appeared in 1926. The English translation, by Redvers Opie, made from a third German edition that was merely a reprint of the second edition, was published by Harvard University Press in 1934.
2. See Gottfried Haberler's discussion of Schumpeter's biographical commentary on his teacher Böhm-Bawerk ("Das wissenschaftliche Lebenswerk Eugen von Böhm-Bawerks," in *Zeitschrift für Volkswirtschaft*, Vienna, 1914, pp. 454–528), in "Joseph Alois Schumpeter, 1883–1950," *Quarterly Journal of Economics*, August 1950, reprinted in Seymour E. Harris, ed., *Schumpeter: Social Scientist* (Cambridge: Harvard University Press, 1951), pp. 24–47. The cited phrase appears on p. 28. An abridged English translation of Schumpeter's essay on Böhm-Bawerk appears in Schumpeter's posthumously published *Ten Great Economists from Marx to Keynes*. (New York: Oxford University Press, 1951), pp. 143–90. In the same source, see also Schumpeter's essay on Carl Menger, p. 87.
3. Joseph A. Schumpeter, "John Maynard Keynes, 1883–1946," *American Economic Review*, September 1946. Reprinted in Seymour E. Harris,

ed., *The New Economics: Keynes' Influence on Theory and Public Policy* (New York: Alfred A. Knopf, 1952), pp. 73–101. The section cited appears on p. 80.

4. Arthur Spiethoff, "Josef Schumpeter, In Memoriam," *Kyklos*, Vol. 3, 1949, p. 290.

5. Schumpeter, *Das Wesen und der Hauptinhalt der theoretischen Nationalökonomie*, Leipzig: 1908.

6. *Epochen der Dogmenund Methodengeschicte*, in Outline of Social Economics (Grundriss der Sozialökonomik), division I, Tubingen, 1914.

7. Spiethoff, "Josef Schumpeter, In Memoriam," p. 291.

8. Arthur Smithies, "Memorial: Joseph Alois Schumpeter, 1883–1950," *American Economic Review*, 1950. Reprinted in Seymour E. Harris, ed., *Schumpeter: Social Scientist*, pp. 11–23.

9. Haberler, "Das wissenschaftliche Lebenswerk," p. 27.

10. Stanley W. Jevons, *Theory of Political Economy* (New York: Kelley and Millman, 1957) [1871]. Carl Menger, *Principles of Economics*. Translated by James Dingwall and Bert F. Hoselitz (Glencoe, Ill.: The Free Press, 1950) [1871]. Leon Walras, *Elements of Pure Economics*. Translated by William Jaffé (Homewood, Ill.: Richard D. Irwin, Inc., 1954) [1874].

11. G.L.S. Shackle, *The Years of High Theory: Invention and Tradition in Economic Theory, 1926–1929* (London: Cambridge University Press, 1967).

12. Piero Sraffa, "The Laws of Returns under Competitive Conditions," *Economic Journal*, Vol. 36, December 1926, pp. 535–50.

13. Joan Robinson, *The Economics of Imperfect Competition* (London: Macmillan, 1961) [1933]. Edward H. Chamberlin, *The Theory of Monopolistic Competition: A Re-orientation of the Theory of Value*, 8th ed. (Cambridge: Harvard University Press, 1962) [1933].

14. John R. Hicks, *Value and Capital* (London: Oxford University Press, 1939).

15. John R. Commons, *Legal Foundations of Capitalism* (New York: Macmillan, 1934); *Institutional Economics: Its Place in Political Economy* (New York: Macmillan, 1934.

16. John M. Keynes, *A Treatise on Money* (New York: Harcourt Brace, 1930); *The General Theory of Employment, Interest, and Money* (New York: Harcourt Brace, 1936).

17. *Business Cycles: A Theoretical, Historical and Statistical Analysis of the Capitalist Process* (New York: McGraw-Hill, 1939).

18. *Capitalism, Socialism, and Democracy* (New York: Harper and Row, 1950) [1942].

19. See *Essays of J.A. Schumpeter*, Richard V. Clemence, ed. (Cambridge: Addison-Wesley Press, 1951).

20. All page numbers in parentheses refer to this Transaction edition of *Economic Development*.

21. Schumpeter distinguished between "static" and "stationary" in the preface to the Japanese edition of *Economic Development*. "A static theory is simply a statement of the conditions of equilibrium and of the

way in which equilibrium tends to re-establish itself after every small disturbance. Such a theory can be useful in the investigation of any kind of reality, however disequilibrated it may be. A stationary process, however, is a process which *actually* does not change of its own initiative, but merely reproduces constant rates of real income as it flows along in time. If it changes at all, it does so under the influence of events which are external to itself, such as natural catastrophes, wars and so on." Cited in Clemence, ed., *Essays of J.A. Schumpeter*, p. 159.

22. Paul Sweezy summarizes this point well in his essay on Schumpeter: "Everyone has equal access to 'capital.'" Under these circumstances, clearly, "no surpluses can accrue to employers of labor; for if they did, the laborers would themselves turn employers and compete the surplus away," Paul M. Sweezy, *The Present as History* (New York: Monthly Review Press, 1953), p. 277.

23. Several of Schumpeter's early German works show a strong influence of Clark's ideas, an influence continuing in *Economic Development*. Notable among these are "Professor Clark's Theory of Distribution" ("Professor Clark's Verteilungstheorie," 1906) and "Recent Economic Theory in the United States" ("Die neuere Wirtschaftstheorie in den Vereinigten Staaten," *Schmollers Jahrbuch*, 1910).

24. Schumpeter expressed his strong intellectual debt to Walras in his preface to the Japanese edition of *Economic Development*, in 1937: "To Walras we owe a concept of the economic system and a theoretical apparatus which for the first time in the history of our science effectively embraced the pure logic of the interdependence between economic quantities." Cited in Clemence, ed., *Essays of J.A. Schumpeter*, p. 159. In the same source, Schumpeter stated that "as an economist," he owed more to "the Walrasian conception and the Walrasian technique . . . than to any other influence." Four years later, in an essay on Alfred Marshall, he called Walras "the greatest of all theorists." Schumpeter, "Marshall's *Principles*: A Semi-Centennial Appraisal," *American Economic Review*, June 1941, p. 239.

25. Under stationary equilibrium conditions, Schumpeter argues, in a manner roughly paralleling Walas before him, "there is no class whose characteristic is that they *possess* produced means of production or consumption goods. . . . If we choose to call the manager or owner of a business 'entrepreneur,' then he would be an entrepreneur *faisant ni bénéfice ni perte*, without special function and without income of a special kind. If the possessors of produced means of production were called 'capitalists,' then they could only be producers, differing in nothing from other producers, and could no more than the others sell their products above the costs given by the total of wages and rents" [45–46].

26. Hayek, "Economics and Knowledge," *Economica*, 1937, pp. 33–54. Reprinted in *Individualism and Economic Order* (Chicago: University of Chicago Press, 1948), pp. 33–56.

27. Pareto, *Manual of Political Economy* [1906], American edition, Ann S. Schwier (New York: Augustus M. Kelley, 1971), pp. 259–63.

28. Schumpeter, *Business Cycles: A Theoretical, Historical, and Statistical Analysis of the Capitalist Process*, Volume 1 (New York: McGraw-Hill, 1939), pp. 68–71.

29. Schumpeter, *Capitalism, Socialism, and Democracy*, p. 62.

30. Consistent with his view of capitalism as an evolutionary process, Schumpeter insisted that it, and the short-run market strategies of business enterprises, must be appraised in terms of a perspective of long-run developmental dynamism. The really "relevant problem," he later noted, is not "how capitalism administers existing structures," but "how it creates and destroys them." Ibid., p. 84.

31. This key methodological point was appreciated by at least some of the early reviewers of *Economic Development*. R.C. McCrea, for example, summarized this matter well: "One's first reaction toward his [Schumpeter's] static analysis is a feeling of vexation. The treatment is so unreal, so like pure mental gymnastic, that it makes the impression of mere logomachy. But Schumpeter himself admits its purely hypothetical quality, nay, seeks to justify it on this ground. . . . In the usual static interpretation there has been too large an implication that the resulting body of principle is a creature of live flesh and bones. Schumpeter, by the rigor of his analysis and the courage with which he has restricted his data, really disembodies this view. The result is . . . virtually a *reductio ad absurdum* of the method of extreme hypothesis as applied to economics." This method, however, McCrea proceeds to observe, is suggestive and is "much more likely to yield fruitful results" precisely because it places the perennial process of change within the domain of an expressly formulated theory of development. McCrea, "Schumpeter's Economic System," *Quarterly Journal of Economics*, May 1913, pp. 527–28.

32. Innovation thus is to be distinguished from "invention" (even where inventor and innovator are the same person), especially when invention is restricted to new ideas of a mechanical or technical nature. Innovation involves the (1) commercial application of (2) any new idea.

33. Schumpeter, *Capitalism, Socialism, and Democracy*, p. 83.

34. "[I]n no sense is his [the entrepreneur's] characteristic motivation of the hedonist kind [i.e.,] capable of being satisfied by the consumption of goods. . . . Hedonistically, . . . the conduct which we usually observe in [entrepreneurs] would be irrational" [92].

35. Böhm-Bawerk, *The Positive Theory of Capital* [1889]. William Smart, trans. (New York: G.E. Stechert, 1891), p. 20.

36. "It should, therefore, be clearly understood that every time the production function itself undergoes a change, we have a case of technical progress brought about by science and that every time the coefficients on production made up of land-services decrease while those of capital-services increase without any change in the production function, we have a case of economic progress resulting from saving." Leon

Walras, *Elements of Pure Economics* [1874]. William Jaffé, trans. (London: Allen and Unwin, 1954), p. 386.

37. Mohd. Shabbir Khan, *Schumpeter's Theory of Capitalist Development* (Delhi: Muslim University, 1957), pp. 54-55.

38. In Clemence, ed., *Essays of J.A. Schumpeter*, p. 159.

39. Ibid., p. 160.

40. In "competitive capitalism," Schumpeter observed shortly after publication of the second edition of *Economic Development*, innovation is "typically embodied in the foundation of new firms [and] the rise of industrial families. . . . All this is different in 'trustified' capitalism" where innovation occurs "within the big units now existing" and where progress becomes "'automatized,' increasingly impersonal and decreasingly a matter of leadership and individual initiative." Schumpeter, "The Instability of Capitalism," *Economic Journal*, September 1928, pp. 361-86. Reprinted in Clemence, ed., *Essays of J.A. Schumpeter*, quotations from pp. 70-71.

41. R.C. McCrea, for example, an early reviewer of *Economic Development*, tempered his clear admiration for Schumpeter's work by observing that entrepreneurial individuals are the "active agents of economic evolution. Schumpeter thus offers a super-man interpretation of economic progress, in main outline quite analogous to the sociological system of Gabriel Tarde." Cf. McCrea, "Schumpeter's Economic System," p. 526.

42. See Footnote 28. See also the useful one-volume edition of *Business Cycles*, abridged by Rendigs Fels (New York: McGraw-Hill, 1964).

43. Schumpeter, *Business Cycles*, Volume 1, p. 137.

44. Hansen, "Schumpeter's Contribution to Business Cycle Theory," in Harris, ed., *The New Economics*, p. 79. The others, as noted earlier, were Wicksell, Tugan-Baranowsky, Spiethoff, and Aftalion.

45. Ibid.

46. See Footnote 16.

47. Hansen, *Business Cycles and National Income* (New York: W.W. Norton, 1951).

48. Haberler, *Prosperity and Depression* [1937] (New York: Antheneum, 1962).

49. Schumpeter, *Capitalism, Socialism, and Democracy*, p. 85.

50. Richard V. Clemence and Francis S. Doody, *The Schumpeterian System* (Cambridge: Addison-Wesley, 1950), p. 13.

51. Schumpeter, *Business Cycles*, Volume 1, p. 150.

52. Ibid, p. 173.

53. Herbert von Beckerath, "Joseph A. Schumpeter as a Sociologist," in Harris, ed., *Schumpeter: Social Scientist*, p. 112.

54. Veblen, *Theory of Business Enterprise* (New York: Charles Scribner's Sons, 1904) and Commons, *Institutional Economics* [1934] (Madison: University of Wisconsin Press, 1961) are representative writings of this

perspective. See also the present author's review essay, "Institutionalism as an Approach to Political Economy," *Journal of Economic Issues*, March 1978, pp. 91-114.

55. Originally published under the titles "Zur Soziologie der Imperialismus," *Archiv für Sozialwissenschaft und Sozialpolitik* (Tubingen: 1919), Volume 46, pp. 1-39, 275-310; and "Die sozialen Klassen im ethnisch homogenen Milieu," *Archiv für Sozialwisssenschaft und Sozialpolitik* (Tubingen: 1927), Volume 57, pp. 1-67. An English translation of these essays, made by Heinz Norden, is available with an editor's introduction by one of Schumpeter's prominent students, Paul M. Sweezy, contemporary Marxist economist and editor of *Monthly Review*. *Imperialism and Social Classes* (New York: Augustus M. Kelley, 1951).

56. Schumpeter, *History of Economic Analysis* (New York: Oxford University Press, 1954).

57. See, e.g., the present author's "Marx and Schumpeter on Capitalism's Creative Destruction," *Quarterly Journal of Economics*, August 1980, pp. 45-68; and Overton H. Taylor, "Schumpeter and Marx: Imperialism and Social Classes in the Schumpeterian System," *Quarterly Journal of Economics*, November 1951, pp. 525-55.

58. "The Communist Manifesto in Sociology and Economics," *Journal of Political Economy*, June 1949, pp. 199-212; in Earl Hamilton, Albert Rees, and Harry Johnson, *Landmarks in Political Economy*, Volume 2 (Chicago: University of Chicago Press, 1962), pp. 337-58; quotations from p. 345.

59. Schumpeter, *History of Economic Analysis*, pp. 20-21.

60. Schumpeter, *Capitalism, Socialism, and Democracy*, p. 20.

61. Böhm-Bawerk, *Karl Marx and the Close of his System* (London: Unwin, 1898). Böhm-Bawerk was the author of the epigrammatic observation that Marx had a past, a present, but certainly no future.

62. Schumpeter, "John Maynard Keynes: 1883-1946," *American Economic Review*, September 1946. Reprinted in Harris, ed., *The New Economics*, pp. 92-93.

63. In addition to this central analytical and methodological critique, there were no doubt important ideological, temperamental, and personal factors which affected Schumpeter's attitude toward Keynes. Ideologically, Keynes is described by Schumpeter as having "smashed . . . into dust . . . the last pillar of the bourgeois argument" by his analysis of aggregate demand and critique of excessive saving, caused fundamentally by an unequal distribution of income. Ibid., p. 99. Temperamentally, Keynes was preeminently interested in public policy, concerned with short-run problems of the day, and disposed to construct theoretical analyses in the light of immediate problems and prospective policy solutions. Schumpeter, by contrast, especially after his return to academic life in 1926, was a sort of analytical esthete, interested in theoretical analysis in its own right, and inclined to focus on the longer-run consequences of changes in policies and institutions.

Personally, Schumpter was deeply disappointed by the fact that the publication of Keynes's *Treatise on Money*, in 1930, anticipated "all the essential ideas" of a volume on "Money and Currency" which Scumpeter was in the process of completing at about the same time, thus forcing Schumpeter to abandon publication of the manuscript and robbing him "of the fruits of many years' labor." Erich Schneider, *Joseph A. Schumpter: Life and Work of a Great Social Scientist*, W.E. Kuhn, trans. (Lincoln: Bureau of Business Research, 1975), pp. 33-34.

64. Schumpeter, "John Maynard Keynes: 1883–1946," Harris, ed., *Schumpeter: Social Scientist*, p. 99.
65. Schumpeter, "The Explanation of the Business Cycle," *Economica*, December 1927, pp. 286-311. Reprinted in Clemence, ed., *Essays of J.A. Schumpeter*, pp. 21-46. The citation appears on p. 29.
66. Schumpeter, *Capitalism, Socialism, and Democracy*, p. 64.
67. Ibid.
68. Ibid., p. 28.
69. Ibid., p. 84.
70. Erich Schneider, *Joseph A. Schumpeter: Life and Work of a Great Social Scientist*, W.E. Kuhn, trans. (Lincoln: Bureau of Business Research, 1975), p. 17.
71. McCrea, "Schumpeter's Economic System," p. 529.
72. B.M. Anderson, Jr., "Schumpeter's Dynamic Economics," *Political Science Quarterly*, 1917, p. 600.
73. Howey, in *American Economic Review*, March 1935, pp. 90-91.
74. McCrea, "Schumpeter's Economic System."
75. Clark, in *American Economic Review*, December 1912, p. 873.
76. Naymier, in *Economic Journal*, March 1913, p. 105.
77. Morgenstern, in *American Economic Review*, June 1927, p. 281.
78. Neisser, in *Social Research*, February 1938, p. 397.
79. Hansen, in *Journal of Political Economy*, August 1936, p. 560.
80. Kuznets, "Schumpeter's Business Cycles," *American Economic Review*, June 1940, p. 271.
81. Sweezy, "Professor Schumpeter's Theory of Innovation," *Review of Economic Statistics*, February 1943, p. 93.
82. Smithies, "Memorial: Joseph Alois Schumpeter, 1883-1950," in Harris, ed., *Schumpeter: Social Scientist*, p. 12.
83. Hansen, *Business Cycles and National Income*.
84. Clark, *Competition as a Dynamic Process*, (Washingon: Brookings Institution, 1961). Mason, *Economic Concentration and the Monopoly Problem* (Cambridge: Harvard University Press, 1957).
85. Sweezy, "Professor Schumpeter's Theory of Innovation," p. 96.
86. Sweezy and Baran, *Monopoly Capital* (New York: Monthly Review Press, 1966).
87. Hagen, *On the Theory of Social Change: How Economic Growth Begins* (Homewood, Ill.: The Dorsey Press, 1962). Hagen expresses his debt to Schumpeter pointedly as follows: "Now it is clear beyond any question that technological creativity is responsible for a far greater share

of increase in productivity than is capital formation. This was apparent to the first great modern student of economic growth, Schumpeter" (p. 49). Indeed, Hagen argues, Schumpeter's statement—that innovative redeployment of existing resources, that is, "doing new things with them," completely overshadows the "slow and continuous increase in time of the national supply of productive means and savings . . ." [68]—"is true not merely in some vague qualitative way but also in a definite quantitative sense" (p. 49).

88. Nelson, "A Diffusion Model of International Productivity Differences in Manufacturing Industry," *American Economic Review*, December 1968, pp. 1219-48.
89. Haberler, "Joseph Alois Schumpeter: 1883–1950," in Harris, ed., *Schumpeter: Social Scientist*, p. 45.
90. Ibid., p. 47.
91. Smithies, "Memorial: Joseph Alois Schumpeter, 1883–1950," p. 15. All of Schumpeter's courses, Haberler observes, "suffererd from one defect: by listening to Schumpeter's lectures and studying his reading assignments and suggestions one could have never found out that he himself had ever written anything on these subjects." Cf. p. 39. See also Paul A. Samuelson, "Schumpeter as a Teacher and Economic Theorist," in Harris, ed., *Schumpeter: Social Scientist*, p. 52.
92. Schumpeter, *Ten Great Economists from Marx to Keynes*, p. 149.
93. Ibid., p. 172.
94. Ibid., p. 76.
95. Ibid., p. 88.
96. Ibid., pp. 97, 102-04.
97. Ibid., pp. 287-90.
98. R.A. Gordon, in Joseph Dorfman, et al., *Institutional Economics: Veblen, Commons, and Mitchell Reconsidered* (Berkeley: University of California Press, 1963), p. 146.
99. Allan G. Gruchy, *Contemporary Economic Thought: The Contribution of Neo-Institutional Economics* (Clifton: Augustus M. Kelley, 1972), p. 44; *Modern Economic Thought: The American Contribution* (New York: Prentice-Hall, 1947).
100. On the possibility of synthesizing elements of Keynes's and Schumpeter's theories, see E.G. Bennion, "Unemployment in the Theories of Schumpeter and Keynes," *American Economic Review*, June 1943, pp. 336-47; and Arthur Smithies, "Schumpeter and Keynes," in Harris, ed., *The New Economics*, pp. 136-42.
101. Smithies, "Memorial: Joseph Alois Schumpeter, 1883–1950," p. 12.
102. Clemence and Doody, *The Schumpeterian System*, p. 30.
103. Böhm-Bawerk, "Eine 'dynamische' Theorie des Kapitalizinses," *Zeitschrift fur Volkswirtschaft Sozialpolitik und Verwaltung*, Vol. 22, 1913. This volume also includes a reply by Schumpeter and a rejoinder by Böhm-Bawerk.
104. In *The Positive Theory of Capital*, pp. 252 ff., Böhm-Bawerk had earlier given three reasons for a premium on present over future: (1) differ-

ent conditions of wants and provision of wants between present and future (e.g., anticipation of higher future income by the young); (2) systematic underestimation of the future because of lack of imagination and will and shortness of life; (3) the greater productivity of more roundabout or more time-consuming methods of production.

105. Robbins, "On a Certain Ambiguity in the Conception of Stationary Equilibrium," *Economic Journal*, June 1930, pp. 213-14.

106. Warriner, "Schumpeter and Static Equilibrium," *Economic Journal*, March 1931, p. 41n.

107. Clemence and Doody, *The Schumpeterian System*, pp. 28-29. Paul A. Samuelson, "Dynamics, Statics, and the Stationary State," *Review of Economic Statistics*, February 1943.

108. Schumpeter's complaint about reaction to Menger's ideas roughly parallels his own experience: "Thus the essential things were accepted, but this acceptance was accompanied not by grateful acknowledgment, but instead by formal rejection based on subsidiary issues." *Ten Great Economists from Marx to Keynes*, p. 89.

109. Schumpeter, "The Instability of Capitalism," *Economic Journal*, September 1928, in Clemence, ed., *Essays of J.A. Schumpeter*, p. 69.

110. Warriner, "Schumpeter and Static Equilibrium," p. 49.

111. Jeffrey B. Nugent and Pan A. Yotopoulos, "What Has Orthodox Development Economics Learned from Recent Experience? *World Development*, Vol. 7, 1979, p. 542.

PREFACE TO THE ENGLISH EDITION

SOME of the ideas submitted in this book go back as far as 1907; all of them had been worked out by 1909, when the general framework of this analysis of the purely economic features of capitalistic society took the shape which has remained substantially unaltered ever since. The book was published for the first time, in German, in the fall of 1911. When, after it had been out of print for ten years, I consented, not without some reluctance, to a second edition, I omitted the seventh chapter, rewrote the second and the sixth, and shortened and added here and there. This was in 1926. The third German edition is merely a reprint of the second, from which also the present English version has been made.

I should be passing a very damaging verdict on what I have done and thought since the book first appeared, if I were to say that my failure to make alterations of other than expository consequence was caused by a belief that it is satisfactory in every detail. Although I do consider both the outlines — what might be termed the "vision" — and the results as correct in the main, there are many points on which I now have another opinion. To mention but one, by way of example: when the theory of the business cycle, which the reader finds in the sixth chapter, was first worked out, I took it for granted that there was a single wave-like movement, viz. that discovered by Juglar. I am convinced now that there are at least three such movements, probably more, and that the most important problem which at present faces theorists of the cycle consists precisely in isolating them and in describing the phenomena incident to their interaction. But this element has not been introduced into the later editions. For books, like children, become independent beings when once they leave the parents' home. They lead their own lives, while the authors lead their own also. It will not do to interfere with those who have become strangers to the house. This book has fought its own way, and rightly or wrongly has won its place in the German literature of its time and field. It had seemed to me best to leave it undisturbed as much as possible. I should hardly have thought of an English translation but for the suggestion and encouragement of my eminent friend Professor Taussig.

For similar reasons, I have not followed the example of my great teacher Böhm-Bawerk, who with infinite care took notice of every objection or critique and embodied his own comments in his later editions. It is not any want of respect towards those who did me the honor of careful criticism of my argument that leads me to limit controversy to the minimum. I have to confess, however, that I have never come across an objection on essential points which carried conviction to my mind.

In aim and method, this book is frankly "theoretical." This is no place for a *professio fidei* on method. Perhaps I think somewhat differently now about the relation between "factual" and "theoretical" research than I did in 1911. But my conviction stands that our science cannot, any more than others, dispense with that refined common-sense which we call "theory" and which provides us with the tools for approaching both facts and practical problems. However important may be the bearing of new masses of unanalysed, especially statistical, facts upon our theoretic apparatus — and undoubtedly increasing wealth of factual material must continually suggest new theoretical patterns, and thereby currently and silently improve any existing theoretical structure — at any given stage *some* theoretical knowledge is a prerequisite to dealing with new facts, that is with facts not already embodied in existing theorems. If this knowledge remains rudimentary and subconscious, it may be bad theory but it will not cease to be theory. I have not been able to convince myself, for example, that such questions as the source of interest are either unimportant or uninteresting. They could be made so, at all events, only by the fault of the author. I hope, however, to supply before long the detailed material which is here missing by more "realistic" studies in money and credit, interest, and cycles.

The argument of the book forms one connected whole. This is not due to any preconceived plan. When I began to work on the theories of interest and of the cycle, nearly a quarter of a century ago, I did not suspect that these subjects would link up with each other and prove closely related to entrepreneurs' profits, money, credit, and the like, in precisely the way in which the current of the argument led me. But it soon became clear that all these phenomena — and many secondary ones — were but incidents of a distinct process, and that certain simple principles which would explain them would explain also that process itself. The conclusion suggested itself that this body of theory might usefully be contrasted with the theory of equilibrium, which explicitly or implicitly always has been and still is the centre of traditional theory. I at first used the terms "statics" and "dynamics" for these two structures, but have now (in deference to Professor Frisch) definitively ceased to use them in this sense. They have been replaced by others, which are perhaps clumsy. But I keep to the distinction, having repeatedly found it helpful in my current work. This has proved to be so even beyond the boundaries of economics, in what may be called the theory of cultural evolution, which in important points presents striking analogies with the economic theory of this book. The distinction itself has met with much adverse criticism. But is it really untrue to life or artificial to keep separate the phenomena incidental to running a firm and the phenomena incidental to creating a new one? And has it necessarily anything to do with a "mechanical analogy"? Those who have a taste for delving into the history of terms should rather, if they feel so inclined, speak of a zoological analogy; for the terms static and dynamic were, although in a different sense, introduced into economics by John Stuart Mill. Mill probably had them from Comte, who, in turn, tells us that he borrowed them from the zoologist de Blainville.

My cordial thanks are due to my friend Dr. Redvers Opie, who with unparalleled kindness undertook the arduous task of translating a text which proved very refractory to the operation. We have decided to omit the two appendices to Chapters I and III of the original, and also passages or paragraphs here and there. In some places, the exposition has been modified and a number of pages have been rewritten. As the argument itself has nowhere been altered, I think it superfluous to give a list of the changes.

JOSEPH A. SCHUMPETER

CAMBRIDGE, MASSACHUSETTS
March, 1934

THE THEORY OF
ECONOMIC DEVELOPMENT

CHAPTER I

THE CIRCULAR FLOW OF ECONOMIC LIFE AS CONDITIONED BY GIVEN CIRCUMSTANCES[1]

THE social process is really one indivisible whole. Out of its great stream the classifying hand of the investigator artificially extracts economic facts. The designation of a fact as economic already involves an abstraction, the first of the many forced upon us by the technical conditions of mentally copying reality. A fact is never exclusively or purely economic; other — and often more important — aspects always exist. Nevertheless, we speak of economic facts in science just as in ordinary life, and with the same right; with the same right, too, with which we may write a history of literature even though the literature of a people is inseparably connected with all the other elements of its existence.

Social facts are, at least immediately, results of human conduct, economic facts results of economic conduct. And the latter may be defined as conduct directed towards the acquisition of goods. In this sense we also speak of an economic motive to action, of economic forces in social and economic life, and so forth. However, since we are concerned only with that economic conduct which is directed towards the acquisition of goods through exchange or production, we shall restrict the concept of it to these types of acquisition, while we shall leave that wider compass to the concepts of economic motive and economic force, because we need both of them outside the narrower field within which we shall speak of economic conduct.

The field of economic facts is thus first of all delimited by the concept of economic conduct. Everyone must, at least in part, act economically; everyone must either be an "economic subject" (Wirtschaftssubjekt) or be dependent upon one. As soon as the members of social groups become occupationally specialised, how-

[1] This title is chosen with reference to an expression used by Philippovich. Cf. his Grundriss II. Bd., Introduction.

ever, we can distinguish classes of people, whose chief activity is
economic conduct or business, from other classes in which the
economic aspect of conduct is overshadowed by other aspects.
In this case, economic life is represented by a special group of
people, although all other members of society must also act
economically. The activity of that group may then be said to
constitute economic life, κατ' ἐξοχὴν, and saying this no longer implies an abstraction, in spite of all the relations of economic life
in this sense to other vital manifestations of the people.

As of economic facts in general, so we speak of economic development. The explanation of it is our object here. Before we
turn to our argument, we shall provide ourselves in this chapter
with the necessary principles, and familiarise ourselves with certain conceptual devices, which we shall need hereafter. Besides,
what follows must be provided, so to speak, with cogs to grip the
wheels of received theory. The armor of methodological commentaries I renounce completely. In this connection let it only be
observed that what this chapter offers is indeed part of the main
body of economic theory, but in essentials requires nothing from
the reader that needs special justification to-day. Further, since
only a few of the results of theory are necessary for our purpose,
I have gladly used the proffered opportunity to convey what I
have to say as simply and non-technically as possible. This involves the sacrifice of absolute correctness. I have, however,
decided on such a course wherever the advantages of more correct
formulation lie in points which are of no further importance for us.
In this connection I refer to another book of mine.[1]

When we inquire about the general forms of economic phenomena, about their uniformities, or about a key to understanding
them, we *ipso facto* indicate that we wish at that moment to consider them as something to be investigated, to be sought for, as
the "unknown"; and that we wish to trace them to the relatively
"known," just as any science deals with its object of inquiry.
When we succeed in finding a definite causal relation between two
phenomena, our problem is solved if the one which plays the

---

[1] Das Wesen und der Hauptinhalt der theoretischen Nationalökonomie, henceforth cited as Wesen.

"causal" rôle is non-economic. We have then accomplished what we, as economists, are capable of in the case in question, and we must give place to other disciplines. If, on the other hand, the causal factor is itself economic in nature, we must continue our explanatory efforts until we ground upon a non-economic bottom. This is true for general theory as well as for concrete cases. If I could say, for example, that the phenomenon ground-rent is founded upon differences in the qualities of land, the economic explanation would be completed. If I can trace particular price movements to political regulations of commerce, then I have done what I can as an economic theorist, because political regulations of commerce do not aim immediately at the acquisition of goods through exchange or production, and hence do not fall within our concept of purely economic facts. Always we are concerned with describing the general forms of the causal links that connect economic with non-economic data. Experience teaches the possibility of this. Economic events have their logic, which every practical man knows, and which we have only consciously to formulate with precision. In doing so we shall, for the sake of simplicity, consider an isolated community; the essence of things, which alone is the concern of this book, we can see as well in this as we could in the more complicated case.

Hence we shall outline the leading characteristics of a mental picture of the economic mechanism. And, to that end, we shall primarily think of a commercially organised state, one in which private property, division of labor, and free competition prevail.

If someone who has never seen or heard of such a state were to observe that a farmer produces corn to be consumed as bread in a distant city, he would be impelled to ask how the farmer knew that this consumer wanted bread and just so much. He would assuredly be astonished to learn that the farmer did not know at all where or by whom it would be consumed. Furthermore, he could observe that all the people through whose hands the corn must go on its way to the final consumer knew nothing of the latter, with the possible exception of the ultimate sellers of bread; and even they must in general produce or buy before they know that this particular consumer will acquire it. The farmer could easily answer the question put to him: long experience,[1] in part inherited, has taught him how much to produce for his greatest advantage; experience has taught him to know the extent and intensity of the demand to be reckoned with. To this quantity he adheres, as well as he can, and only gradually alters it under the pressure of circumstances.

The same holds good for other items in the farmer's calculations, whether he reckons as perfectly as a great industrialist or arrives at his decisions half unconsciously and by force of custom. He knows ordinarily, within certain limits, the prices of the things he must buy; he knows how much of his own labor he must expend (whether he values the latter according to purely economic principles, or whether he looks upon labor on his own land with quite different eyes from any other); he knows the method of cultivation — all from long experience. From experience also all the people from whom he buys know the extent and intensity of his demand. Since the circular flow of the economic periods, this most striking of all economic rhythms, goes relatively fast, and since in every economic period essentially the same thing occurs, the mechanism of the exchange economy operates with great precision. Past economic periods govern the activity of the individual — in a case like ours — not only because they have taught him sternly what he has to do, but also for another reason. During every period the farmer must live, either directly upon the physical product of the preceding period or upon what he can obtain with the proceeds of this product. All the preceding periods have, furthermore, entangled him in a net of social and economic connections which he cannot easily shake off. They have bequeathed him definite means and methods of production. All these hold him in iron fetters fast in his tracks. Here a force appears which is of considerable significance for us and which will soon engage us more closely. Yet at this juncture we shall only state that in the following analysis we shall always assume that everyone lives in each economic period on goods produced in the preceding period — which is possible if production

[1] Cf. Wieser, Der natürliche Wert, where this point was worked out and its meaning elucidated for the first time.

extends into the past, or if the produce of a factor of production flows continuously. This is merely a simplification of the exposition.

The case of the farmer may now be generalised and somewhat refined. Let us suppose that everyone sells all his product and, in so far as he himself consumes, is his own customer, since indeed such private consumption is determined by the market price, that is indirectly by the quantity of other goods obtainable by curtailing private consumption of one's own products; and conversely that the quantity of private consumption operates on market price just as if the quantity in question actually appeared on the market. All businessmen are, therefore, in the position of the farmer. They are all at the same time buyers — for the purposes of their production and consumption — and sellers. In this analysis the workers may be similarly conceived, that is their services may be included in the same category with other marketable things. Now since every one of these businessmen, taken by himself, produces his product and finds his buyers on the basis of his experience, just like our farmer, the same must be true for all taken together. Apart from disturbances, which obviously may occur for all sorts of reasons, all products must be disposed of; for they will indeed only be produced with reference to empirically known market possibilities.

Let us drive this home. How much meat the butcher disposes of depends upon how much his customer the tailor will buy and at what price. That depends, however, upon the proceeds from the latter's business, these proceeds again upon the needs and the purchasing power of his customer the shoemaker, whose purchasing power again depends upon the needs and purchasing power of the people for whom he produces; and so forth, until we finally strike someone whose income derives from the sale of his goods to the butcher. This concatenation and mutual dependence of the quantities of which the economic cosmos consists are always visible, in whichever of the possible directions one may choose to move. Wherever one breaks in and wherever one turns from this point, one must always, after perhaps a great but a finite number of steps, return to the starting point. The analysis neither comes to a natural full stop nor stumbles upon a cause, that is an element which does more to determine other elements than it is by them determined.

Our picture will be more complete if we represent the act of consuming otherwise than is customary. Everyone, for instance, considers himself a consumer of bread, but not of land, services, iron, and so forth. If we consider people as consumers of these other things, however, we can see still more clearly the way taken by individual goods in the circular flow.[1] Now it is obvious that every unit of every commodity does not always travel the same road to the same consumer that its predecessor in the process of production travelled in the preceding economic period. But we may suppose that this *does* happen without altering anything essential. We can imagine that, year in and year out, every recurring employment of permanent sources of productive power endeavors to reach the same consumer. The result of the process is in any case the same as if this happened. Hence it follows that somewhere in the economic system a demand is, so to say, ready awaiting every supply, and nowhere in the system are there commodities without complements, that is other commodities in the possession of people who will exchange them under empirically determined conditions for the former goods. It follows, again from the fact that all goods find a market, that the circular flow of economic life is closed, in other words that the sellers of all commodities appear again as buyers in sufficient measure to acquire those goods which will maintain their consumption and their productive equipment in the next economic period at the level so far attained, and vice versa.

The individual household or firm acts, then, according to empirically given data and in an equally empirically determined manner. Obviously this does not mean that no changes can take place in their economic activity. The data may change, and everyone will act accordingly as soon as it is noticed. But everyone will cling as tightly as possible to habitual economic methods and only submit to the pressure of circumstances as it becomes

[1] Cf. A. Marshall (Principles, bk. VI, as well as his address, "The Old Generation of Economists and the New"), for whom this conception plays the same part.

necessary. Thus the economic system will not change capriciously on its own initiative but will be at all times connected with the preceding state of affairs. This may be called Wieser's principle of continuity.[1]

If the economic system really does not change "of itself," we overlook nothing essential to our present purpose if we simply assume that it remains as it is, but we merely express in so doing a fact with ideal precision. And if we depict a downright changeless system, it is true we make an abstraction, but only for the purpose of exhibiting the essence of what actually happens. Provisionally we shall do this. It is not contrary to orthodox theory, but at the most only to the customary exposition which does not clearly express our point.[2]

The same result may be arrived at by another route. The total of all commodities produced and marketed in a community within an economic period may be called the social product. It is unnecessary for our purpose to go more deeply into the meaning of the concept.[3] The social product does not exist as such. It is just as little the consciously aspired-to result of systematic activity as the economic system as such is an "economy" working according to a uniform plan. But it is a useful abstraction. We can imagine that the products of all individuals form a heap somewhere at the end of the economic period, which is then distributed according to certain principles. Since it involves no essential change in the facts, the assumption is so far quite permissible. We can then say that each individual throws a contribution into this great social reservoir, and later receives something from it. To each contribution there corresponds somewhere in the system a claim of another individual; the share of everyone lies ready somewhere. And since all know from experience how much they must con-

[1] Most recently expounded in the work on the problem of the value of money, Schriften des Vereins für Sozialpolitik, Reports of the Session of 1909.

[2] Cf. Wesen, bk. II.

[3] Cf. on this point especially Adam Smith and A. Marshall. The concept is almost as old as economics and, as is well known, has an eventful past which makes it necessary to use it with caution. For connected concepts cf. also: Fisher, Capital and Income; A. Wagner, Grundlegung; and finally, Pigou, Preferential and Protective Tariffs, where great use is made of the concept "National Dividend." Note also his Economics of Welfare.

tribute in order to get what they want, having regard to the condition that each share involves a certain contribution, the circular flow of the system is closed, and all contributions and shares must cancel out, whatever the principle according to which the distribution is made. The assumption is so far made that all the quantities concerned are empirically given.

This picture may be refined, and made to yield more insight into the functioning of the economic system, by means of a well known device. We assume all this experience to be nonexistent, and reconstruct it *ab ovo*,[1] *as if* the same people, still having the same culture, tastes, technical knowledge, and the same initial stocks of consumers' and producers' goods,[2] but unaided by experience, had to find their way towards the goal of the greatest possible economic welfare by conscious and rational effort. We do not thereby imply that people would in practical life be capable of such an effort.[3] We merely want to bring out the *rationale* of economic behavior irrespective of the actual psychology of the households and firms under observation.[4] Neither do we aim at giving a sketch of economic history. Not how the economic process developed historically to the state in which we actually find it, but the working of its mechanism or organism at any given stage of development, is what we want to analyse.

This analysis suggests, elaborates, and uses those conceptual tools with which we are all familiar by now. Economic activity may have *any* motive, even a spiritual one, but its *meaning* is always the satisfaction of wants. Hence the fundamental importance of those concepts and propositions which we derive from the fact of wants, foremost among which is the concept of

---

[1] This method is due to Léon Walras.

[2] As every reader of J. B. Clark knows, it is strictly speaking necessary to consider these stocks, not in their actual shapes — as so many ploughs, pairs of boots, and so on — but as accumulated productive forces which can at any moment and without loss or friction be turned into any specific commodities wanted.

[3] There is, therefore, misunderstanding in the objection so often levelled at pure theory that it assumes the hedonistic motive and perfectly rational conduct to be the only forces actually at work in economic life.

[4] Psychology, to be sure, comes in later on in order to explain actual conduct and its deviations from the rational picture. Our argument in the following chapters turns largely upon one class of such deviations — force of habit and non-hedonistic motives. But this is another matter.

utility and its derivative, marginal utility, or, to use a more modern term, the "coefficient of choice." We go on to state certain theorems about the distribution of resources over the range of possible uses, about complementariness and rivalry among goods, and rationally we deduce ratios of exchange, prices, and the old empirical "law of supply and demand." We finally arrive at a preliminary idea of a system of values and of the conditions of its equilibrium.[1]

Production is, on one side, conditioned by the physical properties of material objects and natural processes. In this respect it can for economic activity, as John Rae[2] has observed, be only a question of observing the outcome of natural processes and making the most of them. How much of the realm of physical fact may be relevant to economics cannot be stated once for all. According to the type of theory one aims at, such things as the law of decreasing (physical) returns may mean much or little in the way of specifically economic results. There is no relation between the importance of a fact to the welfare of mankind and its importance within the explanatory endeavor of economic theory. But we may of course, as the example of Böhm-Bawerk[3] shows, be driven at any moment to introducing new technical facts into our apparatus. Facts of social organisation are not in the same class. Yet they stand on a par with technical facts in that they are outside the domain of economic theory, and mere "data" for it.[4]

The other side of the matter, the side on which we can penetrate much more deeply into the core of production than on its physical and social side, is the concrete purpose of every act of production. The aim which the economic man pursues when he produces, and which explains why there is any production at all, puts its stamp

[1] I may refer here to the whole literature of the marginal utility theory and its successors.

[2] Cf. the edition of his work by Mixter under the title The Sociological Theory of Capital. The powerful penetration and originality of this work may still repay perusal by the modern student.

[3] His law of returns increasing with the length of the period of production seems to me the one successful attempt to introduce the element of time explicitly into the equations of production.

[4] For this, as for other reasons, the sharp distinction drawn by J. S. Mill between production and distribution seems to me to be less than satisfactory.

clearly on the method and volume of production. Obviously, no argument is required to prove that it must be determining for the "what" and the "why" of production within the framework of given means and objective necessities. This aim can only be the creation of useful things, of objects of consumption. In a non-exchange economy it can only be a question of utilities for consumption within the system. Every individual produces in this case directly for consumption, that is to satisfy his needs. And clearly the nature and intensity of the needs for this product are, within the practical possibilities, decisive. The given external conditions and the needs of the individual appear as the two decisive factors for the economic process, which cooperate in determining the result. Production follows needs; it is so to speak pulled after them. But exactly the same holds good *mutatis mutandis* for an exchange economy.

This second "side" of production makes it at the outset an economic problem. It must be distinguished from the purely technological problem of production. There is a contrast between them which we frequently witness in economic life in the personal opposition between the technical and the commercial manager of an enterprise. We often see changes in the productive process recommended on one side and rejected on another; for example, the engineer may recommend a new process which the commercial head rejects with the argument that it will not pay. The engineer and the businessman can both express their point of view thus: that their aim is to run the business suitably and that their judgment derives from the knowledge of this suitability. Apart from misunderstandings, lack of knowledge of facts, and so forth, the difference in judgment can only come from the fact that each has a different kind of appropriateness in view. What the businessman means when he speaks of appropriateness is clear. He means commercial advantage, and we can express his view thus: the resources which the provision of the machine would require could be employed elsewhere with greater advantage. The commercial director means that in a non-exchange economy the satisfaction of wants would not be increased, but on the contrary reduced, by such an alteration in the productive process. If that is true, what meaning can the technologist's standpoint have, what kind of appropriateness has he in mind? If the satisfaction of wants is the only end of all production, then there is indeed no economic sense in having recourse to a measure which impairs it. The business leader is right in not following the engineer, provided his protest is objectively correct. We disregard the half-artistic joy in technically perfecting the productive apparatus. Actually, in practical life we observe that the technical element must submit when it collides with the economic. But that does not argue against its independent existence and significance, and the sound sense in the engineer's standpoint. For, although the economic purpose governs the technical methods as used in practice, there is good sense in making the inner logic of the methods clear without regard to practical barriers. This is best seen in an example. Suppose a steam engine in all its component parts complies with economic appropriateness. In the light of this appropriateness it is made the most of. There would then be no sense in turning it to greater account in practice by heating it more, by letting more experienced men work it, and by improving it, if this would not pay, that is if it could be foreseen that the fuel, cleverer people, improvements, and increase in raw materials would cost more than they would yield. But there is good sense in considering the conditions under which the engine could do more, and how much more, which improvements are possible with present knowledge, and so forth. For then all these measures will be worked out ready for the time when they become advantageous. And it is also useful to be constantly putting the ideal beside the actual so that the possibilities are passed by, not out of ignorance but on well-considered economic grounds. In short, every method of production in use at a given time bows to economic appropriateness. These methods consist of ideas not only of economic but also of physical content. The latter have their problems and a logic of their own, and consistently to think these through — first of all without considering the economic, and finally decisive factor—is the purport of technology; and in so far as the economic element does not decree otherwise, to put them into practical effect is to produce in the technological sense.

Just as in the last resort expediency governs technological as well as economic production, and the distinction between the two lies in the difference in the nature of this expediency, so a somewhat different line of thought shows us first of all a fundamental analogy and then the same distinction. Technologically as well as economically considered, production "creates" nothing in the physical sense. In both cases it can only influence or control things and processes — or "forces." We now need for what follows a concept which embraces this "utilising" and this "influencing." They include many different methods of using, and of behaving towards, goods; all kinds of locational changes, and changes in mechanical, chemical, and other processes. But it is always a question of changing the existing state of the satisfaction of our wants, of changing the reciprocal relations of things and forces, of uniting some and disconnecting others. Technologically as well as economically considered, to produce means to combine the things and forces within our reach. Every method of production signifies some such definite combination. Different methods of production can only be distinguished by the manner of the combination, that is either by the objects combined or by the relation between their quantities. Every concrete act of production embodies for us, is for us, such a combination. This concept may be extended even to transportation and so forth, in short to everything that is production in the widest sense. An enterprise as such and even the productive conditions of the whole economic system we shall also regard as "combinations." This concept plays a considerable part in our analysis.

But the economic and the technological combinations, the former concerned with existing needs and means, the latter with the basic idea of the methods, do not coincide. The objective of technological production is indeed determined by the economic system; technology only develops productive methods for goods demanded. Economic reality does not necessarily carry out the methods to their logical conclusion and with technological completeness, but subordinates the execution to economic points of view. The technological ideal, which takes no account of economic conditions, is modified. Economic logic prevails over the technological. And in consequence we see all around us in real life faulty ropes instead of steel hawsers, defective draught animals instead of show breeds, the most primitive hand labor instead of perfect machines, a clumsy money economy instead of a cheque circulation, and so forth. The economic best and the technologically perfect need not, yet very often do, diverge, not only because of ignorance and indolence but because methods which are technologically inferior may still best fit the given economic conditions.

"Production coefficients" represent the quantitative relation of production goods in a unit of product, and are therefore an essential characteristic of the combination. At this point the economic element is sharply contrasted with the technological. The economic point of view here will not only decide between two different methods of production, but even within any given method will operate upon the coefficients, since the individual means of production can to a certain extent be substituted for one another, that is deficiencies in one can be compensated for by increases in another without changing the method of production, for example a decrease in steam power by an increase in hand labor and vice versa.[1]

We have characterised the process of production by the concept of combinations of productive forces. The results of these combinations are the products. Now we must define precisely what it is that is to be combined: generally speaking, all possible kinds of objects and "forces." In part they consist of products again, and only in part of objects offered by nature. Also many "natural forces" in the physical sense will assume the character of products for us, as for example in the case of electric current. They comprise partly material, partly immaterial things. Furthermore, it is frequently a matter of interpretation whether one conceives a good as product or as means. Labor, for example, is capable of being regarded as the product of goods consumed by the worker or as an original means of production. We decided for the latter alternative: for us labor is not a product. Frequently

---

[1] These "variations" are very clearly and neatly expounded by Carver, The Distribution of Wealth.

the classification of a good in one or another category depends upon the standpoint of the individual, so that the same good may be consumption good for one person and means of production for another. Likewise the character of a given good may frequently depend upon the use to which it is put. Theoretical literature, especially in earlier times, is full of the discussion of these things. We shall content ourselves with this reference. The following, however, is a more important matter.

It is usual to classify goods in "orders," according to their distance from the final act of consumption.[1] Consumption goods are of the first order, goods from combinations of which consumption goods immediately originate are of the second order, and so on, in continually higher or more remote orders. It must not be forgotten that only goods ready for consumption in the hands of consumers fall in the first order and that bread at the baker's, for example, is strictly speaking only brought into the first order by combining it with the labor of the errand-boy. Goods of lower order, if not immediately the gifts of nature, always originate in a combination of goods of higher order. Although the scheme could be constructed otherwise, it is best for our purposes to rank a good in the highest of the orders in which it ever appears. Accordingly labor is, for example, a good of the highest order, because labor enters at the very beginning of all production, although it is also to be found at all other stages. In successive productive processes or combinations each good matures into a consumption good through the addition of other goods belonging to a greater or lesser number of orders; with the help of such additions it makes its way to the consumer just as a stream, helped by inflowing rivulets of water, breaks its way through the rock ever more deeply into the earth.

The fact must now be taken account of that when we look at the orders from below upwards the goods become increasingly amorphous; more and more they lose that characteristic form, those precise qualities, which predestinate them for one use and exclude them from others. The higher up we go in the orders of goods, the more they lose their specialisation, their efficacy for a particular

[1] Cf. K. Menger's Grundsätze and Böhm-Bawerk's Positive Theorie des Kapitals.

purpose; and the wider their potential uses, the more general their meaning. We meet continually fewer distinguishable kinds of goods, and individual categories become correspondingly more embracing, as when we ascend in a system of logical concepts we come to continually fewer, ever thinner in content but ever wider in compass. The genealogical tree of goods becomes progressively thinner. This simply means that the further away from consumption goods we choose our standpoint, the more numerous the goods of the first order become which descend from similar goods of higher orders. When any goods are wholly or partially combinations of similar means of production, we say they are related in production. Therefore we can say that the productive relationship of goods increases with their order.

Thus, if we ascend in the hierarchy of goods, we finally come to the ultimate elements in production for our purposes. That these ultimate elements are labor and gifts of nature or "land," the services of labor and of land, requires no further argument.[1] All other goods "consist" of at least one and mostly of both of these. We can resolve all goods into "labor and land" in the sense that we can conceive all goods as bundles of the services of labor and land. On the other hand, consumption goods are a special class characterised by their capacity to be consumed. But the remaining products, that is the "produced means of production," are, on the one hand, only the embodiment of those two original production goods, on the other hand "potential" consumption goods, or better, parts of potential consumption goods. So far we have found no reason, and it will appear later that there is no reason at all, why we should see in them an independent factor of production. We "resolve them into labor and land." We can also resolve the consumption goods, and conversely conceive the original productive factors as potential consumption goods. Both views, however, are applicable only to produced means of production; for they have no separate existence.

---

[1] This was particularly sharply emphasised by O. Effertz. When one reflects how one-sidedly the classical economists emphasised labor, how closely this was connected with some of their results, and that really Böhm-Bawerk alone achieved complete consistency on this point, one must recognise Effertz' emphasis of the matter as actually an important service.

The question now arises, in what relation do the two original productive factors stand to each other? Does either of the two take precedence over the other, or are their rôles essentially different? We cannot answer this from a philosophical, physical, or any other general point of view, but only from the economic. For us it is only a question of how their relation is represented for the purposes of the economic system. The answer, however, which ought to be valid in the realm of economic doctrine cannot be valid generally but only with respect to a particular construction of the theoretical system. Thus the Physiocrats, for example, answered the first question in the affirmative, and indeed favorably to land — in itself perfectly correctly. In so far as they would express by their view nothing more than the fact that labor can create no new physical matter, there is nothing to be objected against it. It is only a question of how fruitful this conception is in the economic field. Agreement with the Physiocrats on this point, for example, does not prevent our withholding our approval from their further arguments. Adam Smith also answered the same question affirmatively, but in favor of labor. This also is not false in itself; it would even be proper to take this conception as a starting point. It gives expression to the fact that the use of land demands no sacrifice in disutility from us, and if anything were to be gained by it we might also appropriate this conception. It is true that Adam Smith clearly thought of productive powers offered by nature as free goods, and attributed the fact that they were not actually so considered in the economic system to their occupation by landowners. Clearly he thought that in a community with no private property in land, labor alone would be a factor in economic calculations. Now this is decidedly incorrect, but his point of departure in itself is not on that account untenable. Most of the classical economists put the labor element in the foreground — above all Ricardo. They could do so, because by means of their theory of rent they eliminated land and the determination of its value. If the theory of rent were tenable, then we could certainly content ourselves with this conception. Even as independent a spirit as Rae contented himself with it, precisely because he accepted that theory of rent. Finally, a third group of writers answered our question in the negative. With these we side. For us, the deciding point is that both original productive factors are equally indispensable in production, and indeed for the same reason and in the same manner.

The second question can again be answered variously, quite independently of the answer to the first. Thus Effertz, for example, assigns an active part to labor and a passive one to land. Why he does so is quite clear. He thinks that labor is the motivating element in production, while land represents the object on which labor manifests itself. In this he is right, but his arrangement gives us no new knowledge. On the technical side, the conception of Effertz is hardly one to be adopted, but this aspect is not decisive for us. We are only concerned with the part played by the two original productive factors in the economic deliberations and dealings of individuals, and in this connection the two show up quite equally. Labor as well as land is "economised." Labor as well as land is valued, is used according to economic principles, and both receive equally economic consideration. And in neither case is there anything else involved. Since nothing else is relevant to our purposes with respect to the original factors of production, we shall put them on terms of equality. In this interpretation we agree with the other marginal utility theorists.

While we have nothing further to say about the productive factor, land, it is advisable for us to examine the other factor, labor, somewhat more closely. Passing over the differences between productive and unproductive labor, between labor used directly and indirectly in production, and, as likewise irrelevant, the distinctions between mental and manual and between skilled and unskilled labor, we must comment on two other distinctions which are significant in so far as we can start from them in order to make an observation which is essential for us. These are the distinctions between directing and directed and between independent and wage labor. What distinguishes directing and directed labor appears at first sight to be very fundamental. There are two main characteristics. In the first place directing labor stands higher in the hierarchy of the productive organism. This direction and supervision of the "executing" labor appears to lift the directing labor out of the class of other labor. While the executing labor is simply on a par with the uses of land and from the economic standpoint has absolutely the same function as these, the directing labor is clearly in a governing position in contrast to both the executing labor and the uses of land. It forms, as it were, a third productive factor. And the other characteristic separating it from directed labor appears to constitute its nature: the directing labor has something creative in that it sets itself its own ends. The distinction between independent and wage labor we can. likewise trace to that between directing and directed labor. Independent labor is something peculiar precisely in so far as it possesses the function of directing labor, while for the rest it differs in no way from wage labor. If, therefore, an independent individual produces on his own account and also does executing work, then he splits, so to say, into two individuals, namely a director and a worker in the ordinary sense.

It is easy to see that the characteristic of being in a higher rank, the function of superintendence in itself, constitutes no essential economic distinction. The mere circumstance that ranks one worker above another in the industrial organisation, in a directing and superintending position, does not make his labor into something distinct. Even if the "leader" in this sense does not move a finger or contribute anything directly to production, he still performs indirect labor in the usual sense, exactly as, say, a watchman. Much more importance seems to attach to the other element, which lies in the decision about the direction, method, and quantity of production. Even if one allows that the above-mentioned higher ranking does not signify much economically — though perhaps a lot sociologically — one will still see an essential distinguishing feature in this function of making decisions.

But we see at once that the necessity of making decisions occurs in any work. No cobbler's apprentice can repair a shoe without making some resolutions and without deciding independently some questions, however small. The "what" and the "how" are taught him; but this does not relieve him of the necessity of a certain independence. When a worker from an electrical firm goes into a house to repair the lighting system, even he must decide something of the what and the how. An agent may even have to take part in decisions relative to prices, the setting of the price of his article within certain limits may be left to him — but he is nevertheless neither "leader" nor necessarily "independent." Now the director or independent owner of a business has certainly most to decide and most resolutions to make. But the what and the why are also taught him. He knows first of all the how: he has learned both the technical production and all the economic data concerned. What there is still to be decided only differs in degree from the decisions of the cobbler's apprentice. And the what is prescribed for him by demand. He sets no particular goal, but given circumstances force him to act in a definite way. Certainly the given data may change, and then it will depend upon his ability how quickly and successfully he reacts to it. But so it is in the carrying out of any work. He acts, not on the basis of the prevailing conditions of things, but much more according to certain symptoms of which he has learned to take heed, especially of the tendencies immediately showing in the demand of his customers. And to these tendencies he yields step by step, so that only elements of minor significance can ordinarily be unknown to him. From this consideration, however, it follows that in so far as individuals in their economic conduct simply draw conclusions from known circumstances — and that indeed is what we are here dealing with and what economics has always dealt with — it is of no significance whether they are directing or directed. The conduct of the former is subject to the same rules as that of the latter, and to establish this regularity, to show that the apparently fortuitous is really strictly determined, is a fundamental task of economic theory.

Under our assumptions, therefore, the means of production and the productive process have in general no real leader, or rather the real leader is the consumer. The people who direct business firms only execute what is prescribed for them by wants or demand and by the given means and methods of production. Individuals have influence only in so far as they are consumers, only in so far as they express a demand. In this sense indeed every individual takes part in the direction of production, not only the one to whom the rôle of director in a business has fallen, but everyone, especially the worker in the narrowest sense. In no other sense is there a personal direction of production. The data which have governed the economic system in the past are familiar, and if they remain unchanged the system will continue in the same way. The changes which the data may undergo are not quite so familiar; but in principle the individual follows them as well as he can. He alters nothing spontaneously; he only alters what the conditions are already altering of their own accord; he removes those discrepancies between the data and his conduct which emerge if the given conditions change and people try to continue operating in the same way. Any individual can indeed act otherwise than our view assumes; but in so far as changes result merely from the pressure of objective necessity, any creative rôle in the economic system is absent. If the individual acts differently, then essentially different phenomena appear, as we shall see. But here we are only concerned with stating the logic inherent in economic facts.

From our assumptions it also follows that the quantity of labor is determined by the given circumstances. Here we append the consideration of a question which was left open earlier, namely the magnitude of the supply of labor existing at any time. How much a given number of men work is obviously not rigorously determined at the outset. If we assume for the moment that the best possibilities of employing the labor of all individuals are known, that there is, therefore, a strictly determined scale of such employments, then at every point on this scale the anticipated utility of every concrete employment of labor is compared with the disutility accompanying the employment. Thousands of voices from everyday life remind us that the work concerning our daily bread is a heavy burden, which one only undergoes because one must, and which one throws off if one can. From this emerges unequivocally the amount of work that a worker will perform. At the beginning of each working-day such a comparison naturally always turns out favorably to the work to be undertaken. The further one progresses, however, in the satisfaction of wants, the more the impulse to work declines and at the same time the more the quantity with which it is compared, namely the disutility of work, increases; so that the comparison becomes continually more unfavorable to the continuation of work, until the moment comes for every worker when increasing utility and increasing disutility of work balance each other. Naturally, the strength of both forces varies according to individuals and according to countries. In these variations there lies a fundamental explanatory factor in the shaping of personal and national history. But the essence of the theoretical principle is undisturbed by them.[1]

The services of labor and of land are therefore simply productive powers. The measurement of the quantity of labor of any quality certainly presents difficulties, but it can be effected, just as there would be no difficulties in principle in setting up some physical measure of the services of land however complicated the matter might be in practice. Then if there were only one factor of production, if for example labor of one quality could produce all goods — which is conceivable by assuming that all gifts of nature are free goods, so that no question of economic conduct with respect to them arises — or if both factors of production worked separately, so that each produced distinct goods for itself alone, such a measurement would be all that the practical man required for his economic plans. For example, if the production of a consumption good of definite value required three units of labor and another of the same value required two, then his conduct would be determined. In reality, however, this is not so. The productive factors practically always operate together. Now if, say, three units of labor and two of land were necessary to produce one good of definite value, but two units of labor and three of land to produce another, which alternative should the producer choose? Obviously a standard is necessary to compare the two combinations; a common denominator is required. We may call this question Petty's problem.[2]

[1] For details cf. Wesen, bks. I and II. Obviously the principle is valid only for a given outcome from effort, that is an unequivocal result, such as real wages per hour.

[2] Petty put this problem incidentally in his work Political Arithmetic, which also contains, as is well known, many other germs of later theoretical analysis.

The solution of it gives us the imputation theory. What the individual wishes to measure is the relative significance of quantities of his means of production. He needs a standard with the help of which to regulate his economic conduct; he needs indexes to which he can conform. In short, he requires a standard of value. But he has such a thing directly only for his consumption goods; for only these immediately satisfy his wants, the intensity of which is the basis of the meaning of his goods to him. For his stock of services of labor and land there is in the first instance no such standard, and likewise none, we may now add, for his produced means of production.

It is clear that these other goods also owe their importance merely to the fact that they likewise serve to satisfy wants. They contribute to the satisfaction of wants because they contribute to the realisation of consumption goods. Therefore they receive their value from the latter; the value of the consumption goods, as it were, radiates back to them. It is "imputed" to them, and on the basis of this imputed value they receive their place in each economic scheme. A finite expression for the total value of the stock of means of production or of one of the two original productive factors will thus not always prove possible, because such total value will very often be infinitely large. However, it is not necessary for the practical man or for theory to know this total value. It is never a question of parting with every possibility of production, that is of existence, but simply of assigning certain quantities of productive means to some end or other. An isolated individual, for example, who could not produce (or live) at all without either of the original productive factors could state no finite expression of value for either. To this extent Mill is quite right [1] when he says that the services of labor and of land are indefinite and incommensurable. But he is wrong when he goes on to say also that in the particular case one can never say what are the shares of "nature" and of labor in a product. Physically, indeed, the two will not allow of separation, but this also is not necessary for the purposes of the economic system. What is necessary for the latter every individual knows well enough, namely,

[1] Principles, ed. Ashley, p. 26.

what increase in satisfaction he owes to any small increment of each means of production. However, we shall not go more closely into the problem of the imputation theory here.[1]

In contrast to use value of consumption goods this value of production goods is "return value" (Ertragswert), or as one might also say, productivity value (Produktivitätswert). To the marginal utility of the former corresponds the marginal productive use (Produktivitätsgrenznutzen) of the latter, or, following the usual term, the marginal productivity; the significance of an individual unit of the services of labor or land is given by the marginal productivity of labor or land, which is therefore to be defined as the value of the least important unit of product so far produced with the help of a unit of a given stock of the services of labor or land. This value indicates the share of every individual service of labor or land in the value of the total social product, and can hence be called in a definite sense the "product" of a service of labor or land. To one not completely at home in the theory of value, these meagre statements will not convey what they ought. I refer the reader to J. B. Clark's Distribution of Wealth, where the theory is accurately stated and its meaning elucidated,[2] and merely remark that this is the only precise meaning of the expression "product of labor" for the purposes of a purely economic treatment. In this sense alone we shall use it here. In this sense also we say that the prices of the services of land and labor in an exchange economy, that is rent and wages, are determined by the marginal productivity of land and labor, and therefore that under free competition landlord and laborer receive the product of their means of production. This theorem, which is hardly a controversial one in modern theory, is merely stated here. It will become clearer in later amplifications.

[1] Cf. K. Menger, Wieser, and Böhm-Bawerk, who first treated the problem. Cf. also Wesen, bk. II, and my Bemerkungen zum Zurechnungsproblem, Zeitschrift für Volksw., Sozialpol. und Verw. (1909). We are not concerned with the more difficult problems which arise out of the theory of marginal productivity, and need not, therefore, refer to its present, and much more correct, form.

[2] Misunderstandings arise especially from an inadequate comprehension of the marginal concept. Cf. on this Edgeworth's article "The Theory of Distribution," in the Quarterly Journal of Economics (1904), particularly his reply to Hobson's arguments against Clark.

The following point is also important for us. In reality, the individual uses this value of productive means with such readiness because the consumption goods into which they ripen are empirically familiar. Since the value of the former is dependent upon that of the latter, the former must change when other consumption goods than hitherto are produced. And because we wish to disregard the existence of this given experience, and to allow it to arise before our eyes, in order to investigate its nature, we must start from the point where the individual is not yet clear about the choice between the existing possibilities of employment. Then he will first of all employ his means of production in the production of those goods which satisfy his most pressing needs, and thereafter proceed to produce for continually less urgently felt needs. Moreover, at every step he will consider what other feelings of want must go unsatisfied in consequence of the employment of production goods for the wants preferred at the moment. Each step may only be taken economically provided that the satisfaction of more intensive wants is not thereby made impossible. So long as the choice is not made, the means of production will have no definite value. To each contemplated possibility of employment there will correspond a particular value of every increment. And then, which of these values will be definitely associated with any increment can only appear after the choice has been made and has stood the test of experience. The fundamental condition that a given want will not be satisfied before more intensive wants have been satisfied leads finally to the result that all goods should be so divided amongst their different possible uses that the marginal utility of each good is equal in all its uses. In this arrangement the individual has then found the arrangement which, under the given conditions and from his standpoint, is the best possible. If he so acts, then he can say that, according to his light, he has made the best of these circumstances. He will strive after this distribution of his goods and will vary every conceived or executed economic plan until it is achieved. If no experience is at hand, then he must feel his way step by step to this distribution. If such experience from earlier economic periods is already available, he will try to traverse the same path. And should the conditions of which this experience is the expression change, then he will submit to the pressure of the new conditions and adapt his conduct and his valuations to them.

In all cases there is a definite method of employing every good, hence a definite satisfaction of wants, and so a utility index for the individual increments of the goods which gives expression to them. This utility index characterises the place of each increment in the individual's economy. If a new possibility of employment arises, it must be considered in the light of this value. However, if we return to the individual "acts of choice" which have been made and which result in this utility index, we find that in every case another and not this definitive utility is decisive. If I have divided a certain good amongst three possibilities of employment, I shall esteem it, when a fourth possibility arises, according to the state of satisfaction realised in the first three. For the division between these three, however, this utility is not determining, because it comes into existence only after the division has been decided on. But there finally emerges for every good a definite utility-scale, which reflects the utilities of all its uses and which gives it a definite marginal utility. For a means of production the same is given, as we have said, through its "product," or, according to Wieser's expression, through its "productive contribution."

Since all production involves a choice between competing possibilities and always means the renunciation of the production of other goods, the total value of the product is never a net gain, but only its surplus over the value of the product which would otherwise have been produced. The value of the latter represents a counter-argument against the chosen product and at the same time measures its strength. Here we meet the element of costs. Costs are a value phenomenon. In the final analysis what the production of a good costs the producer is those consumption goods which could otherwise be acquired with the same means of production, and which in consequence of the choice of production cannot now be produced. Therefore the outlay of means of production involves a sacrifice, in the case of labor just as in the case of other means of production. To be sure, in the case of labor there is also another condition which must be fulfilled, viz., that every expenditure of labor must result in a utility which at least compensates for the disutility attaching to that expenditure, of labor. This, however, in no way alters the fact that within the limits of this condition the individual behaves towards the expenditure of labor exactly as towards the expenditure of other productive resources.

Unsatisfied wants are, therefore, by no means without significance. Their impress is noticeable everywhere, and every productive decision must do battle with them. And the further the producer pushes production in a given direction, the harder this battle becomes; that is the more a particular want is satisfied, the less the intensity of the desire for more in the same line, hence the less the increase in satisfaction to be achieved through further production. Moreover, the sacrifice connected with production in this direction also increases simultaneously. For the means of production for this product must be withdrawn from ever more important categories of wants. The gain in value from the production in one direction becomes therefore continually smaller, and finally it vanishes. When that happens, this particular production comes to an end. Thus we can speak here of a law of decreasing returns in production. This has, however, a completely different meaning from the law of decreasing physical product, of which the validity of our proposition is independent.[1] It is obvious that the economic law of increasing costs would finally operate, even if the physical proposition were not valid and even if its contrary were true. For the value of the investment to be made would eventually rise so much that the gain in utility accruing through production would vanish even if the physical amount of this investment progressively sank. If the latter were the case, obviously the condition of satisfaction of the wants of everyone would be at a higher level, but the essential phenomena would not on that account be different.

The consideration which producers actually give to the element

---

[1] In thus turning away from the law of physical decrease we take a decisive step away from the system of the classical economists. Cf. my essay, "Das Rentenprinzip in der Verteilungslehre," Schmoller's Jahrbuch (1906 and 1907). Further: F. X. Weiss, "Abnehmender Ertrag," in the Handwörterbuch der Staatswissenschaften.

of cost of production is therefore nothing but a way of taking account of other possibilities of employing production goods. This consideration constitutes the brake on every productive employment and a guide which every producer follows. But in practice, custom very soon crystallises it into a short handy expression of which every individual makes use, without forming it anew every time. With it the producer works in practice, adapting it to changing circumstances as the necessity arises; in it all the relations between wants and present means are expressed, in a large measure unconsciously; in it all the conditions of his life and his economic horizon are mirrored.

Costs as an expression of the value of other potential employments of means of production constitute the liability items in the social balance sheet. This is the deepest significance of the cost phenomenon. From this expression the value of producers' goods must be distinguished. For it represents the — *ex hypothesi* — higher total value of the actually created product. But at the margin of production, according to the above, both quantities are equal, because these costs rise to the height of the marginal utility of the product, therefore also of the participating combination of productive means. At this point emerges that relatively best position which is usually called the economic equilibrium,[1] and which, as long as the given data are maintained, tends to repeat itself in every period.

This has a very noteworthy consequence. It follows from it, first of all, that the last increment of every product will be produced without a gain in utility above costs. Correctly understood this is, to be sure, simply self-evident. But further, it follows that in production generally no surplus value above the value of producers' goods can be attained. Production realises only the values foreseen in the economic plan, which previously exist potentially in the values of means of production. Also in this sense, not only in the above-mentioned physical sense, production "creates" no values, that is in the course of the productive process no increase in value occurs. The future satisfaction of wants, before production has done its work, is exactly as dependent upon the posses-

[1] Cf. Wesen, bk. II.

sion of the necessary means of production as it is afterwards upon the possession of the product. The individual will try to avert loss of the former just as energetically as of the latter, and renounce the former only for the same compensation as for the latter.

Now the imputation process must go back to the ultimate elements of production, the services of labor and land. It cannot halt at any produced means of production, for the same argument may be repeated for each of them. Hence, no product can so far show a surplus value over the value of the services of labor and land contained in it. Just as we previously resolved produced means of production into labor and land, so we see now that they are only transitory items in the valuation process.

Hence, in an exchange economy — for the moment we anticipate a little — the prices of all products must, under free competition, be equal to the prices of the services of labor and nature embodied in them. For the same price as is obtained for the product after production must have been obtainable beforehand for the complete set of necessary means of production, because exactly as much depends upon them as upon the product. Each producer must give up his total receipts to those who supplied him with means of production, and in so far as they were again producers of some product or other, they must in their turn pass on their receipts until finally the whole original total price falls to the purveyors of the services of labor and of nature. However, we shall return to this later.

Here we come upon a second concept of cost, that of the exchange economy. The businessman considers as his costs those sums of money which he must pay to other individuals, in order to procure his wares or the means of producing them, that is his expenses of production. We complete his calculation in that we also include in costs the money value of his personal efforts.[1] Then costs are in their essence price totals of the services of labor and of nature. And these price totals must always equal the re-

---

[1] Personal labor services are, so to speak, "virtual expenses," as Seager appropriately said; cf. his Introduction to Economics, p. 55. Every businessman who calculates at all correctly now includes the rent of his own land in his expenses.

ceipts obtained for the products. To this extent, therefore, production must flow on essentially profitless. That the economic system in its most perfect condition should operate without profit is a paradox. If we remember the meaning of our statements, the paradox vanishes, at least in part. Of course our assertion does not mean that if it is perfectly balanced the economic system produces without result, but only that the results flow entirely to the original productive factors. As value is a symptom of our poverty, so profit is a symptom of imperfection. However, the paradox remains in part. It seems obvious that producers do as a rule receive more than wages for their labor and rent for the land they may possess. Will there not be a general rate of net profit in the sense of a surplus above costs? Competition may wash away the particular surplus profit of an industry, but it could not destroy profits common to all branches of production. But let it be assumed that producers make such a profit. Then they must value correspondingly the means of production to which they owe it. Now these are either original means of production, viz. personal efforts or natural agents, in which case we are where we were before; or else they are produced means of production, in which case these must be correspondingly more highly prized, that is the services of labor and land embodied in them must be more highly prized than other such services. That, however, is impossible, since laborers and landlords can compete very effectively with these quantities of labor and land which were previously invested. Consequently, net profit cannot exist, because the value and price of the original productive services will always absorb the value and price of the product, even if the productive process is parcelled out among ever so many independent firms. I do not want to tire the reader too much, and have put in a later place further analysis which properly belongs here.[1]

This is not so opposed even to classical doctrine as it may seem to some readers. The cost theory of value and especially the Ricardian labor theory very strongly suggest the same conclusion, and some doctrinal tendencies such as the tendency to label all kinds of revenue, sometimes even interest, as wages are ex-

[1] Cf. Chapter IV, and especially Chapter V.

plained by it. If in classical times it was not expressly stated,[1] it is first because the older economists were not very rigorous in recognising the consequences of their own principles, and secondly because our conclusion appears too blatantly to contradict the facts. Böhm-Bawerk was indeed the first who expressly said that the whole value of the product must in principle be divided between labor and land, if the process of production is to proceed with ideal perfection. This, of course, requires that the whole economic system be accurately adapted to the production undertaken, and that all values be appropriately adjusted to the data; that all economic schemes work harmoniously together and that nothing disturb their execution. Two circumstances, however, so Böhm-Bawerk proceeds, disturb the equilibrium between the values of the product and of the means of production again and again. The first is known under the name of friction. For a thousand reasons the economic organism does not function quite promptly. Error, mishap, indolence, and so forth become, in the well known manner, a continual source of loss, but also of profit.[2]

Before we pass on to the second circumstance alluded to by Böhm-Bawerk, let us insert here a few words about two elements which are of considerable significance. The first is the element of risk. Two kinds of risk may be distinguished, the risk of the technical failure of production, in which we can include the danger of loss from acts of God, and the risk of commercial failure. In so far as these dangers are foreseen they operate immediately upon economic plans. Businessmen will either include premiums for risk in their cost accounting or they will make outlays to guard against certain dangers, or finally they will take account of — and equalise — the differences in risk between the branches of production by simply avoiding the more risky branches until the consequent increase of prices in the latter offers a compensation.[3]

---

[1] Lotz, for example, did this, even if he turned aside from the perception in very weak fashion; see his Handbuch der Staatswissenschaftslehre. Very plain suggestions are to be found in Smith.

[2] Cf. Böhm-Bawerk's exposition, Positive Theorie des Kapitalzinses, 4 ed. pp. 219–316.

[3] Cf. Emery, quoted in my essay, "Die neuere Wirtschaftstheorie in den Vereinigten Staaten," Schmoller's Jahrbuch (1910), and Fisher, Capital and Income.

None of these methods of evening out economic risks, in principle, creates a profit. A producer who takes precautions against risk by whatever measures — the building of dams, insurance of machinery, and so forth — certainly has an advantage in that he protects the fruit of his production, but ordinarily he also has corresponding costs. The risk-premium is no source of gain for the producer — but at the most for an insurance company, which can make an intermediary's profit from it, chiefly by combining many risks — for in the course of time it will be claimed by cases of need arising. And the compensation for greater risk is only apparently a greater return: it has to be multiplied by a probability coefficient, whereby its real value is again reduced — and indeed exactly by the amount of the surplus. Anyone who simply consumes this surplus will atone for it in the course of events. Therefore, there is nothing in the independent rôle often attributed to the element of risk, and in the independent return which is sometimes connected with it. The matter is different, of course, if the risks are not foreseen or at any rate are not taken account of in the economic plan. Then they become on the one hand sources of temporary loss and on the other hand sources of temporary gain.

The chief source of these gains and losses — and this is the second element that I wish to consider here — is spontaneous changes in the data with which the individual is accustomed to reckon. They create new situations, adaptations to which require time. And before that can happen a great many positive or negative discrepancies between cost and receipts occur in the economic system. Adaptation always offers difficulties. The mere knowledge of the changed state of affairs is not attained in most cases with the desirable promptness. To draw conclusions from the knowledge is again a big step, which meets many obstacles in unpreparedness, the lack of means, and so on. But often perfect adaptation relative to the formerly existing products is impossible, and of course especially in the case of durable producers' goods. During the time which must elapse before they are worn out, such changes in conditions unavoidably appear, and this causes one of the peculiarities in the determination of their value which Ricardo considered in Section IV of his first chapter. Returns to them lose all connection with their costs and must be just simply accepted; their appropriate values are altered without the possibility of the corresponding supply being modified. Thus they become, in a certain sense, a special kind of returns and can rise above or fall below the price-total of the services of labor and land contained in them. They appear to the businessman in a light similar to that in which natural agents appear. We call them, with Marshall, quasi-rents.

However, Böhm-Bawerk points to a second circumstance which may alter the result of imputation and may prevent a part of the value of the product from being reflected in the services of labor and nature. This is, as is well known, the lapse of time [1] involved in all production except the instantaneous production of primitive efforts to maintain life. Because of it, the means of production are not merely potential consumption goods, but they are distinguished from the latter by a new essential characteristic, the distance in time which separates them from goods capable of being consumed. The means of production are *future* consumption goods and as such are worth less than consumption goods. Their value does not exhaust the value of the product.

We are here touching upon an exceedingly delicate problem. But as its importance for the argument of this book is limited we shall only ask ourselves one question here. In the normal course of an economic system in which year in and year out the process of production follows the same route and all data remain the same, would there be a systematic undervaluation of means of production as compared with products? This question subdivides into two others: abstracting from objective and personal coefficients of risk, in such an economic system can future satisfactions be systematically and generally valued at less than equal present satisfactions? And in such an economic system, quite apart from the influence of the *passing of time itself* upon valuations, can *what happens* in the course of time establish these differences in value?

---

[1] For the element of time in economic life Böhm-Bawerk is the most important authority. W. S. Jevons and John Rae come next. For a detailed working out of the special element "time-preference," Fisher's Rate of Interest is relevant. Cf. also the treatment of the time element by A. Marshall.

An affirmative answer to the first question sounds plausible enough. Certainly the immediate handing over of some gift is more agreeable than its promise for the future.[1] This, however, is not the question here, but rather the valuation of a regular flow of income. If possible, imagine the following case. Someone enjoys a life-annuity. His wants remain absolutely constant in kind as well as in intensity throughout the rest of his life. The annuity is big and secure enough to relieve him of the necessity of creating funds for special emergencies and for the possibility of loss. He knows himself secure from responsibilities arising towards others and proof against sudden desires. No possibility of investing savings at interest exists — for if we were to grant this we should assume the element of interest beforehand and come dangerously near to circular reasoning. Now will a man in such a position esteem future instalments of his annuity less than those nearer in time? Would he — always abstracting from the personal risk of life — give up future more easily than present instalments? Obviously not, for if he did, that is if he gave up a future instalment for smaller compensation than one nearer in time, he would discover in due course that he had obtained a smaller total satisfaction than he might have done. His conduct would therefore cause him loss; it would be uneconomic. Such a course may nevertheless be taken, just as in other respects offences against the rules of economic reason frequently occur. But it is not an element of these rules themselves that they should occur.[2] Of course most of the exceptions which we meet with in practical life are not "offences," but are to be explained by our assumptions failing to fit the facts. However, where we find quite striking overestimation of present enjoyments, as particularly in the case of children and savages, what we have before us is merely a discrepancy between the economic problem to be solved and the economic out-

---

[1] However, it may be mentioned that even this fact is also not so clear and simple; on the contrary, the reasons for it require analysis, which shall be given briefly below.

[2] My objection is well expressed by the most eminent living exponent of the element of underestimation of future satisfactions, Professor Fisher, when he introduces the term "impatience" for it. Irrational impatience, like error and so on, undoubtedly exists. But it is no element of the normal course of things.

look of the subject: children and primitive men know only instantaneous production. Future wants do not appear smaller to them; they do not see them at all. Therefore they will not stand the test of decisions which require a wider horizon. This is obvious; but ordinarily they have not to make such decisions. He who grasps the double rhythm of wants and means of satisfaction can perhaps in a particular case scorn the conclusion that a one-sided displacement of either means loss of satisfaction, but he cannot reject it in principle.

But what of our second question? Cannot the process of production proceed in ways to which the assumptions of our typical case do not conform? Cannot the continuous flow of goods move sometimes more feebly, sometimes more strongly? But especially, must not the fact that a more fertile method of production demands more time affect the value of present goods, the possession of which alone makes the choice of it possible, and thus constitutes time a factor in the circular flow? The negative answer which we give to this question can easily be misunderstood and will only later acquire its full significance. I do not deny the importance of the element of time in economic life, but only look at it in a different light. The question of the *introduction* of more productive but more time-consuming processes and the question of how the time element affects it are quite distinct problems. We are not now speaking of the *introduction* of new processes, but of the circular flow which consists of given processes already in working order. And here the more fruitful method of production yields its results just as immediately as any other, no matter what the length of its period may be. A method of production will obviously only be called "more fruitful" if it gives more products than the sum of the less fruitful processes which can be executed in the same time by means of the same quantity of productive factors. Given the necessary quantities of labor and natural agents, production by this method will be repeated indefinitely without any exercise of choice, and the stream of products will be continuous. But even if that were not the case, there would be no underestimation of future products. For if the productive process turned out its results in periodic intervals there would still be no waiting, because consumption could adapt itself and run on continuously and at an equal rate per unit of time, so that there would be no motive for underestimating future products.[1] I may quite well prize present goods more highly than future ones if their possession assures me *more* goods for the future. But I shall do this no longer and my present and future valuations must be equalised when I am assured of the richer flow of goods and my conduct has been adapted to it. "More" goods in the future are then no longer dependent upon the possession of present goods. We can also extend the example of our pensioner to this case. Suppose he has received hitherto a thousand dollars a month. Then he is offered, instead, twenty thousand dollars at the end of a year. Now, until the first year's instalment falls due the element of time may make itself felt very unpleasantly. From the time it falls due onwards, however, he will see his position improved, and indeed he will estimate this improvement by the full addition of eight thousand dollars a year, and not by a part of this sum.

A similar argument applies to the element of abstinence,[2] the necessity of waiting, and so forth. And here I refer the reader especially to the exposition of Böhm-Bawerk. For us it is only necessary to formulate our position precisely. This phenomenon also cannot be simply denied out of existence. But it is much more complicated than it has the appearance of being, and it is noteworthy that its nature and its manifestations have as yet found no penetrating analysis. Here also one must distinguish the process of creating a productive apparatus from the process of operating it when once created. Whatever the rôle of abstinence in the former may be — we shall have to speak of this repeatedly, first of all in the discussion of saving in the next chapter — cer-

---

[1] Immediately after the harvest corn is of course cheaper than later. This fact is, however, explicable by storage costs, by the actual existence of interest, and by many other circumstances, all of which change nothing in our principle.

[2] The chief authors are Senior and — on the other side — Böhm-Bawerk in his Geschichte und Kritik der Kapitalzinstheorien; and most recently the American writer McVane. Cf. also the article "Abstinence" in Palgrave's Dictonary and the literature specified there. For the carelessness with which this element is often treated, Cassel, The Nature and Necessity of Interest, is typical. Our position is near to Wieser's Natürlicher Wert, and John B. Clark's Distribution of Wealth. Cf. also Wesen, bk. III.

tainly in the latter the necessity of waiting does not recur every
time a process of production is repeated. One need not "wait"
for the regular returns, since one receives them as a matter of
course just when they are needed. In the normal circular flow one
has not periodically to withstand a temptation to instantaneous
production, because one would *immediately* fare worse by suc-
cumbing. Therefore there can be no question of abstinence in the
sense of non-consumption of the sources of returns, because by
our assumptions there are no other sources of returns than labor
and land. Could not, finally, the element of abstinence play a
part in the normal circular flow, because if it is necessary to the
initial creation of the productive apparatus it has to be paid for
afterwards out of the regular output of production? In the first
place it will appear in the course of our investigation that abstinence plays only a very secondary part in the provision of the
necessary factors; that, speaking concretely, the introduction of
new methods of production requires on the whole no previous
accumulation of goods. And secondly, considering abstinence as
an independent element of cost involves in this case counting the
same item twice, as Böhm-Bawerk has shown.[1] Whatever may be
the nature of waiting, it is certainly not an element of the economic process which we are here considering, because the circular
flow, once established, leaves no gaps between outlay or productive effort and the satisfaction of wants. Both are, following Professor Clark's conclusive expression, automatically synchronised.[2]

The theory of imputation explains the values of all individual
goods. It only remains to be added that the individual values are
not independent, but mutually condition one another. The only
exception to the rule is in the case of a commodity which cannot
be replaced by another, which has only such means of production
as are incapable of substitution and moreover are not employable

---

[1] Fisher's treatment of the same subject (Rate of Interest, pp. 43–51) is vitiated
by his considering time discount as a primary fact the existence of which is almost
self-evident.

[2] Clark, it is true, attributes to capital the merit of bringing about this "syn-
chronisation." As will appear, we do not follow him in this. I emphasise once more:
outlay and return are *automatically* synchronised with one another under the ac-
celerating and retarding influence of profit and loss.

elsewhere. Such instances are imaginable; they can occur, for example, in the case of consumption goods offered immediately by nature; but they are a negligible exception. All other quantities of goods and their values stand in a strict mutual relation. It is expressed by their relation as complements, by the possibility of alternative employment, and by the substitutive relation. Even if two goods have only a single agent of production in common, their values are still connected; for the quantities and hence the values of both goods, depending upon the cooperation of this one agent, will follow the rule of equi-marginal utility with respect to the agent of production common to both. It need hardly be pointed out that the productive relationship resulting from the productive factor labor in particular embraces practically all goods. The determination of the quantity of each good and hence its value is under the influence of the values of all other goods and is completely explicable only by having regard to them. Therefore we can say that the values of individual goods for everyone form a value system, the separate elements of which are mutually dependent.

In this system of values a person's whole economy is expressed, all the relations of his life, his outlook, his method of production, his wants, all his economic combinations. The individual is never equally conscious of all parts of this value system; rather at any moment the greater part of it lies beneath the threshold of consciousness. Also, when he makes decisions concerning his economic conduct he does not pay attention to all the facts given expression to in this value system, but only to certain indices ready at hand. He acts in the ordinary daily round according to general custom and experience, and in every use of a given good he starts from its value, which is given to him by experience. But the structure and nature of this experience are given in the value system. The values, as adjusted to each other, are realised by the individual year in and year out. Now this value system, as already mentioned, exhibits a very noteworthy stability. In every economic period the tendency exists to turn again into the former well-worn tracks, and to realise once more the same values. And even when this constancy is interrupted, some continuity always remains; for even if the external conditions change, it is never a question of doing something completely new, but only of adapting what was previously done to the new conditions. The value system once established and the combinations once given are always the starting point for every new economic period and have so to speak a presumption in their favor.

This stability is indispensable for the economic conduct of individuals. In practice they could not, in by far the majority of the cases, do the mental labor necessary to create this experience anew. We also see, in fact, that the quantity and value of goods in past periods partly determine the quantities and values of goods in the following ones, but this alone does not explain the stability. The salient fact is obviously that these rules of behavior have stood the test of experience and that individuals are of the opinion that on the whole they cannot do better than go on acting according to them. And our analysis of the value system, the geology, as it were, of this mountain of experience, has also shown us that actually these quantities and these values of goods are explicable, given the wants and the horizons of the people, as rational consequences of the given conditions in the surrounding world.

This empirical way of acting in the individual is therefore no accident, but has a rational basis. There is one kind of economic conduct which, under given conditions, establishes the equilibrium between means on hand and wants to be satisfied in the best way possible. The value system that we have described corresponds to a position of economic equilibrium whose constituent parts cannot be altered (if all the data remain the same) without the individual's having the experience that he is worse off than before. In so far, therefore, as it is a question of adapting himself to the conditions and of simply complying with the objective necessities of the economic system without wishing to change them, one and only one particular way of acting commends itself to the individual,[1] and the results of this action will remain the same as long as the given conditions remain the same.

---

[1] This is universally recognised, indeed, only for the cases of free competition and unilateral monopoly in the technical sense of both words. Yet it is sufficient for our

Assuming the reader to be familiar with the general theory of both competitive and monopolistic exchange and prices, we may notice in passing that the ubiquitous possibility of exchange will naturally alter everyone's system of values. The fundamental theorem, according to which units of resources are distributed among possible uses so as to yield equal marginal satisfactions, will of course still hold. In an exchange economy we may express it by saying that for all households prices must be proportional to marginal utilities of consumers' goods and that for all firms prices of producers' goods must be proportional to their marginal productivities. But a new phenomenon presents itself in the fact that products will be estimated by their producers no longer according to any "value-in-use" which they might have for them, but according to the utility of those commodities which producers ultimately acquire for them.[1] Everyone's scale of valuation of his products, and hence everyone's scale of valuation of the means of production he may happen to have, will be composed of the scale of valuation of the goods received in exchange or bought with the income derived from selling the services of those means of production. The most advantageous way of performing these operations will be found by experience, and every commodity or productive service will be valued accordingly.

All the innumerable exchanges which we can observe in an exchange economy in each period constitute in their totality the external form of the circular flow of economic life. The laws of exchange show us how this circular flow is explicable from given conditions, and also teach us why it does not alter so long as these conditions remain the same, and why and how it changes in adapting itself to changes in these conditions. Under the assumption of constant conditions, consumers' and producers' goods of the same

purposes. And it has been shown of late that Cournot was not wrong, after all, in holding that there are important cases of determinateness even in the field of "monopolistic competition."

[1] This is what the Austrians used to call "subjective exchange value." Readers who are familiar with the history of theoretical discussions of the last fifty years will recall how this phenomenon gave rise to an indictment of circular reasoning implied, as many opponents of the Austrian theory held, in any argument which tries to explain prices of producers' goods by "utility." To-day, it would hardly be worth while to go out of our way in order to show why this objection fails.

kind and quantity would be produced and consumed in every successive period because of the fact that in practice people act in accordance with well-tried experience, and that in theory we regard them as acting in accordance with a knowledge of the best combination of present means under the given conditions. But there is also another connection between the successive periods because every period operates with goods which an earlier period prepared for it, and in every period goods are produced for use in the next. We shall now, to simplify the statement, express this fact by assuming that in every period only products which were produced in the previous period are consumed, and that only products which will be consumed in the following period are produced. This dovetailing of the economic periods does not change anything essential, as may easily be seen. According to it, every consumption good requires two economic periods, neither more nor less, for its completion.

Now we shall classify the exchanges which are necessary to carry out this simplified economic process in every period. First, we discard those which are carried out merely in order to hand on again whatever is so received. Theory demonstrates that such exchanges must exist in great numbers in every trading economy, yet these purely technical transactions do not interest us here.[1] Then there is the exchange of the services of labor and land against consumption goods, which occurs in every trading economy. No doubt this class of exchanges embodies the bulk of the economic system's stream of goods and connects its source with its mouth. But laborer and landlord sell their productive services, which only yield their product at the end of each period, for consumption goods which are already on hand. Further, they sell their productive services for consumption goods, even though some of their services go towards the production of producers' goods. In every period those services of labor and land which are not already embodied in means of production to be employed in the period under consideration are exchanged for consumption goods which were completed in the previous period. Whatever in this assertion is contrary to fact serves merely to simplify the ex-

[1] Cf. Wesen, bk. ii.

position and does not affect the principle. It is clear who possess the services of labor and land before this exchange. But who constitute the other party in the transaction? In whose hands, before the exchange, are the consumption goods for paying for the services? The answer is, simply those people who need the services of labor and land in this period, that is those who wish to transform the means of production produced in the previous period into consumption goods by the addition of more services of labor and land or who wish to produce new means of production. Let us assume, for simplicity's sake, that both categories do the same in all periods to be considered, that is keep on producing either consumption goods or production goods — which conforms to the principle of a trading economy with division of labor. Then we can say that those individuals who produced consumption goods in the preceding period give up a part of them in the present period to workers and landlords whose services they require for the production of new consumption goods for the following period. Those individuals who produced production goods in the preceding period and who wish to do likewise in the present will give up these production goods to the producers of consumption goods in return for those consumption goods which they want in order to acquire new productive services.

Therefore workers and landlords always exchange their productive services for present consumption goods only, whether the former are employed directly or only indirectly in the production of consumption goods. There is no necessity for them to exchange their services of labor and land for future goods or for promises of future consumption goods or to apply for any "advances" of present consumption goods. It is simply a matter of exchange, and not of credit transactions. The element of time plays no part. All products are *only* products and nothing more. For the individual firm it is a matter of complete indifference whether it produces means of production or consumption goods. In both cases the product is paid for immediately and at its full value. The individual need not look beyond the current period, even though he always works for the next. He simply follows the dictates of demand, and the mechanism of the economic process sees to it that he also provides for the future at the same time. He is not concerned with what happens further to his products, and he would probably never begin the process of production if he had to follow it to the end. Consumption goods in particular are also only products and nothing more, products to which nothing more happens than their sale to consumers. They form in nobody's hands a "fund" for the maintenance of laborers, and so on; they serve neither directly nor indirectly further productive ends. Hence every question of the accumulation of such stocks disappears. How such a mechanism, which, once adjusted, continually maintains itself, comes into existence is another question. How it develops is a different problem from how it functions.

It follows, again, that everywhere, even in a trading economy, produced means of production are nothing but transitory items. Nowhere do we find a stock of them fulfilling any functions, as it were, in their own right. No claim on the national dividend is made by them beyond wages and rent for the services of labor and land contained in them. No element of net income attaches finally to them. No independent demand issues from them. On the contrary, in each period all the consumption goods on hand will go to the services of labor and land employed in this period; hence all incomes are absorbed under the title of wages or rent of natural agents.[1] Thus we come to the conclusion that the process of exchange between labor and land on the one side and consumption goods on the other side not only supplies the chief direction of the stream of economic life, but that under our assumptions this would be the only one. Labor and land share the whole national dividend, and there are just as many consumption goods on hand as are necessary to satisfy their effective demand, and no more. And this is in accordance with the ultimate pair of data in economics: wants and the means for their satisfaction. It is also a true picture of that part of economic reality of which we have been taking account so far. It was mutilated by theory and from it a great number of fictions and sham problems were arti-

[1] The first fundamental theorem of the theory of distribution lies in this statement.

ficially created — including the problem of what is the "fund" out of which the services of labor and land are remunerated.

The organisation of an exchange economy therefore presents itself to us in the following manner. Individual businesses appear to us now as places of production for the requirements of other people, and the output of the whole production of a nation will in the first place be "distributed" among these units. Within the latter, however, there are no other functions than that of combining the two original factors of production, and this function is performed in every period mechanically as it were, of its own accord, without requiring a personal element distinguishable from superintendence and similar things. Thus, if we suppose that the services of land are in private hands, then abstracting from monopolists there are no people with any claims upon the product except those who perform some kind of labor or place the services of land at the disposal of production. Under these conditions there is no other class of people in the economic system, in particular there is no class whose characteristic is that they *possess* produced means of production or consumption goods. We have already seen that the idea that somewhere there is an accumulated stock of such goods is absolutely false. It is chiefly evoked by the fact that very many produced means of production last through a series of economic periods. However, this is not an essential element, and we alter nothing fundamental if we limit the use of such means of production to one economic period. The idea of a stock of consumption goods has not even this support; on the contrary consumption goods are generally only in the hands of retailers and consumers in the quantity necessary to meet the requirements of the moment. We find a continuous flow of goods and a continuously moving economic process, but we find no stocks which are either constant in their component parts or constantly replaced. It also makes no difference to an individual firm whether it produces consumption or production goods. In both cases it disposes of its products in the same way, receives, under the hypothesis of completely free competition, a payment corresponding to the value of its land or labor services, and nothing else. If we choose to call the manager or owner of a business "entrepreneur," then he would be an *entrepreneur faisant ni bénéfice ni perte*,[1] without special function and without income of a special kind. If the possessors of produced means of production were called "capitalists," then they could only be producers, differing in nothing from other producers, and could no more than the others sell their products above the costs given by the total of wages and rents.

From the standpoint of this interpretation, therefore, we see a stream of goods being continually renewed.[2] Only for a single moment is there anything like a stock of certain individual goods; moreover one can actually speak of "stocks" only in an abstract sense, namely in the sense that goods of a certain kind and quantity always appear through the mechanism of production and exchange at definite places in the economic system. Stocks in this sense are comparable to a river-bed rather than to the water which flows through it. The stream is fed from the continually flowing springs of labor-power and land, and flows in every economic period into the reservoirs which we call income, in order there to be transformed into the satisfaction of wants. We shall not enlarge upon this, but only observe shortly that it involves accepting a definite concept of income, namely Fetter's, and excluding from its scope all those goods which are not regularly consumed. In one sense the circular flow ends at this place. In another sense, however, it does not, for consumption begets the desire to repeat it and this desire again begets economic activity. We shall be pardoned if we have not in this connection spoken of quasi-rent as we ought to have done. More serious at first sight appears to be the absence of any mention of saving. Yet this point will also be explained. In any case, saving would not play a great part in economic systems displaying no change.

The exchange value of every quantity of a commodity for

---

[1] A construction of Walras. It is true, however, that interest exists as an income in his equilibrium system.

[2] Sharply separating "funds" and "flows" and making the separation fruitful constitute one of the merits of the too little appreciated book of S. Newcomb, Principles of Political Economy. In contemporary literature the point is particularly emphasised by Fisher. The circular flow of money is nowhere more clearly described than in Newcomb, p. 316 ff.

every individual depends upon the value of the goods which he can procure and actually intends to procure with it. As long as the latter is undecided, this exchange value will undoubtedly fluctuate according to the possibilities conceived at the time, and likewise it will alter if the individual alters the direction of his demand. Yet, when the best employment in exchange is found for any good, the exchange value remains at one and only one definite height, given constancy in the conditions. Obviously, taken in this sense, the exchange value of any unit of one and the same commodity is different for different individuals, and indeed not only in consequence of the differences, firstly of their tastes, and secondly of their economic situations as a whole, but also thirdly, quite independently of these facts, in consequence of differences in the goods which the individual exchanges.[1] But the relation of the quantities in which any two goods are exchanged in the market, or of their reciprocals, the price of each good, is the same for all individuals rich or poor — as we said before. That the price of every good is connected with the prices of all other goods will only become quite clear if we reduce them all to a common denominator.[2]

Let us now introduce this denominator of price and medium of exchange and let us choose gold for the rôle of "money commodity." While for our purposes we require very little of the familiar theory of exchange and hence could treat it quite briefly, we must go rather further into the theory of money. But here also we shall confine ourselves to those points which will be significant for us later, and we shall consider even them only so far as is necessary for what follows. Therefore we shall leave on one side problems which will not crop up again in this book, for example the problem of bimetallism or of the international value of money. And theories whose merits lie in directions which we shall have no opportunity of following, we shall replace without scruple by simpler or better known ones, provided they will

---

[1] I mean: in consequence of the differences in taste and in the total economic situation, each individual values differently even the same goods which other individuals likewise exchange. But the individuals also exchange different goods.

[2] Cf. Wesen, bk. II.

serve us as well, even if they are in other respects much more incomplete.[1]

Experience shows that every individual values his stock of money. And in the market all these individual value-estimates lead to the establishment of a definite exchange relation between the unit of money and quantities of all other goods, in principle just as we asserted earlier of other goods. From the competition between individuals and between possibilities of employment there issue, under given conditions, as many definite "prices" of money as there are other goods. These prices of money — an expression which is completely defined by the preceding statements and which we shall often use in what follows — are, therefore, like any other price, founded upon individual value-estimates. But upon what do these rest? The question obtrudes itself, because here in the case of money we have not the simple explanation which for any other commodity lies in the satisfaction of wants obtained by the individual from his consumption. We answer the question after Wieser:[2] the use value of the material commodity of course provides the historical foundation upon which money acquires a definite exchange relation to other goods, but its value for every individual and its price on the market may and actually do move from this basis. Of course it is obvious that neither the individual marginal utility nor the price of gold as money can deviate from its individual marginal utility and its market price as a commodity. For if this happened, a continual tendency would exist to remove the difference by coining gold from the arts or by melting down gold coin. This is correct. Only it proves nothing. Because a commodity fetches the same price in two different uses it cannot be concluded that the one use

---

[1] The reader will find the leading features of my ideas on money and its value in "Das Sozialprodukt und die Rechenpfennige," Archiv für Sozialwissenschaft, Bd. 44 (1918). The concept of money employed there is an entirely different one.

[2] Schriften des Vereins für Sozialpolitik. Reports of the Session of 1909. On this see Mises, Theorie des Geldes und der Umlaufsmittel, 2 ed., and earlier, Weiss, "Die moderne Tendenz in der Lehre vom Geldwert," Zeitschrift für Volksw., Sozialpol. und Verw. (1910). To Professor von Mises' book the reader may also be referred in case he should suspect that the above argument implies circular reasoning. Although it does not, the author wishes to state that he would not now consider this way of introducing the element of money to be satisfactory, even within the limits of the purposes of this chapter.

determines the price and that the other simply follows it. On the contrary it is clear that both employments together form the value scale of the good and that its price would be different if one ceased to exist. The money commodity is in this position. It serves two different possibilities of employment, and although the marginal utilities and the prices must certainly be equal in both if the good can move freely from one to the other, yet its value is never explicable from the employment in the arts alone. This becomes especially clear if we imagine that the whole stock of money commodity is coined, which would indeed be possible. Money would even then have value and a price, but the above explanation would obviously break down. The suspension of coinage on the one hand and the prohibition of melting on the other likewise offer us examples from experience of the independent character of the value of money.

Therefore the value of money as money can be completely separated theoretically from the value of the material. To be sure, the latter is the historical source of the former. But in principle we can neglect the value of the material in explaining a concrete instance of the value of money, just as in considering the lower course of a great stream we can neglect the contribution to its volume which comes from its source. We can imagine that individuals receive, in proportion to their possession of goods, or more correctly to the latter expressed in prices, an allotted portion of units of some medium of exchange without use value, for which all goods must be disposed of in each economic period. Then this medium would be valued only as a medium of exchange. Its value *ex hypothesi* can be only an exchange value.[1] Every individual, as we asserted earlier of all goods produced for the market, will value this medium of exchange according to the value of the goods which he can obtain with it. Every individual will therefore value his money differently, and even if each expresses his value estimates of other goods in money, these estimates will have a different significance from individual to individual even if

---

[1] Money will be esteemed for its exchange function. And this is obviously analogous to the function of means of production. If one conceives money simply as "bene istrumentale" (as do many Italians) the matter is clearer.

they are numerically equivalent. In the market, it is true, every good will have only one price in money, and also there can be only one price of money in the market at any moment. All individuals calculate with these prices and meet on common ground at this point. But only superficially, for while equal for all, the prices have a different implication for each; they signify for each different limits to the acquisition of goods.

How is this personal exchange value of money formed, then? At this point we shall link up the theory of money with what we have just said about the flow of the economic process. We see at once that according to our conception, personal exchange value must go right back to producers' goods. We said that producers' goods are transitory items and that they involve no independent formation of value in an exchange economy. We said also that no stream of income flows to those who possess them at any time. Therefore there is no occasion here for the construction of an independent personal exchange value of money. As in the economic process, so in the money calculations of the businessman produced means of production are transitory items under our assumptions. These individuals will not esteem money according to its personal exchange value, since they procure no goods for their own consumption by means of it but simply pass it on. Hence we cannot seek here for the determination of the personal exchange value of money; on the contrary the exchange value which is reflected in these transactions must originate elsewhere. Hence, only the primary stream of goods remains, only the exchange between services of labor and land on the one hand and consumption goods on the other. Solely according to the values of the consumption goods which can be obtained with money does one value one's stock of money. The exchange between money income and real income is therefore the salient point, is the place in the economic process where personal exchange value and hence the price of money is formed. The result is now easy to state: the exchange value of money for everyone depends upon the use value of the consumption goods which he can obtain for his income. The total effective demand in terms of goods in a period serves as the value scale for the units of income available in this economic process. Therefore, under given conditions, there is for every individual an unequivocally determined value scale and definite marginal utility of his stock of money.[1] The absolute magnitude of this stock of money in the economic system is irrelevant. In principle a smaller total performs the same service as a larger. If we assume the existing quantity of money to be constant, then there will be the same demand for money year in and year out, and the same value of money will emerge for every individual. Money will be so distributed in the economic system that a uniform price of money emerges. This is the case when all consumption goods are disposed of and all services of labor and land paid for. The exchange between services of labor and land on the one hand and consumption goods on the other is divided into two parts: the exchange between services of labor and land and money, and that between money and consumption goods. Since the values and prices of money must be equal on the one hand to the values and prices of consumption goods and on the other hand to the values and prices of services of labor and land,[2] it is clear that the essential lines of our picture are not altered by the insertion of intermediate links, that money only performs the function of a technical instrument, but adds nothing new to the phenomena. To employ a customary expression, we can say that money thus far represents only the cloak of economic things and nothing essential is overlooked in abstracting from it.

At first sight money appears as a general order upon different quantities of goods [3] or as we may say as "general purchasing power." Every individual regards money first of all as a means of obtaining goods in general; if he sells his services of labor or land,

[1] With a given technique of the market exchange and given habits of payment. Cf. on this Marshall's Money, Credit and Commerce or Keynes' Tract on Monetary Reform, and also Schlesinger, Theorie der Geld- und Kreditwirtschaft.

[2] We are considering here for simplicity's sake, I repeat, an isolated economic system, since the inclusion of international relations would complicate the exposition without contributing anything essential. Similarly we are considering an economic system in which all individuals reckon perfectly in money and are connected with each other.

[3] This conception is to be found as early as Berkeley. It has never been lost, and J. S. Mill more recently gave it currency. In contemporary German literature it is found chiefly in Bendixen. It contradicts neither the quantity theory, nor the cost of production nor the "balance" theory.

he sells them not for definite goods but, as it were, for goods in general. If one looks more closely, however, things take on a different aspect. For every individual values his money income really according to the goods which he actually obtains with it and not according to goods in general. When he speaks of the value of money, the range of goods he customarily purchases floats more or less plainly before his eyes. If whole classes of buyers were suddenly to change the expenditure of their incomes, then obviously the price of money and also the personal exchange value of money would undoubtedly have to change. Ordinarily, however, this does not happen. In general, a definite plan of expenditure is adhered to as being the best, and it does not change quickly. This is why, in practice, everyone can normally reckon with a constant value and price of money and he need only gradually adjust them to changed conditions. Therefore, one can also say of money what we said earlier of all other goods, namely that for every part of the existing purchasing power there lies ready somewhere in the economic system a demand for it, a supply of goods for it, and that the bulk of the money, just as the bulk of the means of production and consumption goods, goes the same way year in and year out. Here too we can assert that we change nothing essential if we imagine that every individual piece of money travels exactly the same route in every economic period. This relation of real income and money income also determines the changes in the value of money.[1]

We have so far considered money solely as a circulating medium. We have had in view the determination of the value of only those quantities of money which are actually used for the movement of the mass of commodities periodically. Obviously there are also in every economic system, for well known reasons, noncirculating quantities of money, and the determination of their value is not yet explained. For so far we have not learned of any employment of money which necessitates an accumulation beyond the measure that enables the individual to pay for his current purchases. To this point we must return later. We shall not go into it further here, but content ourselves with having ex-

[1] Cf. Wieser, loc. cit.

plained the circulation and determination of the value of those quantities of money which correspond to the chief exchange transactions which we have depicted. In any case, in the normal circular flow, which we have in view here, no holding of important stocks of money for other purposes would be necessary.

We have also neglected another element. Purchasing power is employed not only to carry out the exchange of consumption goods against the services of labor and land, but also to transfer the possession of landed property itself, and furthermore purchasing power itself is transferred. We could easily take account of all these elements, but they have an essentially different significance for us from that of those which we can analyse within the framework of our present argument. We may only briefly point out that within the continually recurring economic process which we have been describing there would be little room for these things. Transfers of purchasing power as such are not necessary elements of this process. It rather flows along as it were of its own accord and in its essence makes no kind of credit transactions necessary. We have already pointed out that no advances are made to laborers and landlords, but that their means of production are simply bought from them. This is not altered by the intervention of money, and an advance payment of money is no more necessary than an advance of consumption goods or means of production. Obviously we need not exclude the case in which individuals obtain purchasing power from others and transfer to them in return a part of their original productive powers, land for example. Such is the case of borrowing for purposes of consumption, to which no special interest attaches. Similarly, as we shall show below, in the case of transfers of labor and land in general, and therefore we can say that money has, in the circular flow, no other rôle than that of facilitating the circulation of commodities.

It may also be added that for a similar reason we have not spoken of credit instruments. Of course not only a part but the whole of the exchange process can be settled by such credit media. It is not uninteresting even to imagine that, instead of actual metal money, only, say, bills of exchange circulate. For example, this teaches us that the assertion about an *original* necessity of money's having a commodity value does not mean that the particular money commodity must actually circulate. For indeed nothing more is necessary to put money in a fixed relation to the values of other goods than that it should be *connected* with something of definite value. The economic process could, therefore, be carried out without the intervention of metal money. Anyone who supplies services of labor and land would receive a bill for a determined amount of monetary units, then buy consumption goods with it, in order to receive again in the next period — if we adhere to our conception of the identity of the routes travelled by money periodically — the same amount of units in the shape of another bill of exchange. Assuming smooth functioning and general acceptability, such a medium of exchange fills the rôle of money perfectly, and because it does, it will be valued by individuals just as metal money, and change hands at the same "prices" expressed in commodities. This is true even if there is never any question of redemption, but simply of a continuous process of claims to legal tender being offset against each other. There will therefore be a demand for this medium of exchange, which will under our assumptions always be met by a corresponding supply. But since we have seen that the price of the unit of metal money simply mirrors the price of consumption goods and hence of production goods, it follows that the price of our hypothetical bills of exchange will do the same. Hence they will be negotiated at their full nominal value, or, in other words, will always be at par. For no motive exists to allow a discount. This argument teaches us in a somewhat more practical manner than an earlier has already done that no interest would appear in the economic system under our assumptions, and that therefore the logic of economic things as here described does not explain the phenomenon of interest.

But apart from this, there is no reason for us to occupy ourselves further in this place with credit means of payment. If credit instruments only replace some already existing metal money, then their use will not of itself produce any new phenomena. If a particular exchange transaction is settled year in and year out by means of such credit instruments, then the latter play the same part as the corresponding amount of metal money would and there is no incentive so far to the sudden introduction of credit into the circular flow, which we should have to consider. For this reason, but also because the element of credit will later become very important for us and because we want very much to contrast this sharply with the function of money described here, we shall assume that our money circulation so far consists only of metal money [1] and indeed, to simplify matters, of gold. In order to keep the two elements separate, we shall in general understand by money only metal money. And we include this concept, together with such credit instruments as do not simply replace previously existing quantities of money, in the concept of means of payment. The problem of whether "credit means of payment" are money will be dealt with later.[2]

Thus, corresponding to the stream of goods there is a stream of money, the direction of which is opposite to that of the stream of goods, and the movements of which, upon the assumption that no increase of gold or any other one-sided change occurs, are only reflexes of the movement of goods. With this we have closed the description of the circular flow. For an exchange economy as a whole there is the same continuity, and under the same assumptions, the same changelessness as for a non-exchange economy — continuity and constancy not only of the processes but also of values. It would indeed be a misrepresentation of the facts to speak of social valuations. Psychic values must live in a consciousness, hence if the word is to have any meaning at all they must be by nature individual. The values with which we have to do here carry meaning not with reference to the point of view of

---

[1] The quantity of "metal money" in such an economic system corresponds not only to a definite price level, but also to a definite rapidity of circulation of money. If all incomes were paid yearly, then obviously a greater amount of money would be required, or all prices must be lower, than if they were paid weekly. We assume this rapidity of circulation to be constant, since we quite agree, within the limits of this argument, with Wieser when he says (loc. cit., p. 522 f.) that changes in the rapidity of circulation, like the quantity of the credit means of payment, are not independent causes of changes in the price level, since they — it is better from our standpoint to say "in so far as they" — are induced by commodity movements. Cf. also Aupetit, Théorie de la monnaie; Del Vecchio, "Teoria della moneta," Giornale degli Economisti (1909).

[2] Cf. on the concept of "purchasing power," amongst others, Davenport, Value and Distribution.

the whole economic system but only to that of the individual. The social fact, here as in all valuations, is in the circumstance that individual values are interrelated and are not independent of each other. The totality of the economic relations constitutes the economic system, just as the totality of social relations constitutes society. If one may not speak of social values, there is yet a social value system, a social system of individual values. These values are interrelated similarly with the values within the individual's economy. They operate upon one another through the exchange relation so that they influence and are influenced by all the values of other individuals.[1] In this social value system all the conditions of life in a country are mirrored, in particular all "combinations" are expressed in it. The sediment of the social value system is the price system. It is a unit in the same sense. To be sure, prices do not express a kind of estimate of the social value of a good. Indeed they are not at all the immediate expression of a definite value, but only the results of processes which work under the pressure of many individual valuations.

[1] There is general interdependence between them. Cf. Wesen, bk. II, for more extensive details on this point.

CHAPTER II

THE FUNDAMENTAL PHENOMENON OF
ECONOMIC DEVELOPMENT

I

THE social process, which rationalises [1] our life and thought, has led us away from the metaphysical treatment of social development and taught us to see the possibility of an empirical treatment; but it has done its work so imperfectly that we must be careful in dealing with the phenomenon itself, still more with the concept in which we comprehend it, and most of all with the word by which we designate the concept and whose associations might lead us astray in all manner of undesirable directions. Closely connected with the metaphysical preconception — more precisely with the ideas which grow out of metaphysical roots and become preconceptions if, neglecting unbridgeable gulfs, we make them do the work of empirical science — even if not itself such a metaphysical preconception, is every search for a "meaning" of history. The same is true of the postulate that a nation, a civilisation, or even the whole of mankind, must show some kind of uniform unilinear development, as even such a matter-of-fact mind as Roscher assumed and as the innumerable philosophers and theorists of history in the long brilliant line from Vico to Lamprecht took and still take for granted. Here, too, belong all kinds of evolutionary thought that centre in Darwin — at least if this means no more than reasoning by analogy — and also the psychological prejudice which consists in seeing more in motives and acts of volition than a reflex of the social process. But the evolutionary idea is now discredited in our field, especially with his-

---

[1] This is used here in Max Weber's sense. As the reader will see, "rational" and "empirical" here mean, if not identical, yet cognate, things. They are equally different from, and opposed to, "metaphysical," which implies going beyond the reach of both "reason" and "facts," beyond the realm, that is, of science. With some it has become a habit to use the word "rational" in much the same sense as we do "metaphysical." Hence some warning against misunderstanding may not be out of place.

torians and ethnologists, for still another reason. To the reproach of unscientific and extra-scientific mysticism that now surrounds the "evolutionary" ideas, is added that of dilettantism. With all the hasty generalisations in which the word "evolution" plays a part, many of us have lost patience.

We must get away from such things. Then two facts still remain: first the fact of historical change, whereby social conditions become historical "individuals" in historical time. These changes constitute neither a circular process nor pendulum movements about a centre. The concept of social development is defined by these two circumstances, together with the other fact: that whenever we do not succeed in adequately explaining a given historical state of things from the preceding one, we do indeed recognise the existence of an unsolved but not insoluble problem. This holds good first of all for the individual case. For example, we understand Germany's internal political history in 1919 as one of the effects of the preceding war. It also holds good, however, for more general problems.

Economic development is so far simply the object of economic history, which in turn is merely a part of universal history, only separated from the rest for purposes of exposition. Because of this fundamental dependence of the economic aspect of things on everything else, it is not possible to explain *economic* change by previous *economic* conditions alone. For the economic state of a people does not emerge simply from the preceding economic conditions, but only from the preceding total situation. The expository and analytical difficulties which arise from this are very much diminished, practically if not in principle, by the facts which form the basis of economic interpretation of history; without being compelled to take a stand for or against this view, we can state that the economic world is relatively autonomous because it takes up such a great part of a nation's life, and forms or conditions a great part of the remainder; wherefore writing economic history by itself is obviously a different thing from writing, say, military history. To this must be added still another fact which facilitates the separate description of any of the divisions of the social process. Every sector of social life is, as it were, inhabited by a distinct set of people. The heteronomous elements generally do not affect the social process in any such sector directly as the bursting of a bomb "affects" all things which happen to be in the room in which it explodes, but only through its data and the conduct of its inhabitants; and even if an event occurs like the one suggested by our metaphor of a bursting bomb, the effects only occur in the particular garb with which those primarily concerned dress them. Therefore, just as describing the effects of the Counter Reformation upon Italian and Spanish painting always remains history of art, so describing the economic process remains economic history even where the true causation is largely non-economic.

The economic sector, again, is open to an endless variety of points of view and treatments, which one can array, for example, according to the breadth of their scope — or we might just as well say according to the degree of generalisation which they imply. From an exposition of the nature of the economic life of the Niederaltaich monastery in the thirteenth century to Sombart's exposition of the development of economic life in western Europe, there runs a continuous, logically uniform thread. Such an exposition as Sombart's is theory, and indeed theory of economic development in the sense in which we intend it for the moment. But it is not economic theory in the sense in which the contents of the first chapter of this book are economic theory, which is what has been understood by "economic theory" since Ricardo's day. Economic theory in the latter sense, it is true, plays a part in a theory like Sombart's, but a wholly subordinate one: namely, where the connection of historical facts is complicated enough to necessitate methods of interpretation which go beyond the analytic powers of the man in the street, the line of thought takes the form offered by that analytical apparatus. However, where it is simply a question of making development or the historical outcome of it intelligible, of working out the elements which characterise a situation or determine an issue, economic theory in the traditional sense contributes next to nothing.[1]

[1] If economists, nevertheless, have always had something to say on this theme, this is only because they did not restrict themselves to economic theory, but — and

We are not concerned here with a theory of development in this sense. No historical evolutionary factors will be indicated — whether individual events like the appearance of American gold

indeed quite superficially as a rule — studied historical sociology or made assumptions about the economic future. Division of labor, the origin of private property in land, increasing control over nature, economic freedom, and legal security — these are the most important elements constituting the "economic sociology" of Adam Smith. They clearly relate to the social framework of the economic course of events, not to any immanent spontaneity of the latter. One can also consider this as Ricardo's theory of development (say in Bücher's sense), which, moreover, exhibits the line of thought which earned the characterisation of "pessimist" for him: namely the "hypothetical prognosis" that in consequence of the progressive increase of population together with the progressive exhaustion of the powers of the soil (which can according to him only temporarily be interrupted by improvements in production) a position of rest would eventually appear — to be distinguished *toto coelo* from the ideal momentary position of rest of the equilibrium of modern theory — in which the economic situation would be characterised by an hypertrophy of rent, which is something totally different from what is understood above by a theory of development, and still more different from what we shall understand by it in this book. Mill worked out the same line of thought more carefully, and also distributed color and tone differently. In essence, however, his Book IV, "Influence of the Progress of Society on Production and Distribution," is just the same thing. Even this title expresses how much "progress" is considered as something non-economic, as something rooted in the data that only "exercises an influence" upon production and distribution. In particular his treatment of improvements in the "arts of production" is strictly "static." Improvement, according to this traditional view, is something which just happens and the effects of which we have to investigate, while we have nothing to say about its occurrence *per se*. What is thereby passed over is the subject matter of this book, or rather the foundation stone of its construction. J. B. Clark (Essentials of Economic Theory), whose merit is in having consciously separated "statics" and "dynamics," saw in the dynamic elements a disturbance of the static equilibrium. This is likewise our view, and also from our standpoint an essential task is to investigate the effect of this disturbance and the new equilibrium which then emerges. But while he confines himself to this and just like Mill sees therein the meaning of dynamics, we shall first of all give a theory of these causes of disturbances in so far as they are more than mere disturbances for us and in so far as it seems to us that essential economic phenomena depend upon their appearance. In particular: two of the causes of disturbance enumerated by him (increase of capital and population) are for us, as for him, merely causes of disturbance, however important as "factors of change" they may be for another kind of problem just indicated in the text. The same is true of a third (changes in the direction of consumers' tastes) which will later be substantiated in the text. But the other two (changes in technique and in productive organisation) require special analysis and evoke something different again from disturbances in the theoretical sense. The non-recognition of this is the most important single reason for what appears unsatisfactory to us in economic theory. From this insignificant-looking source flows, as we shall see, a new conception of the economic process, which overcomes a series of fundamental difficulties and thus justifies the new statement of the problem in the text. This statement of the problem is more nearly parallel to that of Marx. For according to him there is an *internal* economic development and no mere adaptation of economic life to changing data. But my structure covers only a small part of his ground.

production in Europe in the sixteenth century, or "more general" circumstances like changes in the mentality of economic men, in the area of the civilised world, in social organisation, in political constellations, in productive technique, and so forth — nor will their effects be described for individual cases or for groups of cases.[1] On the contrary, the economic theory the nature of which was sufficiently expounded to the reader in the first chapter will simply be improved for its own purposes, by building onto it. If this were also to enable this theory to perform better than hitherto its service to the other kind of theory of development, the fact would still remain that the two methods lie in different planes.

Our problem is as follows. The theory of the first chapter describes economic life from the standpoint of a "circular flow," running on in channels essentially the same year after year — similar to the circulation of the blood in an animal organism. Now this circular flow and its channels do alter in time, and here we abandon the analogy with the circulation of the blood. For although the latter also changes in the course of the growth and decline of the organism, yet it only does so continuously, that is by steps which one can choose smaller than any assignable quantity, however small, and always within the same framework. Economic life experiences such changes too, but it also experiences others which do not appear continuously and which change the framework, the traditional course itself. They cannot be understood by means of any analysis of the circular flow, although they are purely economic and although their explanation is obviously among the tasks of pure theory. Now such changes

---

[1] Therefore one of the most annoying misunderstandings that arose out of the first edition of this book was that this theory of development neglects all historical factors of change except one, namely the individuality of entrepreneurs. If my representation were intended to be as this objection assumes, it would obviously be nonsense. But it is not at all concerned with the concrete factors of change, but with the method by which these work, with the *mechanism of change*. The "entrepreneur" is merely the bearer of the mechanism of change. And I have taken account not of one factor of historical change, but of none. We have still less to do here with the factors which in particular explain the changes in the economic organisation, economic custom, and so on. This is still another problem, and although there are points at which all these methods of treatment collide, it means spoiling the fruit of all if they are not kept apart and if each is not allowed the right to grow by itself.

and the phenomena which appear in their train are the object of our investigation. But we do not ask: what changes of this sort have actually made the modern economic system what it is? nor: what are the conditions of such changes? We only ask, and indeed in the same sense as theory always asks: how do such changes take place, and to what economic phenomena do they give rise?

The same thing may be put somewhat differently. The theory of the first chapter describes economic life from the standpoint of the economic system's tendency towards an equilibrium position, which tendency gives us the means of determining prices and quantities of goods, and may be described as an adaptation to data existing at any time. In contrast to the conditions of the circular flow this does not mean in itself that year after year "the same" things happen; for it only means that we conceive the several processes in the economic system as partial phenomena of the tendency towards an equilibrium position, but not necessarily towards the same one. The position of the ideal state of equilibrium in the economic system, never attained, continually "striven after" (of course not consciously), changes, because the data change. And theory is not weaponless in the face of these changes in data. It is constructed so as to be able to deal with the consequences of such changes; it has special instruments for the purpose (for example the instrument called quasi-rent). If the change occurs in the non-social data (natural conditions) or in non-economic social data (here belong the effects of war, changes in commercial, social, or economic policy), or in consumers' tastes, then to this extent no fundamental overhaul of the theoretical tools seems to be required. These tools only fail — and here this argument joins the preceding — where economic life itself changes its own data by fits and starts. The building of a railway may serve as an example. Continuous changes, which may in time, by continual adaptation through innumerable small steps, make a great department store out of a small retail business, come under the "static" analysis. But "static" analysis is not only unable to predict the consequences of discontinuous changes in the traditional way of doing things; it can neither explain the occurrence of such productive revolutions nor the phenomena which accompany them. It can only investigate the new equilibrium position after the changes have occurred. It is just this occurrence of the "revolutionary" change that is our problem, the problem of economic development in a very narrow and formal sense. The reason why we so state the problem and turn aside from traditional theory lies not so much in the fact that economic changes, especially, if not solely, in the capitalist epoch, have actually occurred thus and not by continuous adaptation, but more in their fruitfulness.[1]

By "development," therefore, we shall understand only such changes in economic life as are not forced upon it from without but arise by its own initiative, from within. Should it turn out that there are no such changes arising in the economic sphere itself, and that the phenomenon that we call economic development is in practice simply founded upon the fact that the data change and that the economy continuously adapts itself to them, then we should say that there is *no* economic development. By this we should mean that economic development is not a phenomenon to be explained economically, but that the economy, in itself without development, is dragged along by the changes in the surrounding world, that the causes and hence the explanation of the development must be sought outside the group of facts which are described by economic theory.

Nor will the mere growth of the economy, as shown by the growth of population and wealth, be designated here as a process of development. For it calls forth no qualitatively new phenomena, but only processes of adaptation of the same kind as the changes in the natural data. Since we wish to direct our attention to other phenomena, we shall regard such increases as changes in data.[2]

---

[1] The problems of capital, credit, entrepreneurial profit, interest on capital, and crises (or business cycles) are the ones in which this fruitfulness will be demonstrated here. Yet it is not thereby exhausted. For the expert theorist I point, for example, to the difficulties which surround the problem of increasing return, the question of multiple points of intersection between supply and demand curves, and the element of time, which even Marshall's analysis has not overcome.

[2] We do this because these changes are small per annum and therefore do not stand in the way of the applicability of the "static" method. Nevertheless, their appearance is frequently a condition of development in our sense. But even though they often make the latter possible, yet they do not create it out of themselves.

Every concrete process of development finally rests upon preceding development. But in order to see the essence of the thing clearly, we shall abstract from this and allow the development to arise out of a position without development. Every process of development creates the prerequisites for the following. Thereby the form of the latter is altered, and things will turn out differently from what they would have been if every concrete phase of development had been compelled first to create its own conditions. However, if we wish to get at the root of the matter, we may not include in the data of our explanation elements of what is to be explained. But if we do not do this, we shall create an apparent discrepancy between fact and theory, which may constitute an important difficulty for the reader.

If I have been more successful than in the first edition in concentrating the exposition upon essentials and in guarding against misunderstandings, then further special explanations of the words "static" and "dynamic," with their innumerable meanings, are not necessary. Development in our sense is a distinct phenomenon, entirely foreign to what may be observed in the circular flow or in the tendency towards equilibrium. It is spontaneous and discontinuous change in the channels of the flow, disturbance of equilibrium, which forever alters and displaces the equilibrium state previously existing. Our theory of development is nothing but a treatment of this phenomenon and the processes incident to it.[1]

---

[1] In the first edition of this book, I called it "dynamics." But it is preferable to avoid this expression here, since it so easily leads us astray because of the associations which attach themselves to its various meanings. Better, then, to say simply what we mean: economic life changes; it changes partly because of changes in the data, to which it tends to adapt itself. But this is not the only kind of economic change; there is another which is not accounted for by influence on the data from without, but which arises from within the system, and this kind of change is the cause of so many important economic phenomena that it seems worth while to build a theory for it, and, in order to do so, to isolate it from all the other factors of change. The author begs to add another more exact definition, which he is in the habit of using: what we are about to consider is that kind of change arising from within the system *which so displaces its equilibrium point that the new one cannot be reached from the old one by infinitesimal steps.* Add successively as many mail coaches as you please, you will never get a railway thereby.

II

These spontaneous and discontinuous changes in the channel of the circular flow and these disturbances of the centre of equilibrium appear in the sphere of industrial and commercial life, not in the sphere of the wants of the consumers of final products. Where spontaneous and discontinuous changes in consumers' tastes appear, it is a question of a sudden change in data with which the businessman must cope, hence possibly a question of a *motive* or an opportunity for other than gradual adaptations of his conduct, but not of such other conduct itself. Therefore this case does not offer any other problems than a change in natural data or require any new method of treatment; wherefore we shall neglect any spontaneity of consumers' needs that may actually exist, and assume tastes as "given." This is made easy for us by the fact that the spontaneity of wants is in general small. To be sure, we must always start from the satisfaction of wants, since they are the end of all production, and the given economic situation at any time must be understood from this aspect. Yet innovations in the economic system do not as a rule take place in such a way that first new wants arise spontaneously in consumers and then the productive apparatus swings round through their pressure. We do not deny the presence of this nexus. It is, however, the producer who as a rule initiates economic change, and consumers are educated by him if necessary; they are, as it were, taught to want new things, or things which differ in some respect or other from those which they have been in the habit of using. Therefore, while it is permissible and even necessary to consider consumers' wants as an independent and indeed the fundamental force in a theory of the circular flow, we must take a different attitude as soon as we analyse *change*.

To produce means to combine materials and forces within our reach (cf. *supra*, Chapter I). To produce other things, or the same things by a different method, means to combine these materials and forces differently. In so far as the "new combination" may in time grow out of the old by continuous adjustment in small steps, there is certainly change, possibly growth, but neither a new phenomenon nor development in our sense. In so far as this is not the case, and the new combinations appear discontinuously, then the phenomenon characterising development emerges. For reasons of expository convenience, henceforth, we shall only mean the latter case when we speak of new combinations of productive means. Development in our sense is then defined by the carrying out of new combinations.

This concept covers the following five cases: (1) The introduction of a new good — that is one with which consumers are not yet familiar — or of a new quality of a good. (2) The introduction of a new method of production, that is one not yet tested by experience in the branch of manufacture concerned, which need by no means be founded upon a discovery scientifically new, and can also exist in a new way of handling a commodity commercially. (3) The opening of a new market, that is a market into which the particular branch of manufacture of the country in question has not previously entered, whether or not this market has existed before. (4) The conquest of a new source of supply of raw materials or half-manufactured goods, again irrespective of whether this source already exists or whether it has first to be created. (5) The carrying out of the new organisation of any industry, like the creation of a monopoly position (for example through trustification) or the breaking up of a monopoly position.

Now two things are essential for the phenomena incident to the carrying out of such new combinations, and for the understanding of the problems involved. In the first place it is not essential to the matter — though it may happen — that the new combinations should be carried out by the same people who control the productive or commercial process which is to be displaced by the new. On the contrary, new combinations are, as a rule, embodied, as it were, in new firms which generally do not arise out of the old ones but start producing beside them; to keep to the example already chosen, in general it is not the owner of stage-coaches who builds railways. This fact not only puts the discontinuity which characterises the process we want to describe in a special light, and creates so to speak still another kind of discontinuity in addition to the one mentioned above, but it also explains important features of the course of events. Especially in a competitive economy, in which new combinations mean the competitive elimination of the old, it explains on the one hand the process by which individuals and families rise and fall economically and socially and which is peculiar to this form of organisation, as well as a whole series of other phenomena of the business cycle, of the mechanism of the formation of private fortunes, and so on. In a non-exchange economy, for example a socialist one, the new combinations would also frequently appear side by side with the old. But the economic consequences of this fact would be absent to some extent, and the social consequences would be wholly absent. And if the competitive economy is broken up by the growth of great combines, as is increasingly the case to-day in all countries, then this must become more and more true of real life, and the carrying out of new combinations must become in ever greater measure the internal concern of one and the same economic body. The difference so made is great enough to serve as the water-shed between two epochs in the social history of capitalism.

We must notice secondly, only partly in connection with this element, that whenever we are concerned with fundamental principles, we must never assume that the carrying out of new combinations takes place by employing means of production which happen to be unused. In practical life, this is very often the case. There are always unemployed workmen, unsold raw materials, unused productive capacity, and so forth. This certainly is a contributory circumstance, a favorable condition and even an incentive to the emergence of new combinations; but great unemployment is only the consequence of non-economic events — as for example the World War — or precisely of the development which we are investigating. In neither of the two cases can its existence play a fundamental rôle in the explanation, and it cannot occur in a well balanced circular flow from which we start. Nor would the normal yearly increment meet the case, as it would be small in the first place, and also because it would normally be absorbed by a corresponding expansion of production within the circular flow, which, if we admit such increments, we must think of as adjusted to this rate of growth.[1] As a rule the new combinations must draw the necessary means of production from some old combinations — and for reasons already mentioned we shall assume that they *always* do so, in order to put in bold relief what we hold to be the essential contour line. The carrying out of new combinations means, therefore, simply the different employment of the economic system's existing supplies of productive means —which might provide a second definition of development in our sense. That rudiment of a pure economic theory of development which is implied in the traditional doctrine of the formation of capital always refers merely to saving and to the investment of the small yearly increase attributable to it. In this it asserts nothing false, but it entirely overlooks much more essential things. The slow and continuous increase in time of the national supply of productive means and of savings is obviously an important factor in explaining the course of economic history through the centuries, but it is completely overshadowed by the fact that development consists primarily in employing existing resources in a different way, in doing new things with them, irrespective of whether those resources increase or not. In the treatment of shorter epochs, moreover, this is even true in a more tangible sense. Different methods of employment, and not saving and increases in the available quantity of labor, have changed the face of the economic world in the last fifty years. The increase of population especially, but also of the sources from which savings can be made, was first made possible in large measure through the different employment of the then existing means.

The next step in our argument is also self-evident: command over means of production is necessary to the carrying out of new combinations. Procuring the means of production is one distinct problem for the established firms which work within the circular flow. For they *have* them already procured or else can procure them currently with the proceeds of previous production as was explained in the first chapter. There is no fundamental gap here

---

[1] On the whole it is much more correct to say that population grows slowly up to the possibilities of any economic environment than that it has any tendency to outgrow it and to become thereby an independent cause of change.

between receipts and disbursements, which, on the contrary, necessarily correspond to one another just as both correspond to the means of production offered and to the products demanded. Once set in motion, this mechanism works automatically. Furthermore, the problem does not exist in a non-exchange economy even if new combinations are carried out in it; for the directing organ, for example a socialist economic ministry, is in a position to direct the productive resources of the society to new uses exactly as it can direct them to their previous employments. The new employment may, under certain circumstances, impose temporary sacrifices, privations, or increased efforts upon the members of the community; it may presuppose the solution of difficult problems, for example the question from which of the old combinations the necessary productive means should be withdrawn; but there is no question of procuring means of production not already at the disposal of the economic ministry. Finally, the problem also does not exist in a competitive economy in the case of the carrying out of new combinations, if those who carry them out have the necessary productive means or can get them in exchange for others which they have or for any other property which they may possess. This is not the privilege of the possession of property *per se*, but only the privilege of the possession of disposable property, that is such as is employable either immediately for carrying out the new combination or in exchange for the necessary goods and services.[1] In the contrary case — and this is the rule as it is the fundamentally interesting case — the possessor of wealth, even if it is the greatest combine, must resort to credit if he wishes to carry out a new combination, which cannot like an established business be financed by returns from previous production. To provide this credit is clearly the function of that category of individuals which we call "capitalists." It is obvious that this is the characteristic method of the capitalist type of society — and important enough to serve as its *differentia specifica* — for forcing the economic system into new channels, for putting its means at

---

[1] A privilege which the individual can also achieve through saving. In an economy of the handicraft type this element would have to be emphasised more. Manufacturers' "reserve funds" assume an existing development.

the service of new ends, in contrast to the method of a non-exchange economy of the kind which simply consists in exercising the directing organ's power to command.

It does not appear to me possible to dispute in any way the fore-going statement. Emphasis upon the significance of credit is to be found in every textbook. That the structure of modern industry could not have been erected without it, that it makes the individual to a certain extent independent of inherited possessions, that talent in economic life "rides to success on its debts," even the most conservative orthodoxy of the theorists cannot well deny. Nor is the connection established here between credit and the carrying out of innovations, a connection which will be worked out later, anything to take offence at. For it is as clear *a priori* as it is established historically that credit is primarily necessary to new combinations and that it is from these that it forces its way into the circular flow, on the one hand because it was originally necessary to the founding of what are now the old firms, on the other hand because its mechanism, once in existence, also seizes old combinations for obvious reasons.[1] First, *a priori*: we saw in the first chapter that borrowing is not a necessary element of production in the normal circular flow within accustomed channels, is not an element without which we could not understand the essential phenomena of the latter. On the other hand, in carrying out new combinations, "financing" as a special act is fundamentally necessary, in practice as in theory. Second, historically: those who lend and borrow for industrial purposes do not appear early in history. The pre-capitalistic lender provided money for other than business purposes. And we all remember the type of industrialist who felt he was losing caste by borrowing and who therefore shunned banks and bills of exchange. The capitalistic credit system has grown out of and thrived on the financing of new combinations in all countries, even though in a different way in each (the origin of German joint stock banking is especially characteristic). Finally there can be no stumblingblock in our speak-

---

[1] The most important of which is the appearance of productive interest, as we shall see in Chapter V. As soon as interest emerges somewhere in the system, it expands over the whole of it.

ing of receiving credit in "money or money substitutes." We certainly do not assert that one can produce with coins, notes, or bank balances, and do not deny that services of labor, raw materials, and tools are the things wanted. We are only speaking of a method of procuring them.

Nevertheless there is a point here in which, as has already been hinted, our theory diverges from the traditional view. The accepted theory sees a problem in the existence of the productive means, which are needed for new, or indeed any, productive processes, and this accumulation therefore becomes a distinct function or service. We do not recognise this problem at all; it appears to us to be created by faulty analysis. It does not exist in the circular flow, because the running of the latter presupposes given quantities of means of production. But neither does it exist for the carrying out of new combinations,[1] because the productive means required in the latter are drawn from the circular flow whether they already exist there in the shape wanted or have first to be produced by other means of production existing there. Instead of this problem another exists for us: the problem of detaching productive means (already employed somewhere) from the circular flow and allotting them to new combinations. This is done by credit, by means of which one who wishes to carry out new combinations outbids the producers in the circular flow in the market for the required means of production. And although the meaning and object of this process lies in a movement of goods from their old towards new employments, it cannot be described entirely in terms of goods without overlooking something essential, which happens in the sphere of money and credit and upon which depends the explanation of important phenomena in the capitalist form of economic organisation, in contrast to other types.

Finally one more step in this direction: whence come the sums

---

[1] Of course the productive means do not fall from heaven. In so far as they are not given by nature or non-economically, they were and are created at some time by the individual waves of development in our sense, and henceforth incorporated in the circular flow. But every individual wave of development and every individual new combination itself proceeds again from the supply of productive means of the existing circular flow — a case of the hen and the egg.

needed to purchase the means of production necessary for the new combinations if the individual concerned does not happen to have them? The conventional answer is simple: out of the annual growth of social savings plus that part of resources which may annually become free. Now the first quantity was indeed important enough before the war — it may perhaps be estimated as one-fifth of total private incomes in Europe and North America — so that together with the latter sum, which it is difficult to obtain statistically, it does not immediately give the lie quantitatively to this answer. At the same time a figure representing the range of all the business operations involved in carrying out new combinations is also not available at present. But we may not even start from total "savings." For its magnitude is explicable only by the results of previous development. By far the greater part of it does not come from thrift in the strict sense, that is from abstaining from the consumption of part of one's regular income, but it consists of funds which are themselves the result of successful innovation and in which we shall later recognise entrepreneurial profit. In the circular flow there would be on the one hand no such rich source, out of which to save, and on the other hand essentially less incentive to save. The only big incomes known to it would be monopoly revenues and the rents of large landowners; while provision for misfortunes and old age, perhaps also irrational motives, would be the only incentives. The most important incentive, the chance of participating in the gains of development, would be absent. Hence, in such an economic system there could be no great reservoirs of free purchasing power, to which one who wished to form new combinations could turn — and his own savings would only suffice in exceptional cases. All money would circulate, would be fixed in definite established channels.

Even though the conventional answer to our question is not obviously absurd, yet there is another method of obtaining money for this purpose, which claims our attention, because it, unlike the one referred to, does not presuppose the existence of accumulated results of previous development, and hence may be considered as the only one which is available in strict logic. This method of obtaining money is the creation of purchasing power by banks. The form it takes is immaterial. The issue of bank-notes not fully covered by specie withdrawn from circulation is an obvious instance, but methods of deposit banking render the same service, where they increase the sum total of possible expenditure. Or we may think of bank acceptances in so far as they serve as money to make payments in wholesale trade. It is always a question, not of transforming purchasing power which already exists in someone's possession, but of the creation of new purchasing power out of nothing — out of nothing even if the credit contract by which the new purchasing power is created is supported by securities which are not themselves circulating media — which is added to the existing circulation. And this is the source from which new combinations *are* often financed, and from which they would have to be financed *always*, if results of previous development did not actually exist at any moment.

These credit means of payment, that is means of payment which are created for the purpose and by the act of giving credit, serve just as ready money in trade, partly directly, partly because they can be converted immediately into ready money for small payments or payments to the non-banking classes — in particular to wage-earners. With their help, those who carry out new combinations can gain access to the existing stocks of productive means, or, as the case may be, enable those from whom they buy productive services to gain immediate access to the market for consumption goods. There is never, in this nexus, granting of credit in the sense that someone must wait for the equivalent of his service in goods, and content himself with a claim, thereby fulfilling a special function; not even in the sense that someone has to accumulate means of maintenance for laborers or land-owners, or produced means of production, all of which would only be paid for out of the final results of production. Economically, it is true, there is an essential difference between these means of payment, if they are created for new ends, and money or other means of payment of the circular flow. The latter may be conceived on the one hand as a kind of certificate for completed production and the increase in the social product effected through it, and on the other hand as a kind of order upon, or claim to, part of this social product. The former have not the first of these two characteristics. They too are orders, for which one can immediately procure consumption goods, but not certificates for previous production. Access to the national dividend is usually to be had only on condition of some productive service previously rendered or of some product previously sold. This condition is, in this case, not yet fulfilled. It will be fulfilled only after the successful completion of the new combinations. Hence this credit will in the meantime affect the price level.

The banker, therefore, is not so much primarily a middleman in the commodity "purchasing power" as a *producer* of this commodity. However, since all reserve funds and savings to-day usually flow to him, and the total demand for free purchasing power, whether existing or to be created, concentrates on him, he has either replaced private capitalists or become their agent; he has himself become the capitalist par excellence. He stands between those who wish to form new combinations and the possessors of productive means. He is essentially a phenomenon of development, though only when no central authority directs the social process. He makes possible the carrying out of new combinations, authorises people, in the name of society as it were, to form them. He is the ephor of the exchange economy.

III

We now come to the third of the elements with which our analysis works, namely the "new combination of means of production," and credit. Although all three elements form a whole, the third may be described as the fundamental phenomenon of economic development. The carrying out of new combinations we call "enterprise"; the individuals whose function it is to carry them out we call "entrepreneurs." These concepts are at once broader and narrower than the usual. Broader, because in the first place we call entrepreneurs not only those "independent" businessmen in an exchange economy who are usually so designated, but all who actually fulfil the function by which we define the concept, even if they are, as is becoming the rule, "dependent" employees of a company, like managers, members of boards of directors, and so forth, or even if their actual power to perform the entrepreneurial function has any other foundations, such as the control of a majority of shares. As it is the carrying out of new combinations that constitutes the entrepreneur, it is not necessary that he should be permanently connected with an individual firm; many "financiers," "promotors," and so forth are not, and still they may be entrepreneurs in our sense. On the other hand, our concept is narrower than the traditional one in that it does not include all heads of firms or managers or industrialists who merely may operate an established business, but only those who actually perform that function. Nevertheless I maintain that the above definition does no more than formulate with greater precision what the traditional doctrine really means to convey. In the first place our definition agrees with the usual one on the fundamental point of distinguishing between "entrepreneurs" and "capitalists" — irrespective of whether the latter are regarded as owners of money, claims to money, or material goods. This distinction is common property to-day and has been so for a considerable time. It also settles the question whether the ordinary shareholder as such is an entrepreneur, and disposes of the conception of the entrepreneur as risk bearer.[1] Furthermore, the ordinary characterisation of the entrepreneur type by such expressions as "initiative," "authority," or "foresight" points entirely in our direction. For there is little scope for such qualities within the routine of the circular flow, and if this had been sharply separated

[1] Risk obviously always falls on the owner of the means of production or of the money-capital which was paid for them, hence never on the entrepreneur *as such* (see Chapter IV). A shareholder *may* be an entrepreneur. He may even owe to his holding a controlling interest the power to act as an entrepreneur. Shareholders *per se*, however, are never entrepreneurs, but merely capitalists, who in consideration of their submitting to certain risks participate in profits. That this is no reason to look upon them as anything but capitalists is shown by the facts, first, that the average shareholder has normally no power to influence the management of his company, and secondly, that participation in profits is frequent in cases in which everyone recognises the presence of a loan contract. Compare, for example, the Graeco-Roman *foenus nauticum*. Surely this interpretation is more true to life than the other one, which, following the lead of a faulty legal construction — which can only be explained historically — attributes functions to the average shareholder which he hardly ever thinks of discharging.

from the occurrence of changes in this routine itself, the emphasis in the definition of the function of entrepreneurs would have been shifted automatically to the latter. Finally there are definitions which we could simply accept. There is in particular the well known one that goes back to J. B. Say: the entrepreneur's function is to combine the productive factors, to bring them together. Since this is a performance of a special kind only when the factors are combined for the first time — while it is merely routine work if done in the course of running a business — this definition coincides with ours. When Mataja (in Unternehmergewinn) defines the entrepreneur as one who receives profit, we have only to add the conclusion of the first chapter, that there is no profit in the circular flow, in order to trace this formulation too back to ours.[1] And this view is not foreign to traditional theory, as is shown by the construction of the *entrepreneur faisant ni bénéfice ni perte*, which has been worked out rigorously by Walras, but is the property of many other authors. The tendency is for the entrepreneur to make neither profit nor loss in the circular flow — that is he has no function of a special kind there, he simply does not exist; but in his stead, there are heads of firms or business managers of a different type which we had better not designate by the same term.

It is a prejudice to believe that the knowledge of the historical origin of an institution or of a type immediately shows us its sociological or economic nature. Such knowledge often leads us to understand it, but it does not directly yield a theory of it. Still more false is the belief that "primitive" forms of a type are also *ipso facto* the "simpler" or the "more original" in the sense that they show their nature more purely and with fewer complications than later ones. Very frequently the opposite is the case, amongst other reasons because increasing specialisation may allow functions and qualities to stand out sharply, which are more difficult to recognise in more primitive conditions when mixed with others.

---

[1] The definition of the entrepreneur in terms of entrepreneurial profit instead of in terms of the function the performance of which creates the entrepreneurial profit is obviously not brilliant. But we have still another objection to it: we shall see that entrepreneurial profit does not fall to the entrepreneur by "necessity" in the same sense as the marginal product of labor does to the worker.

So it is in our case. In the general position of the chief of a primitive horde it is difficult to separate the entrepreneurial element from the others. For the same reason most economists up to the time of the younger Mill failed to keep capitalist and entrepreneur distinct because the manufacturer of a hundred years ago was both; and certainly the course of events since then has facilitated the making of this distinction, as the system of land tenure in England has facilitated the distinction between farmer and landowner, while on the Continent this distinction is still occasionally neglected, especially in the case of the peasant who tills his own soil.[1] But in our case there are still more of such difficulties. The entrepreneur of earlier times was not only as a rule the capitalist too, he was also often — as he still is to-day in the case of small concerns — his own technical expert, in so far as a professional specialist was not called in for special cases. Likewise he was (and is) often his own buying and selling agent, the head of his office, his own personnel manager, and sometimes, even though as a rule he of course employed solicitors, his own legal adviser in current affairs. And it was performing some or all of these functions that regularly filled his days. The carrying out of new combinations can no more be a *vocation* than the making and execution of strategical decisions, although it is this function and not his routine work that characterises the military leader. Therefore the entrepreneur's essential function must always appear mixed up with other kinds of activity, which as a rule must be much more conspicuous than the essential one. Hence the Marshallian definition of the enterpreneur, which simply treats the entrepreneurial function as "management" in the widest meaning, will naturally appeal to most of us. We do not accept it, simply because it does not bring out what we consider to be the salient point and the only one which specifically distinguishes entrepreneurial from other activities.

[1] Only this neglect explains the attitude of many socialistic theorists towards peasant property. For smallness of the individual possession makes a difference only for the petit-bourgeois, not for the socialist. The criterion of the employment of labor other than that of the owner and his family is economically relevant only from the standpoint of a kind of exploitation theory which is hardly tenable any longer.

Nevertheless there are types — the course of events has evolved them by degrees — which exhibit the entrepreneurial function with particular purity. The "promoter," to be sure, belongs to them only with qualifications. For, neglecting the associations relative to social and moral status which are attached to this type, the promoter is frequently only an agent intervening on commission, who does the work of financial technique in floating the new enterprise. In this case he is not its creator nor the driving power in the process. However, he *may* be the latter also, and then he is something like an "entrepreneur by profession." But the modern type of "captain of industry" [1] corresponds more closely to what is meant here, especially if one recognises his identity on the one hand with, say, the commercial entrepreneur of twelfth-century Venice — or, among later types, with John Law — and on the other hand with the village potentate who combines with his agriculture and his cattle trade, say, a rural brewery, an hotel, and a store. But whatever the type, everyone is an entrepreneur only when he actually "carries out new combinations," and loses that character as soon as he has built up his business, when he settles down to running it as other people run their businesses. This is the rule, of course, and hence it is just as rare for anyone always to remain an entrepreneur throughout the decades of his active life as it is for a businessman never to have a moment in which he is an entrepreneur, to however modest a degree.

Because being an entrepreneur is not a profession and as a rule not a lasting condition, entrepreneurs do not form a social class in the technical sense, as, for example, landowners or capitalists or workmen do. Of course the entrepreneurial function will *lead* to certain class positions for the successful entrepreneur and his family. It can also put its stamp on an epoch of social history, can form a style of life, or systems of moral and aesthetic values; but in itself it signifies a class position no more than it presupposes one. And the class position which may be attained is not as such an entrepreneurial position, but is characterised as landowning or

---

[1] Cf. for example the good description in Wiedenfeld, Das Persönliche im modernen Unternehmertum. Although it appeared in Schmoller's Jahrbuch in 1910 this work was not known to me when the first edition of this book was published.

capitalist, according to how the proceeds of the enterprise are used. Inheritance of the pecuniary result and of personal qualities may then both keep up this position for more than one generation and make further enterprise easier for descendants, but the function of the entrepreneur itself cannot be inherited, as is shown well enough by the history of manufacturing families.[1]

But now the decisive question arises: why then is the carrying out of new combinations a special process and the object of a special kind of "function"? Every individual carries on his economic affairs as well as he can. To be sure, his own intentions are never realised with ideal perfection, but ultimately his behavior is moulded by the influence on him of the results of his conduct, so as to fit circumstances which do not as a rule change suddenly. If a business can never be absolutely perfect in any sense, yet it in time approaches a relative perfection having regard to the surrounding world, the social conditions, the knowledge of the time, and the horizon of each individual or each group. New possibilities are continuously being offered by the surrounding world, in particular new discoveries are continuously being added to the existing store of knowledge. Why should not the individual make just as much use of the new possibilities as of the old, and, according to the market position as he understands it, keep pigs instead of cows, or even choose a new crop rotation, if this can be seen to be more advantageous? And what kind of special new phenomena or problems, not to be found in the established circular flow, can arise there?

While in the accustomed circular flow every individual can act promptly and rationally because he is sure of his ground and is supported by the conduct, as adjusted to this circular flow, of all other individuals, who in turn expect the accustomed activity from him, he cannot simply do this when he is confronted by a new task. While in the accustomed channels his own ability and experience suffice for the normal individual, when confronted with innovations he needs guidance. While he swims with the stream in the circular flow which is familiar to him, he swims against the

---

[1] On the nature of the entrepreneurial function also compare my statement in the article "Unternehmer" in the Handwörterbuch der Staatswissenschaften.

stream if he wishes to change its channel. What was formerly a help becomes a hindrance. What was a familiar datum becomes an unknown. Where the boundaries of routine stop, many people can go no further, and the rest can only do so in a highly variable manner. The assumption that conduct is prompt and rational is in all cases a fiction. But it proves to be sufficiently near to reality, if things have time to hammer logic into men. Where this has happened, and within the limits in which it has happened, one may rest content with this fiction and build theories upon it. It is then not true that habit or custom or non-economic ways of thinking cause a hopeless difference between the individuals of different classes, times, or cultures, and that, for example, the "economics of the stock exchange" would be inapplicable say to the peasants of to-day or to the craftsmen of the Middle Ages. On the contrary the same theoretical picture [1] in its broadest contour lines fits the individuals of quite different cultures, whatever their degree of intelligence and of economic rationality, and we can depend upon it that the peasant sells his calf just as cunningly and egotistically as the stock exchange member his portfolio of shares. But this holds good only where precedents without number have formed conduct through decades and, in fundamentals, through hundreds and thousands of years, and have eliminated unadapted behavior. Outside of these limits our fiction loses its closeness to reality.[2] To cling to it there also, as the traditional theory does, is to hide an essential thing and to ignore a fact which, in contrast with other deviations of our assumptions from reality, is theoretically important and the source of the explanation of phenomena which would not exist without it.

[1] The same *theoretical* picture, obviously not the same sociological, cultural, and so forth.

[2] How much this is the case is best seen to-day in the economic life of those nations, and within our civilisation in the economics of those individuals, whom the development of the last century has not yet completely drawn into its stream, for example, in the economy of the Central European peasant. This peasant "calculates"; there is no deficiency of the "economic way of thinking" (Wirtschaftsgesinnung) in him. Yet he cannot take a step out of the beaten path; his economy has not changed at all for centuries, except perhaps through the exercise of external force and influence. Why? Because the choice of new methods is not simply an element in the concept of rational economic action, nor a matter of course, but a distinct process which stands in need of special explanation.

Therefore, in describing the circular flow one must treat combinations of means of production (the production-functions) as data, like natural possibilities, and admit only small [1] variations at the margins, such as every individual can accomplish by adapting himself to changes in his economic environment, without materially deviating from familiar lines. Therefore, too, the carrying out of new combinations is a special function, and the privilege of a type of people who are much less numerous than all those who have the "objective" possibility of doing it. Therefore, finally, entrepreneurs are a special type,[2] and their behavior a special

[1] Small disturbances which may indeed, as mentioned earlier, in time add up to great amounts. The decisive point is that the businessman, if he makes them, never alters his routine. The usual case is one of small, the exception one of great (*uno actu* great), disturbances. Only in this sense is emphasis put upon "smallness" here. The objection that there can be no difference in principle between small and large disturbances is not effective. For it is false in itself, in so far as it is based upon the disregard of the principle of the infinitesimal method, the essence of which lies in the fact that one can assert of "small quantities" under certain circumstances what one cannot assert of "large quantities." But the reader who takes umbrage at the large-small contrast may, if he wishes, substitute for it the contrast adapting-spontaneous. Personally I am not willing to do this because the latter method of expression is much easier to misunderstand than the former and really would demand still longer explanations.

[2] In the first place it is a question of a type of *conduct* and of a type of *person* in so far as this conduct is accessible in very unequal measure and to relatively few people, so that it constitutes their outstanding characteristic. Because the exposition of the first edition was reproached with exaggerating and mistaking the peculiarity of this conduct, and with overlooking the fact that it is more or less open to every businessman, and because the exposition in a later paper ("Wellenbewegung des Wirtschaftslebens," Archiv für Sozialwissenschaft) was charged with introducing an intermediate type ("half-static" businessmen), the following may be submitted. The conduct in question is peculiar in two ways. First, because it is directed towards something different and signifies doing something different from other conduct. One may indeed in this connection include it with the latter in a higher unity, but this does not alter the fact that a theoretically relevant difference exists between the two, and that only one of them is adequately described by traditional theory. Secondly, the type of conduct in question not only differs from the other in its object, "innovation" being peculiar to it, but also in that it presupposes aptitudes differing *in kind* and not only in degree from those of mere rational economic behavior.

Now these aptitudes are presumably distributed in an ethically homogeneous population just like others, that is the curve of their distribution has a maximum ordinate, deviations on either side of which become rarer the greater they are. Similarly we can assume that every healthy man can sing if he will. Perhaps half the individuals in an ethically homogeneous group have the capacity for it to an average degree, a quarter in progressively diminishing measure, and, let us say, a quarter in a measure above the average; and within this quarter, through a series of continually increasing singing ability and continually diminishing number of people problem, the motive power of a great number of significant phenomena. Hence, our position may be characterised by three corresponding pairs of opposites. First, by the opposition of two real processes: the circular flow or the tendency towards equilibrium on the one hand, a change in the channels of economic routine or a spontaneous change in the economic data arising from within the system on the other. Secondly, by the opposition of two theoretical *apparatuses*: statics and dynamics.[1] Thirdly, by the opposi-

who possess it, we come finally to the Carusos. Only in this quarter are we struck in general by the singing ability, and only in the supreme instances can it become the characterising mark of the person. Although practically all men can sing, singing ability does not cease to be a distinguishable characteristic and attribute of a minority, indeed not exactly of a type, because this characteristic — unlike ours — affects the total personality relatively little.

Let us apply this: Again, a quarter of the population may be so poor in those qualities, let us say here provisionally, of economic initiative that the deficiency makes itself felt by poverty of their moral personality, and they play a wretched part in the smallest affairs of private and professional life in which this element is called for. We recognise this type and know that many of the best clerks, distinguished by devotion to duty, expert knowledge, and exactitude, belong to it. Then comes the "half," the "normal." These prove themselves to be better in the things which even within the established channels cannot simply be "dispatched" (erledigen) but must also be "decided" (entscheiden) and "carried out" (durchsetzen). Practically all business people belong here, otherwise they would never have attained their positions; most represent a selection — individually or hereditarily tested. A textile manufacturer travels no "new" road when he goes to a wool auction. But the situations there are never the same, and the success of the business depends so much upon skill and initiative in buying wool that the fact that the textile industry has so far exhibited no trustification comparable with that in heavy manufacturing is undoubtedly partly explicable by the reluctance of the cleverer manufacturers to renounce the advantage of their own skill in buying wool. From there, rising in the scale we come finally into the highest quarter, to people who are a type characterised by super-normal qualities of intellect and will. Within this type there are not only many varieties (merchants, manufacturers, financiers, etc.) but also a continuous variety of degrees of intensity in "initiative." In our argument types of every intensity occur. Many a one can steer a safe course, where no one has yet been; others follow where first another went before; still others only in the crowd, but in this among the first. So also the great political leader of every kind and time is a type, yet not a thing unique, but only the apex of a pyramid from which there is a continuous variation down to the average and from it to the sub-normal values. And yet not only is "leading" a special function, but the leader also something special, distinguishable — wherefore there is no sense in our case in asking: "Where does that type begin then?" and then to exclaim: "This is no type at all!"

[1] It has been objected against the first edition that it sometimes defines "statics" as a theoretical construction, sometimes as the picture of an actual state of economic life. I believe that the present exposition gives no ground for this opinion. "Static" theory does not assume a stationary economy; it also treats of the effects of changes in data. In itself, therefore, there is no necessary connection between static theory and stationary reality. Only in so far as one can exhibit the fundamental form of the

tion of two types of conduct, which, following reality, we can picture as two types of individuals: mere managers and entrepreneurs. And therefore the "best method" of producing in the theoretical sense is to be conceived as "the most advantageous among the methods which have been empirically tested and become familiar." But it is not the "best" of the methods "possible" at the time. If one does not make this distinction, the concept becomes meaningless and precisely those problems remain unsolved which our interpretation is meant to provide for.

Let us now formulate precisely the characteristic feature of the conduct and type under discussion. The smallest daily action embodies a huge mental effort. Every schoolboy would have to be a mental giant, if he himself had to create all he knows and uses by his own individual activity. And every man would have to be a giant of wisdom and will, if he had in every case to create anew all the rules by which he guides his everyday conduct. This is true not only of those decisions and actions of individual and social life the principles of which are the product of tens of thou-

economic course of events with the maximum simplicity in an unchanging economy does this assumption recommend itself to theory. The stationary economy is for uncounted thousands of years, and also in historical times in many places for centuries, an incontrovertible fact, apart from the fact, moreover, which Sombart emphasised, that there is a tendency towards a stationary state in every period of depression. Hence it is readily understood how this historical fact and that theoretical construction have allied themselves in a way which led to some confusion. The words "statics" and "dynamics" the author would not now use in the meaning they carry above, where they are simply short expressions for "theory of the circular flow" and "theory of development." One more thing: theory employs two methods of interpretation, which may perhaps make difficulties. If it is to be shown how all the elements of the economic system are determined in equilibrium by one another, this equilibrium system is considered as not yet existing and is built up before our eyes *ab ovo*. This does not mean that its coming into being is genetically explained thereby. Only its existence and functioning are made logically clear by mental dissection. And the experiences and habits of individuals are assumed as existing. How just these productive combinations have come about is not thereby explained. Further, if two contiguous equilibrium positions are to be investigated, then sometimes (not always), as in Pigou's Economics of Welfare, the "best" productive combination in the first is compared with the "best" in the second. And this again need not, but may, mean that the two combinations in the sense meant here differ not only by small variations in quantity but in their whole technical and commercial structure. Here too the coming into being of the second combination and the problems connected with it are not investigated, but only the functioning and the outcome of the already existing combination. Even though justified as far as it goes, this method of treatment passes over our problem. If the assertion were implied that this is also settled by it, it would be false.

sands of years, but also of those products of shorter periods and of a more special nature which constitute the particular instrument for performing vocational tasks. But precisely the things the performance of which according to this should involve a supreme effort, in general demand no special individual effort at all; those which should be especially difficult are in reality especially easy; what should demand superhuman capacity is accessible to the least gifted, given mental health. In particular within the ordinary routine there is no need for leadership. Of course it is still necessary to set people their tasks, to keep up discipline, and so forth; but this is easy and a function any normal person can learn to fulfil. Within the lines familiar to all, even the function of directing other people, though still necessary, is mere "work" like any other, comparable to the service of tending a machine. All people get to know, and are able to do, their daily tasks in the customary way and ordinarily perform them by themselves; the "director" has his routine as they have theirs; and his directive function serves merely to correct individual aberrations.

This is so because all knowledge and habit once acquired becomes as firmly rooted in ourselves as a railway embankment in the earth. It does not require to be continually renewed and consciously reproduced, but sinks into the strata of subconsciousness. It is normally transmitted almost without friction by inheritance, teaching, upbringing, pressure of environment. Everything we think, feel, or do often enough becomes automatic and our conscious life is unburdened of it. The enormous economy of force, in the race and the individual, here involved is not great enough, however, to make daily life a light burden and to prevent its demands from exhausting the average energy all the same. But it is great enough to make it possible to meet the ordinary claims. This holds good likewise for economic daily life. And from this it follows also for economic life that every step outside the boundary of routine has difficulties and involves a new element. It is this element that constitutes the phenomenon of leadership.

The nature of these difficulties may be focussed in the following three points. First, outside these accustomed channels the individual is without those data for his decisions and those rules of conduct which are usually very accurately known to him within them. Of course he must still foresee and estimate on the basis of his experience. But many things must remain uncertain, still others are only ascertainable within wide limits, some can perhaps only be "guessed." In particular this is true of those data which the individual strives to alter and of those which he wants to create. Now he must really to some extent do what tradition does for him in everyday life, viz. consciously plan his conduct in every particular. There will be much more conscious rationality in this than in customary action, which as such does not need to be reflected upon at all; but this plan must necessarily be open not only to errors greater in degree, but also to other kinds of errors than those occurring in customary action. What has been done already has the sharp-edged reality of all the things which we have seen and experienced; the new is only the figment of our imagination. Carrying out a new plan and acting according to a customary one are things as different as making a road and walking along it.

How different a thing this is becomes clearer if one bears in mind the impossibility of surveying exhaustively all the effects and counter-effects of the projected enterprise. Even as many of them as could in theory be ascertained if one had unlimited time and means must practically remain in the dark. As military action must be taken in a given strategic position even if all the data potentially procurable are not available, so also in economic life action must be taken without working out all the details of what is to be done. Here the success of everything depends upon intuition, the capacity of seeing things in a way which afterwards proves to be true, even though it cannot be established at the moment, and of grasping the essential fact, discarding the unessential, even though one can give no account of the principles by which this is done. Thorough preparatory work, and special knowledge, breadth of intellectual understanding, talent for logical analysis, may under certain circumstances be sources of failure. The more accurately, however, we learn to know the natural and social world, the more perfect our control of facts becomes; and the greater the extent, with time and progressive rationalisation, within which things can be simply calculated, and indeed quickly and reliably calculated, the more the significance of this function decreases. Therefore the importance of the entrepreneur type must diminish just as the importance of the military commander has already diminished. Nevertheless a part of the very essence of each type is bound up with this function.

As this first point lies in the task, so the second lies in the psyche of the businessman himself. It is not only objectively more difficult to do something new than what is familiar and tested by experience, but the individual feels reluctance to it and would do so even if the objective difficulties did not exist. This is so in all fields. The history of science is one great confirmation of the fact that we find it exceedingly difficult to adopt a new scientific point of view or method. Thought turns again and again into the accustomed track even if it has become unsuitable and the more suitable innovation in itself presents no particular difficulties. The very nature of fixed habits of thinking, their energy-saving function, is founded upon the fact that they have become subconscious, that they yield their results automatically and are proof against criticism and even against contradiction by individual facts. But precisely because of this they become drag-chains when they have outlived their usefulness. So it is also in the economic world. In the breast of one who wishes to do something new, the forces of habit rise up and bear witness against the embryonic project. A new and another kind of effort of will is therefore necessary in order to wrest, amidst the work and care of the daily round, scope and time for conceiving and working out the new combination and to bring oneself to look upon it as a real possibility and not merely as a day-dream. This mental freedom presupposes a great surplus force over the everyday demand and is something peculiar and by nature rare.

The third point consists in the reaction of the social environment against one who wishes to do something new. This reaction may manifest itself first of all in the existence of legal or political impediments. But neglecting this, any deviating conduct by a member of a social group is condemned, though in greatly varying degrees according as the social group is used to such conduct or not. Even a deviation from social custom in such things as dress or manners arouses opposition, and of course all the more so in the graver cases. This opposition is stronger in primitive stages of culture than in others, but it is never absent. Even mere astonishment at the deviation, even merely noticing it, exercises a pressure on the individual. The manifestation of condemnation may at once bring noticeable consequences in its train. It may even come to social ostracism and finally to physical prevention or to direct attack. Neither the fact that progressive differentiation weakens this opposition — especially as the most important cause of the weakening is the very development which we wish to explain — nor the further fact that the social opposition operates under certain circumstances and upon many individuals as a stimulus, changes anything in principle in the significance of it. Surmounting this opposition is always a special kind of task which does not exist in the customary course of life, a task which also requires a special kind of conduct. In matters economic this resistance manifests itself first of all in the groups threatened by the innovation, then in the difficulty in finding the necessary cooperation, finally in the difficulty in winning over consumers. Even though these elements are still effective to-day, despite the fact that a period of turbulent development has accustomed us to the appearance and the carrying out of innovations, they can be best studied in the beginnings of capitalism. But they are so obvious there that it would be time lost for our purposes to dwell upon them.

There is leadership *only* for these reasons — leadership, that is, as a special kind of function and in contrast to a mere difference in rank, which would exist in every social body, in the smallest as in the largest, and in combination with which it generally appears. The facts alluded to create a boundary beyond which the majority of people do not function promptly by themselves and require help from a minority. If social life had in all respects the relative immutability of, for example, the astronomical world, or if mutable this mutability were yet incapable of being influenced by human action, or finally if capable of being so influenced this type of action were yet equally open to everyone, then there would be no special function of leadership as distinguished from routine work.

The specific problem of leadership arises and the leader type appears only where new possibilities present themselves. That is why it is so strongly marked among the Normans at the time of their conquests and so feebly among the Slavs in the centuries of their unchanging and relatively protected life in the marshes of the Pripet. Our three points characterise the nature of the *function* as well as the *conduct* or behavior which constitutes the leader type. It is no part of his function to "find" or to "create" new possibilities. They are always present, abundantly accumulated by all sorts of people. Often they are also generally known and being discussed by scientific or literary writers. In other cases, there is nothing to discover about them, because they are quite obvious. To take an example from political life, it was not at all difficult to see how the social and political conditions of France at the time of Louis XVI could have been improved so as to avoid a breakdown of the *ancien régime*. Plenty of people as a matter of fact did see it. But nobody was in a position to *do* it. Now, it is this "doing the thing," without which possibilities are dead, of which the leader's function consists. This holds good of all kinds of leadership, ephemeral as well as more enduring ones. The former may serve as an instance. What is to be done in a casual emergency is as a rule quite simple. Most or all people may see it, yet they want someone to speak out, to lead, and to organise. Even leadership which influences merely by example, as artistic or scientific leadership, does not consist simply in finding or creating the new thing but in so impressing the social group with it as to draw it on in its wake. It is, therefore, more by will than by intellect that the leaders fulfil their function, more by "authority," "personal weight," and so forth than by original ideas.

Economic leadership in particular must hence be distinguished from "invention." As long as they are not carried into practice, inventions are economically irrelevant. And to carry any improvement into effect is a task entirely different from the inventing of it, and a task, moreover, requiring entirely different kinds of aptitudes. Although entrepreneurs of course *may* be inventors just as they may be capitalists, they are inventors not by nature of their function but by coincidence and vice versa. Besides, the innovations which it is the function of entrepreneurs to carry out need not necessarily be any inventions at all. It is, therefore, not advisable, and it may be downright misleading, to stress the element of invention as much as many writers do.

The entrepreneurial kind of leadership, as distinguished from other kinds of economic leadership such as we should expect to find in a primitive tribe or a communist society, is of course colored by the conditions peculiar to it. It has none of that glamour which characterises other kinds of leadership. It consists in fulfilling a very special task which only in rare cases appeals to the imagination of the public. For its success, keenness and vigor are not more essential than a certain narrowness which seizes the immediate chance and *nothing else.* "Personal weight" is, to be sure, not without importance. Yet the personality of the capitalistic entrepreneur need not, and generally does not, answer to the idea most of us have of what a "leader" looks like, so much so that there is some difficulty in realizing that he comes within the sociological category of leader at all. He "leads" the means of production into new channels. But this he does, not by convincing people of the desirability of carrying out his plan or by creating confidence in his leading in the manner of a political leader — the only man he has to convince or to impress is the banker who is to finance him — but by buying them or their services, and then using them as he sees fit. He also leads in the sense that he draws other producers in his branch after him. But as they are his competitors, who first reduce and then annihilate his profit, this is, as it were, leadership against one's own will. Finally, he renders a service, the full appreciation of which takes a specialist's knowledge of the case. It is not so easily understood by the public at large as a politician's successful speech or a general's victory in the field, not to insist on the fact that he seems to act — and often harshly — in his individual interest alone. We shall understand, therefore, that we do not observe, in this case, the emergence of all those affective values which are the glory of all other kinds of social leadership. Add to this the precariousness of the economic position both of the individual entrepreneur and of entrepreneurs as a group, and the fact that when his economic success raises him socially he has no cultural tradition or attitude to fall back upon, but moves about in society as an upstart, whose ways are readily laughed at, and we shall understand why this type has never been popular, and why even scientific critique often makes short work of it.[1]

We shall finally try to round off our picture of the entrepreneur in the same manner in which we always, in science as well as in practical life, try to understand human behavior, viz. by analysing the characteristic motives of his conduct. Any attempt to do this must of course meet with all those objections against the economist's intrusion into "psychology" which have been made familiar by a long series of writers. We cannot here enter into the fundamental question of the relation between psychology and economics. It is enough to state that those who on principle object to *any* psychological considerations in an economic argument may leave out what we are about to say without thereby losing contact with the argument of the following chapters. For none of the results to which our analysis is intended to lead stands or falls with our "psychology of the entrepreneur," or could be vitiated by any errors in it. Nowhere is there, as the reader will easily satisfy himself, any necessity for us to overstep the frontiers of observable behavior. Those who do not object to *all* psychology but only to the *kind* of psychology which we know from the traditional textbook, will see that we do not adopt any part of the time-honored picture of the motivation of the "economic man."

In the theory of the circular flow, the importance of examining motives is very much reduced by the fact that the equations of the system of equilibrium may be so interpreted as not to imply any psychic magnitudes at all, as shown by the analysis of Pareto

---

[1] It may, therefore, not be superfluous to point out that our analysis of the rôle of the entrepreneur does not involve any "glorification" of the type, as some readers of the first edition of this book seemed to think. We do hold that entrepreneurs *have* an economic function as distinguished from, say, robbers. But we neither style every entrepreneur a genius or a benefactor to humanity, nor do we wish to express any opinion about the comparative merits of the social organisation in which he plays his rôle, or about the question whether what he does could not be effected more cheaply or efficiently in other ways.

and of Barone. This is the reason why even very defective psychology interferes much less with results than one would expect. There may be rational *conduct* even in the absence of rational *motive*. But as soon as we really wish to penetrate into motivation, the problem proves by no means simple. Within given social circumstances and habits, most of what people do every day will appear to them primarily from the point of view of duty carrying a social or a superhuman sanction. There is very little of conscious rationality, still less of hedonism and of *individual* egoism about it, and so much of it as may safely be said to exist is of comparatively recent growth. Nevertheless, as long as we confine ourselves to the great outlines of constantly repeated economic action, we may link it up with wants and the desire to satisfy them, on condition that we are careful to recognise that economic motive so defined varies in intensity very much in time; that it is society that shapes the particular desires we observe; that wants must be taken with reference to the group which the individual thinks of when deciding his course of action — the family or any other group, smaller or larger than the family; that action does not promptly follow upon desire but only more or less imperfectly corresponds to it; that the field of individual choice is always, though in very different ways and to very different degrees, fenced in by social habits or conventions and the like: it still remains broadly true that, within the circular flow, everyone adapts himself to his environment so as to satisfy certain *given* wants — of himself or others — as best he can. In *all* cases, the *meaning* of economic action is the satisfaction of wants in the sense that there would be no economic action if there were no wants. In the case of the circular flow, we may also think of satisfaction of wants as the normal *motive*.

The latter is not true for our type. In one sense, he may indeed be called the most rational and the most egotistical of all. For, as we have seen, conscious rationality enters much more into the carrying out of new plans, which themselves have to be worked out before they can be acted upon, than into the mere running of an established business, which is largely a matter of routine. And the typical entrepreneur is more self-centred than other types, because he relies less than they do on tradition and connection and because his characteristic task — theoretically as well as historically — consists precisely in breaking up old, and creating new, tradition. Although this applies primarily to his economic action, it also extends to the moral, cultural, and social consequences of it. It is, of course, no mere coincidence that the period of the rise of the entrepreneur type also gave birth to Utilitarianism.

But his conduct and his motive are "rational" in no other sense. And in *no* sense is his characteristic motivation of the hedonist kind. If we define hedonist motive of action as the wish to satisfy one's wants, we may indeed make "wants" include any impulse whatsoever, just as we may define egoism so as to include all altruistic values too, on the strength of the fact that they also mean something in the way of self-gratification. But this would reduce our definition to tautology. If we wish to give it meaning, we must restrict it to such wants as are capable of being satisfied by the consumption of goods, and to that kind of satisfaction which is expected from it. Then it is no longer true that our type is acting on a wish to satisfy his wants.

For unless we assume that individuals of our type are driven along by an insatiable craving for hedonist satisfaction, the operations of Gossen's law would in the case of business leaders soon put a stop to further effort. Experience teaches, however, that typical entrepreneurs retire from the arena only when and because their strength is spent and they feel no longer equal to their task. This does not seem to verify the picture of the economic man, balancing probable results against disutility of effort and reaching in due course a point of equilibrium beyond which he is not willing to go. Effort, in our case, does not seem to weigh at all in the sense of being felt as a reason to stop. And activity of the entrepreneurial type is obviously an obstacle to hedonist enjoyment of those kinds of commodity which are usually acquired by incomes beyond a certain size, because their "consumption" presupposes leisure. Hedonistically, therefore, the conduct which we usually observe in individuals of our type would be irrational.

This would not, of course, prove the absence of hedonistic motive. Yet it points to another psychology of non-hedonist character, especially if we take into account the indifference to hedonist enjoyment which is often conspicuous in outstanding specimens of the type and which is not difficult to understand.

First of all, there is the dream and the will to found a private kingdom, usually, though not necessarily, also a dynasty. The modern world really does not know any such positions, but what may be attained by industrial or commercial success is still the nearest approach to medieval lordship possible to modern man. Its fascination is specially strong for people who have no other chance of achieving social distinction. The sensation of power and independence loses nothing by the fact that both are largely illusions. Closer analysis would lead to discovering an endless variety within this group of motives, from spiritual ambition down to mere snobbery. But this need not detain us. Let it suffice to point out that motives of this kind, although they stand nearest to consumers' satisfaction, do not coincide with it.

Then there is the will to conquer: the impulse to fight, to prove oneself superior to others, to succeed for the sake, not of the fruits of success, but of success itself. From this aspect, economic action becomes akin to sport — there are financial races, or rather boxing-matches. The financial result is a secondary consideration, or, at all events, mainly valued as an index of success and as a symptom of victory, the displaying of which very often is more important as a motive of large expenditure than the wish for the consumers' goods themselves. Again we should find countless nuances, some of which, like social ambition, shade into the first group of motives. And again we are faced with a motivation characteristically different from that of "satisfaction of wants" in the sense defined above, or from, to put the same thing into other words, "hedonistic adaptation."

Finally, there is the joy of creating, of getting things done, or simply of exercising one's energy and ingenuity. This is akin to a ubiquitous motive, but nowhere else does it stand out as an independent factor of behavior with anything like the clearness with which it obtrudes itself in our case. Our type seeks out difficulties, changes in order to change, delights in ventures. This group of motives is the most distinctly anti-hedonist of the three.

Only with the first groups of motives is private property as the result of entrepreneurial activity an essential factor in making it operative. With the other two it is not. Pecuniary gain is indeed a very accurate expression of success, especially of *relative* success, and from the standpoint of the man who strives for it, it has the additional advantage of being an objective fact and largely independent of the opinion of others. These and other peculiarities incident to the mechanism of "acquisitive" society make it very difficult to replace it as a motor of industrial development, even if we would discard the importance it has for creating a fund ready for investment. Nevertheless it is true that the second and third groups of entrepreneurial motives may in principle be taken care of by other social arrangements not involving private gain from economic innovation. What other stimuli could be provided, and how they could be made to work as well as the "capitalistic" ones do, are questions which are beyond our theme. They are taken too lightly by social reformers, and are altogether ignored by fiscal radicalism. But they are not insoluble, and may be answered by detailed observation of the psychology of entrepreneurial activity, at least for given times and places.

CHAPTER III

CREDIT AND CAPITAL

The Nature and Function of Credit [1]

The fundamental notion that the essence of economic development consists in a *different* employment of *existing* services of labor and land leads us to the statement that the carrying out of new combinations takes place through the withdrawal of services of labor and land from their previous employments. For every form of economy in which the leader has no direct power of disposal over these services, this again leads us to two heresies: first to the heresy that money, and then to the second heresy that also other means of payment, perform an essential function, hence that processes in terms of means of payment are not merely reflexes of processes in terms of goods. In every possible strain, with rare unanimity, even with impatience and moral and intellectual indignation, a very long line of theorists have assured us of the opposite.

Economics, almost since it became a science, has continually resisted the popular errors which cling to the phenomenon of money — quite rightly. This has been one of its fundamental services. And whoever thinks through what has been said so far

[1] The line of thought that is expounded fundamentally unchanged in the following has in the meantime received valuable substantiation and improvement from the investigations of A. Hahn in his Volkswirtschaftliche Theorie des Bankkredits (1 ed. 1920, 2 ed. 1926). The reader is expressly referred to this original and meritorious book, which has essentially advanced our knowledge of the problem. Also in many respects parallel is W. G. Langworthy Taylor in The Credit System. Perhaps the post-war phenomena and the discussions of the rôle of bank credit in boom and depression have removed from what I have to say much of the appearance of a paradox. To-day every theory of the business cycle considers the fact of "additional credit" in prosperity and takes account of the question, raised by Keynes, whether the cycle may be mitigated by being influenced from the money side. This does not yet mean the acceptance of my point of view. But it must lead to it. Cf. also my article "Kreditkontrolle" in the Archiv für Sozialwissenschaft und Sozialpolitik (1925). Recently Robertson, in Banking Policy and the Price Level, has arrived at similar results (cf. on this Pigou, Economic Journal, June, 1926).

will easily be convinced that none of these errors is maintained in it. Of course if one were to say that money is only a medium for facilitating the circulation of goods and that no important phenomena can be connected with it, this would be false. If one would forge out of this an objection against our argument, then it would be at once refuted by our proof that in our case a different employment of the system's productive powers cannot be achieved otherwise than by a disturbance in the relative purchasing power of individuals. We saw that, in principle, a loan of the services of labor and land by workers and landlords is not possible. Nor can the entrepreneur himself borrow produced means of production. For in the circular flow there would be no idle stocks for the needs of the entrepreneur. If somewhere or other exactly such produced means of production as the entrepreneur needs happen to exist, then of course he can buy them; for this, however, he again needs purchasing power. But he cannot simply borrow them, for they are needed for the purposes for which they were produced, and the possessor cannot and will not wait for his return — which the entrepreneur could indeed reimburse him for, but only later — and also can and will bear no risk. If someone nevertheless does this, then two transactions occur, a purchase and an extension of credit. Both are not only two legally distinct parts of one and the same economic process, but two very different economic processes, to each of which very different economic phenomena adhere, as will be seen later. Finally the entrepreneur also cannot "advance" [1] consumption goods to workers and landlords, simply because he has none. If he buys them, then he needs purchasing power for *that* purpose. We cannot get over this point, since it is always a question of drawing goods out of the circular flow. With respect to the loan of consumption goods, the same holds true as for the loan of produced means of production. Thus we are asserting nothing mysterious or strange.

It is clear that there would be no sense in objecting that nothing essential "can" depend upon money. Actually purchasing power

---

[1] The theoretical construction which this unreal conception has enforced since Quesnay's day thus refutes itself. And it is so important that one may speak of "advances-economics" (Vorschussökonomie).

is the vehicle of an essential process; of this there can be no doubt. Moreover the objection cannot really be made at all, because everyone acknowledges the analogous phenomenon that changes in the quantity or distribution of money can have very far-reaching effects. But this observation has stood on a side-track so far. Yet the comparison is quite instructive. Here too there is not necessarily a change in the sphere of goods, a preceding cause on the commodity side, which could be resorted to for explanation. Goods behave quite passively in any case. Nevertheless their kind and quantity are, as everybody knows, very much influenced by such changes.

Our second heresy is also far from being as dangerous as it seems. It also rests, in the ultimate analysis, on a fact that is not merely demonstrable and even obvious but also generally acknowledged. Means of payment are created in the economic system which are, in their external form, it is true, represented as mere *claims* to money, but which differ essentially from claims to other goods in that they perform exactly the same service — at least temporarily — as the good in question itself, so that they may under certain circumstances take its place.[1] Not only is this recognised in the literature on money and banking, but also in theory in the narrower sense. This can be seen in any textbook. We have nothing to add to the observation, but only to the analysis. The problems the discussion of which had most to do with the recognition of the fact were the questions of the concept and value of money. When the quantity theory set up its formula for the value of money, the critics first seized upon the fact of other means of payment. It is well known too that the old question whether these means of payment, more especially bank credits, are money has been answered affirmatively by many of the best writers. But it is sufficient that it was put. In any case the fact with which we are concerned has been recognised without exception so far as I know, even by those writers who

---

[1] Although one may not in general add up claims to goods and the goods themselves — any more than the ear and the grains of corn — yet the matter is clearly somewhat different here. While I cannot ride on a claim to a horse, I can, under certain conditions, do exactly the same with claims to money as with money itself, namely buy.

answered the question negatively. It was also always explained, in more or less detail, how and in what forms the matter is technically possible.

This implies recognising that the circulating media so created do not merely represent an equal quantity of metal money, but that they exist in such quantities that they could not possibly all be redeemed at once; and further, that they not only replace, for the sake of convenience, sums of money which previously circulated, but also appear newly created side by side with the existing sums. Likewise the point, by no means essential for us, but which we maintain for purposes of exposition, that this creation of means of payment centres in the banks and constitutes their fundamental function, we find agrees with the prevailing conception. The creation of money by the banks establishing claims against themselves, which is described by Adam Smith, and indeed by still earlier authors in a way quite free from popular errors, has become a commonplace to-day; whereupon I hasten to add that for our purposes it is all the same whether or not one regards the expression "creation of money" as theoretically correct. Our deductions are completely independent of the particulars of any monetary theory.

Finally, there can be no doubt that these circulating media come into being in the process of granting credit and are created especially — neglecting the cases in which it is only a question of avoiding the transport of metal money — for the *purpose* of granting credit. A bank is, according to Fetter (Principles of Economics, p. 462), "a business whose income is derived chiefly from lending its promises to pay." So far I have said nothing controversial and so far I do not even see the possibility of a difference of opinion. No one can reproach me with offending against, say, Ricardo's statement that "banking operations" cannot increase a country's wealth, or with making myself guilty of, say, a "vapory speculation"[1] in Law's sense. Furthermore, who would

---

[1] Cf. J. S. Mill. Moreover, every economist will admit that Ricardo's statement is not quite correct, even if he is ever so conservative on this point. Cf. for example J. L. Laughlin, who says in his Principles of Money: "Credit does not increase capital (that is means of production) but mobilises it and makes it more efficient and thereby leads to an increase in product." We shall have something similar to say.

deny the fact that, in some countries, perhaps three-quarters of bank deposits are simply credits,[1] and that the businessman as a rule first becomes the bank's debtor in order to become its creditor, that he first "borrows" what he *uno actu* "deposits," to say nothing of the fact that only a negligible fraction of all transactions are and can be effected by money in the strict sense? Therefore I shall not consider these things more closely. There is really no purpose in advancing explanations here which anyone to whom they offer anything new can find in every elementary book. That all forms of credit, from the bank-note to book-credits, are essentially the same thing, and that in all these forms credit increases the means of payment, is also held to be uncontroversial.[2]

So far only one point can be controversial. Most of these circulating media obviously cannot be created without a basis consisting of legal tender or commodities. I believe I do not err when I say that to the businessman as well as to the theorist the producer's bill of exchange appears as the typical example of such circulating media. The producer, after completing his production and selling the product, draws on his customers, in order to turn his claim into "money" immediately. Then these products serve as the "basis" — *in concreto* say bills of lading — and even if the bill is not backed by existing money, it is based instead upon existing goods and so still in a certain sense upon existing "purchasing power." The deposits mentioned above obviously also arise to a great extent from the discounting of commercial paper of this kind. This could well be considered as the normal case of

[1] Only a few banks show in their periodical statements what part of their deposits consists of real deposits. The above estimate is based upon English statements, which show it at least indirectly, and probably amounts to a *communis opinio*. This does not hold good for Germany, for example, because there it is not the practice simply to credit a customer with the amount of the loan. However, the essence of the theory is not on this account different. Strictly speaking, moreover, all bank deposits are based upon mere credits, as Hahn rightly emphasised — only that credits which arise out of "sums paid in" are covered in a special manner and do not increase the purchasing power of the depositors.

[2] Of course there are always theorists who take the layman's standpoint, who regard with astonishment "the gigantic sums in the banks." It is more surprising that financial writers sometimes take a similar line too. As an example, see the otherwise very serviceable book of Clare, A Money Market Primer, which indeed does not accept this standpoint outright, but yet defines the sums available for granting credit as "other peoples' money," which is of course only true for a part, and even then only in a figurative sense.

granting credit or putting credit instruments into the channels of commerce, and every other case might be called abnormal.[1] But even in those cases where there is no question of settling a normal commodity transaction, collateral is usually demanded, and therefore what we call "creation" would only be a question of the mobilisation of existing assets. At this point we should therefore come back again to the traditional conception. In fact the latter seems to triumph, because then there would not only be no circulating media without a basis, but even money could be abstracted from and hence everything would be traced back to the exchange of commodities for commodities, that is, purely to processes in the sphere of goods. This interpretation also explains why it is generally believed that the "creation of money" is merely a technical matter, with no deeper significance for the general theory of economic life, which can safely be relegated to a chapter on banking methods.

We do not wholly agree with this. For the time being it need only be emphasised that what practice designates as "abnormal" is only the creation of circulating media which pretend to be the result of regular commodity transactions, without such being the case. Apart from this, finance bills are not simply something "abnormal." They are, it is true, not creations of credit for financing new combinations, but they frequently come to much the same thing. As regards the collateral, which in such cases cannot be existing products but only other things, its significance, in principle, is not that the assets constituting the collateral are "mobilised" by the granting of credit. This is not a good characterisation of the nature of the thing. On the contrary we must distinguish two cases. First, the entrepreneur may have some kind of security which he can mortgage at the bank.[2] This cir-

---

[1] In this I am neglecting from the outset the case in which the regular business of an economic system is dispatched with credit means of payment and the producer receives a bill or other credit instrument from his customers and buys producers' goods with it immediately. Here there is no granting of credit at all in any relevant sense, and the case is not fundamentally different from cash transactions by means of metal currency. This case, of which we shall say no more here, was mentioned in the first chapter.

[2] Moreover, if it is a question of things like land or shares, which do not circulate — or are not in the market for goods — then the creation of money has just the

cumstance certainly makes it much easier for him in practice to obtain credit. But it does not belong to the nature of the thing in its purest form. The entrepreneurial function is not, in principle, connected with the possession of wealth, as analysis and experience equally teach, even though the accidental fact of the possession of wealth constitutes a practical advantage. In view of the cases in which the latter circumstance is absent, this interpretation can hardly be challenged, and it follows then that the statement that credit as it were "coins property" is not a sufficient formulation of the matter. Or secondly, the entrepreneur may mortgage goods, which he acquires with the borrowed purchasing power. The granting of credit comes first and collateral must be dispensed with, at least in principle, for however short an interval. From this case the conception of putting existing assets into circulation receives still less support than from the first. On the contrary it is perfectly clear that purchasing power is created to which in the first case no new goods correspond.

From this it follows, therefore, that in real life total credit must be greater than it could be if there were only fully covered credit. The credit structure projects not only beyond the existing gold basis, but also beyond the existing commodity basis. Again, this fact as such cannot very well be denied. Only its theoretical significance can be in doubt. The distinction between normal and abnormal credit is, however, important for us. Normal credit creates claims to the social dividend, which represent and may be thought of as certifying services rendered and previous delivery of existing goods. That kind of credit, which is designated by traditional opinion as abnormal, also creates claims to the social product, which, however, in the absence of past productive services could only be described as certificates of future services or of goods yet to be produced. Thus there is a fundamental differ-

---

same effect in the sphere of commodities and upon prices as an uncovered issue. This is often overlooked. Cf. the analogous error in the case of government fiat money when this money is "based" upon land. The frequent foundation of this category of means of payment upon some kind of collateral only eliminates the insecurity which would otherwise exist, but does not alter the fact that there is no new supply of products corresponding to the new demand for products proceeding from it. Cf. Chapter II.

ence between the two categories, in their nature as well as in their effects. Both serve the same purpose as means of payment and are externally indistinguishable. But the one embraces means of payment to which there is a corresponding contribution to the social product, the other means of payment to which so far nothing corresponds — at least no contribution to the social product, even though this deficiency is often made up by other things.

After these introductory remarks, the shortness of which it is hoped will cause no misunderstanding, I proceed to the theme of this chapter. First we must prove the statement, so strange at first sight, that in principle no one other than the entrepreneur needs credit — or the corollary but at once much less strange statement that credit serves industrial development. It has already been established that the entrepreneur—in principle and as a rule — does need credit, in the sense of a temporary transfer to him of purchasing power, in order to produce at all, to be able to carry out his new combinations, to *become* an entrepreneur. And this purchasing power does not flow towards him automatically, as to the producer in the circular flow, by the sale of what he produced in preceding periods. If he does not happen to possess it — and if he did then it would simply be the consequence of former development — he must borrow it. If he does not succeed, then obviously he cannot become an entrepreneur. In this there is nothing fictitious; it is merely the formulation of generally known facts. He can only become an entrepreneur by previously becoming a debtor. He becomes a debtor in consequence of the logic of the process of development, or, to put it in still another way, his becoming a debtor arises from the necessity of the case and is not something abnormal, an accidental event to be explained by particular circumstances. What he first wants is credit. Before he requires any goods whatever, he requires purchasing power. He is the typical debtor in capitalist society.[1]

[1] The entrepreneur is also a debtor in a deeper sense, as may be emphasised here; he receives goods from the social stream — again in principle — before he has contributed anything to it. In this sense he is so to speak a debtor of society. Goods are transferred to him, to which he has not that claim which alone gives access to the national dividend in other cases. Cf. Chapter II.

The argument must now be completed by the negative proof that the same cannot be said of any other type and that no one else is a debtor by the nature of his economic function. Of course there are in reality many other motives for borrowing or lending. But the point is that the granting of credit does not then appear as an essential element of the economic process. This holds good first of all for consumptive credit. Neglecting the fact that its significance can only be a limited one, it is not an element in the fundamental forms and necessities of industrial life. It is not part of the economic nature of any individual that he should contract consumptive loans or of the nature of any productive process that the participators should incur debts for the purposes of their consumption. Therefore the phenomenon of consumptive credit is of no further interest for us here, and in spite of all its practical importance we exclude it from our consideration. This involves no abstraction — we recognise it as a fact, only we have nothing particular to say about it. Exactly the same holds good for those cases in which a credit requirement arises solely for the maintenance of a business which has been disturbed, perhaps by misfortunes. These cases, which I embrace under the concept of "consumptive-productive credits," are also no part of the nature of an economic process in the sense that their treatment appertains to the understanding of the life of the economic organism. They too are of no further interest to us here.

Since every kind of extension of credit for purposes of "innovations" is by definition the granting of credit to the *entrepreneur,* and forms an element of economic development, then the only kind of granting of credit left for consideration here is credit for running a business in the circular flow (Betriebskredit). Our proof is achieved if we can explain it as "unessential" in our sense. What of it then?

We saw in the first chapter that it is not part of the nature of the circular flow that credit (Betriebskredit) is currently taken and given: [1] when the producer has finished his products, then accord-

---

[1] It is to be hoped that the reader will not confuse *this* "current credit" (in the circular flow) with the sum which must also be supplied to the entrepreneur for "running" in contrast to founding the business, that is especially for the purpose of current wage payments.

ing to our conception he sells them immediately and begins his production anew with the proceeds. To be sure, things do not always happen thus. It may be that he wishes to begin producing before he has delivered the products to his customer. But the decisive point is that we can, without overlooking anything essential, represent the process within the circular flow as if production were currently financed by receipts. Credit in the ordinary routine of established business owes its practical importance solely to the fact that there is development and that this development carries with it the possibility of employing sums of money which are temporarily idle. Hence every businessman will turn these receipts to account as promptly as possible and will then borrow what purchasing power he may require. If there were no development, then the sums of money necessary to carry out transactions would normally have to be actually kept in every firm and household, and during the time when they were not needed would have to lie idle. It is development that alters this. It soon sweeps away those types whose pride it was that they never took any credit. And when in the end all businesses — old as well as new ones — are drawn into the circle of the credit phenomenon, bankers will even prefer this kind of credit on account of the smaller risk it involves. Many banks, particularly of the "deposit" type and also almost all old-established houses, actually do this and restrict themselves more or less to such "current" credit. But this is only a consequence of development already in full swing.

This interpretation does not place us in opposition to the prevailing one as much as might be thought.[1] On the contrary, we assert by it, in complete agreement with the usual view, that we can dispense with credit if we want to grasp the economic process of the circular flow. Only because the prevailing theory takes the same view, and like us sees in the financing by credit of current

[1] Moreover, it is directly verified by the facts. For many centuries there was practically only consumptive credit. Then there was no more than credit for founding a business. And the circular flow went on without it. Current credit only attained its present importance in modern times. And since a modern factory differs economically from a medieval workshop in no other fundamental respect, the conclusion is reached that the former needs no credit in principle.

commodity transactions nothing essential to the understanding of the matter, can it eliminate this proceeding from its treatment of the main features of the economic process. Only on this account can it restrict its view to the sphere of goods. Within the world of goods something like credit transactions may of course be found, but we have already come to an understanding on this. At all events the prevailing theory recognises the necessity of creating new purchasing power at this point just as little as we do, and the fact that it also does not see such a necessity at any other point shows again that it is merely static.

This current credit can therefore be eliminated from our treatment with the same justification as consumptive credit. From the knowledge that it involves only a question of a technical expedient of exchange — in the circular flow, of course, because with development it would be something different for the reason mentioned — an expedient which has no further effect upon the economic process, we come to the following conclusion. In order to contrast current credit sharply with that credit which does play a fundamental rôle and without which complete understanding of the economic process is impossible, we shall assume in the case of the circular flow that all exchanges are effected by metal money which exists once for all in given quantities and with a given rapidity of circulation. Obviously the whole circulation of an economy without development may also consist of credit means of payment. Since these means of payment, however, would function just like metal money in that they are "certificates" for existing goods and past services, and since there is therefore no essential difference between them and metallic money, by using this expository device we merely indicate that what we regard as the essential element in the credit phenomenon is not to be found in current credit within the circular flow.

By this we have both proved our thesis and precisely formulated the sense in which it is meant. Only the entrepreneur then, in principle, needs credit; only for industrial development does it play a fundamental part, that is a part the consideration of which is essential to an understanding of the whole process. Furthermore, it is seen at once from the arguments of the second chapter that the correlative of the thesis also holds good, namely the statement that where there is no direct power of disposal by leaders over means of production, development is in principle impossible without credit.

The essential function of credit in our sense consists in enabling the entrepreneur to withdraw the producers' goods which he needs from their previous employments, by exercising a demand for them, and thereby to force the economic system into new channels. Our second thesis now runs: in so far as credit cannot be given out of the results of past enterprise or in general out of reservoirs of purchasing power created by past development, it can only consist of credit means of payment created *ad hoc*, which can be backed neither by money in the strict sense nor by products already in existence. It can indeed be covered by other assets than products, that is by any kind of property which the entrepreneur may happen to own. But this is in the first place not necessary and in the second place does not alter the nature of the process, which consists in creating a new demand for, without simultaneously creating, a new supply of goods. This thesis needs no further proof here, but follows from the arguments of the second chapter. It provides us with the connection between lending and credit means of payment, and leads us to what I regard as the nature of the credit phenomenon.

Since credit in the one case in which it is essential to the economic process can only be granted from such newly created means of payment (provided there are no results of previous development); and since, conversely, only in this one case does the creation of such credit means of payment play more than a merely technical rôle, then to this extent giving credit involves creating purchasing power, and newly created purchasing power is of use only in giving credit to the entrepreneur, is necessary for this purpose alone. This is the only case in which we cannot, without impairing the truth of our theoretical picture, substitute metal money for credit means of payment. For we can assume that a certain quantity of metal money exists at any time, since nothing depends upon its absolute magnitude; but we cannot assume an increase of it to appear just at the right time and place. Therefore if we exclude from lending as well as from the creation of credit instruments those cases in which credit transactions and credit instruments play no essential part, then the two must coincide, if we neglect the results of previous development.

In this sense, therefore, we define the kernel of the credit phenomenon in the following manner: credit is essentially the creation of purchasing power for the purpose of transferring it to the entrepreneur, but not simply the transfer of existing purchasing power. The creation of purchasing power characterises, in principle, the method by which development is carried out in a system with private property and division of labor. By credit, entrepreneurs are given access to the social stream of goods before they have acquired the normal claim to it. It temporarily substitutes, as it were, a fiction of this claim for the claim itself. Granting credit in this sense operates as an order on the economic system to accommodate itself to the purposes of the entrepreneur, as an order on the goods which he needs: it means entrusting him with productive forces. It is only thus that economic development could arise from the mere circular flow in perfect equilibrium. And this function constitutes the keystone of the modern credit structure.

Hence, while granting credit is not essential in the normal circular flow, because in it no necessary gap exists between products and means of production, and because it can be assumed there that all purchases of production goods by producers are cash transactions or that in general whoever is a buyer previously sold goods of the same money value, it is certain that there is such a gap to bridge in the carrying out of new combinations. To bridge it is the function of the lender, and he fulfils it by placing purchasing power created *ad hoc* at the disposal of the entrepreneur. Then those who supply production goods need not "wait" and yet the entrepreneur need advance them neither goods nor existing money. Thus the gap is closed which would otherwise make development extraordinarily difficult, if not impossible in an exchange economy where private property prevails. That the function of lenders lies in this is denied by no one. Differences of opinion exist only about the nature of the "bridge." I believe that our conception, far from being more audacious and foreign to reality than others, is nearest to reality and makes a whole network of fictions superfluous.

In the circular flow, from which we always start, the same products are produced every year in the same way. For every supply there waits somewhere in the economic system a corresponding demand, for every demand the corresponding supply. All goods are dealt in at determined prices with only insignificant oscillations, so that every unit of money may be considered as going the same way in every period. A given quantity of purchasing power is available at any moment to purchase the existing quantity of original productive services, in order then to pass into the hands of their owners and then again to be spent on consumption goods. There is no market for the bearers of the original productive services themselves, especially for land, and there is also no price for them within the normal circular flow.[1]

If we neglect, as unessential, the value of the material of the monetary units, the purchasing power then really represents nothing but existing goods. Its total tells us nothing, but the shares of households and firms in this total do. If now credit means of payment, new purchasing power in our sense, are created and placed at the entrepreneur's disposal, then he takes his place beside the previous producers and his purchasing power its place beside the total previously existing. Obviously this does not increase the quantity of productive services existing in the economic system. Yet "new demand" becomes possible in a very obvious sense. It causes a rise in the prices of productive services. From this ensues the "withdrawal of goods" from their previous use, to which we have referred.[2] The process amounts to compress-

---

[1] Cf. the construction in Chapter I, from which it is clear why I do not mention produced means of production with the services of labor and land, although purchasing power is obviously applied to them too and not only to the services of labor and land.

[2] On this point I differ from Spiethoff. His three articles: "Die äussere Ordnung des Kapital- und Geldmarktes," "Das Verhältnis von Kapital, Geld, und Güterwelt," and "Der Kapitalmangel in seinem Verhältnisse zur Güterwelt" in Schmoller's Jahrbuch (1909) (also independently under the title Kapital Geld und Güterwelt) have above all the merit of having attacked the problem. At a number of points they anticipated what is said in this chapter. The possibility of "creating new money substitutes" was also expressly emphasised (for example, in the second

ing [1] the existing purchasing power. In one sense no goods and certainly no new goods correspond to the newly created purchasing power. But room for it is squeezed out at the cost of previously existing purchasing power.

This explains the manner in which the creation of purchasing power works. The reader can see that there is nothing illogical or mystical in it.[2] The external form of the credit instruments is quite irrelevant. To be sure, the matter is seen most plainly in the case of the uncovered bank-note. But also a bill, which does not replace existing money, and which is not based upon goods already produced, is of the same character, if it actually circulates. Of course this is not true if it merely records the entrepreneur's obligation to his creditor or if it is merely discounted, but only when it is used in paying for goods. And all other forms of credit instruments, even simple credits in the books of a bank, may be considered from the same point of view. Just as when additional gas streams into a vessel the share of the space occupied by each molecule of the previously existing gas is diminished by compression, so the inflow of new purchasing power into the economic system will compress the old purchasing power. When the price changes which thus become necessary are completed, any given commodities exchange for the new units of purchasing power on the same terms as for the old, only the units of purchasing power now existing are all smaller than those existing before and their distribution among individuals has been shifted.

This may be called credit inflation. But it is distinguished from

article, p. 85). But to this there is an "insurmountable economic limit, in the existing supply of goods. Only in so far as these artificial measures can put hitherto idle goods in circulation are they able to work." If this limit is exceeded prices rise. The latter is certainly correct — but the salient point for us is precisely here. Of course we agree that tightness of money cannot be eliminated by creating purchasing power — or at any rate can only be when it is a matter of a momentary panic.

[1] In the first place, the purchasing power of previous producers in the market for producers' goods will be compressed, then the purchasing power in the market for consumption goods of those people who receive no share or no adequate share in the increased money incomes resulting from the entrepreneur's demand. This explains rising prices in periods of boom. If I am not mistaken it was von Mises who coined the extremely happy expression "forced saving" (erzwungenes Sparen) for this process.

[2] Cf. also A. Hahn, the article "Kredit" in the Handwörterbuch der Staatswissenschaften.

credit inflation for consumptive purposes by a very essential element. In these cases also new purchasing power takes its place beside the old, prices rise, a withdrawal of goods results in favor of the credit receiver or of those to whom the latter pays out the borrowed sums. There the process breaks off: the goods withdrawn are consumed, the means of payment created remain in circulation, the credit must be continually renewed, and prices have risen permanently. It may be then that the loan is paid off out of the normal income stream — for example by an increase in taxation. But this is a new, special operation (deflation), which, proceeding in the well known way, again restores the health of the monetary system, which but for it would not return to its previous state.

In our case, however, the process goes *vi impressa* further. The entrepreneur must not only legally repay money to his banker, but he must also economically repay commodities to the reservoir of goods — the equivalent of borrowed productive means; or, as we have expressed it, he must ultimately fulfil the condition upon which goods may normally be taken out of the social stream. The result of the borrowing enables him to fulfil this condition. After completing his business — in our conception, therefore, after a period at the end of which his products are on the market and his productive goods used up — he has, if everything has gone according to expectations, enriched the social stream with goods whose total price is greater than the credit received and than the total price of the goods directly and indirectly used up by him. Hence the equivalence between the money and commodity streams is more than restored, the credit inflation more than eliminated, the effect upon prices more than compensated for,[1] so that it may be said that there is no credit inflation at all in this case — rather deflation — but only a non-synchronous appearance of purchasing power and of the commodities corresponding to it, which temporarily produces the semblance of inflation.

Furthermore, the entrepreneur can now repay his debt (amount

---

[1] This alone would explain falling prices in periods of depression and actually explains the secular fall in the price level in times when no other causes, for example gold discoveries, prevent it, as we shall see in Chapter VI.

credited plus interest) at his bank, and normally still retain a credit balance (= entrepreneurial profit) that is withdrawn from the purchasing-power fund of the circular flow. Only this profit and interest necessarily remain in circulation; the original bank credit has disappeared, so that the deflationary effect in itself — and especially if new and bigger enterprises are not continually being financed — would be much more severe than that just indicated. It is true that in practice two reasons prevent the prompt disappearance of the newly created purchasing power: first the fact that most enterprises are not terminated in one period but in most cases only after a series of years. The essence of the matter is not altered by this, but the newly created purchasing power remains longer in circulation and the "redemption" at the legal date then often takes the form of a "prolongation." In this case it is economically no redemption at all but a method of periodically testing the soundness of the enterprise. Economically this should really be called "presentation for audit" instead of "presentation for payment" — whether the thing to be redeemed is a bill or a personal loan. Moreover, if it is true that long-term enterprises are financed by short-term credit, every entrepreneur and every bank will try for obvious reasons to exchange this basis as soon as possible for a more permanent one, indeed will regard it as an achievement if the first stage can be completely jumped in an individual case. In practice this approximately coincides with replacing purchasing power created *ad hoc* by that existing already. And this generally happens in the case of development in full swing which has already accumulated reserves of purchasing power — thus for reasons which our theory itself explains and which do not argue against it — and indeed in two steps. In the first place, shares or bonds are created and their amounts are credited to the enterprise, which means that banking resources still finance the enterprise. Then these shares and bonds are disposed of and gradually are paid for — not always at once, on the contrary the accounts of the subscribing customers are often only debited — by the subscribers out of existing supplies of purchasing power or reserves or savings. Thus, as it may be expressed, they are resorbed by the community's savings. The redemption of the credit instruments is thus accomplished and they are replaced by existing money. But this is not yet the final redemption of the entrepreneur's debt, the redemption in goods. The latter only comes later, even in this case.

Secondly, still another fact prevents the prompt disappearance of the new purchasing power. Credit instruments may disappear in the case of final success, they have so to say the tendency to do so automatically. But even if they do not disappear, no disturbance occurs either in the individual or in the social economy — for now the commodities are there which constitute a counterbalance to and the only really significant kind of "cover." for the new purchasing power, which is precisely what is always absent in the case of consumptive credit. And so the process of production can always be repeated anew with the help of renewal of credit, although this is no longer "new enterprise" within our meaning. The credit instruments thus not only have no further influence upon prices, but they even lose that which they originally exercised. Indeed, this is the most important of the ways in which bank credit forces its way into the circular flow, until it has so established itself there that analytical effort is necessary in order to recognise that its source is not there. If this were not so the received theory would not only be false — which it is in any case — but inexcusable and incomprehensible.

If the possibility of giving credit is therefore not limited by the quantity of liquid resources existing independently of creation for the very purpose of granting credit, nor by the existing — idle or total — quantity of goods, by what is it limited?

First as regards practice: let us assume that we have a free gold standard, that is redemption of bank-notes in gold upon demand, the obligation to purchase gold at a legal price, and free export of gold. Assume also that we have a banking system grouped around a central note-issuing bank, but that there are no other legal barriers and rules for the gestation of banking business — for example no note-reserve regulations and so on for the central bank or deposit-reserve regulations and so on for the other banks. This represents the leading case, the treatment of which is easily applicable to other cases. Then every new creation of purchasing power which precedes the appearance of the corresponding quantities of goods and hence raises prices will have the tendency to raise the value of the gold contained in gold coin above the value of the monetary unit. This will lead to a diminution of the quantity of gold in circulation, but above all to the presentation of bank means of payment for redemption, first bank-notes, then directly and indirectly all others, in another sense, for another purpose and for another reason than that which we have just described. And if the solvency of the banking system in this sense is not to be endangered, the banks can only give credit in such a way that the resulting inflation is really temporary and moreover remains moderate. But it can only remain temporary if the commodity complement of the newly created purchasing power comes on the market at the right time, and if, in cases of failure where it does not appear on the market at all and in cases of lengthy production where it appears only after long years, the banker intervenes with purchasing power drawn from the circular flow, for example with money saved by other people. Hence the necessity of maintaining a reserve, which acts as a brake on the central bank as well as on the other banks. Competing with this nexus is the circumstance that all credits given are finally resolved into small sums in daily trade, and in order to serve in the latter must be changed into coin or small state notes — at least in most countries — which cannot be created by the banks. Finally, the credit inflation must start an outflow of gold abroad — hence a further danger of insolvency. It may happen, however, and is indeed sometimes approximately realised, that the banks of all countries extend their credits almost simultaneously. Therefore, even if we cannot, in the nature of things, state the limit to the creation of purchasing power under the assumptions made as accurately as, say, the limit to the production of a commodity, and even if the limit must vary according to the mentality of the people, legislation, and so on, yet we can state that there is such a limit at any time and what circumstances normally guarantee its maintenance. Its existence neither excludes the creation of purchasing power in our sense nor alters its significance. But it makes its volume at any time an elastic, though nevertheless a definite, magnitude.

The fundamental question under consideration here is of course only very superficially answered by the above; just as the question regarding the reasons for a rate of exchange is answered superficially by saying it must lie between the gold points in the case of a universal free gold standard. However, just as we look at essentials in the latter case if we omit the gold mechanism and look at the "commodity points" underneath, so in our case, by the same principle, we arrive at a more fundamental explanation of the fact that the creation of purchasing power has definite, even though elastic, limits if we consider a country with a paper standard or let us say outright with nothing but bank means of payment. Since the case of countries trading with one another offers nothing fundamentally new we leave the analysis of it to the reader. Here, then, the limit is given by the condition that credit inflation in favor of new enterprises should be only temporary, or that there should be no inflation at all in the sense of permanently raising the price level. And the brake which guarantees the maintenance of this limit is the fact that any other conduct in the face of the rush of entrepreneurs seeking credit would mean a loss for the bank concerned. This loss always occurs if the entrepreneur does not succeed in producing commodities at least equal in value to the credit plus interest. Only when he succeeds in so doing has the bank done good business — then and only then, however, is there also no inflation, as we have shown, that is no infraction of the limit. From this the rules may be derived which determine in individual cases the magnitude of the possible creation of purchasing power.

Only in one other case could the banking world, if it were released from the obligation of redeeming its means of payment in gold and if the regard for international exchange were suspended, start inflation and arbitrarily determine the price level, not only without loss but even with profit: namely, if it pumped credit means of payment into the circular flow either by making bad commitments good by a further creation of new circulating media or by giving credits which really serve consumptive ends. In general no single bank could do this. For while its issue of means of payment would not appreciably affect the price level, the bad commitment would remain bad and the consumptive credit become bad if it did not lie within the limits in which it could be repaid by the debtor out of his income. But all banks together could do it. They could, under our assumptions, continually give additional credit and precisely through its effect upon prices make good that given previously. And that this is possible to a certain extent even outside these assumptions is the chief reason why special legal restrictions and special safety-valves are actually necessary in practice.

This last statement is really self-evident. Just as the state, under certain circumstances, can print notes without any assignable limit, so the banks could do likewise if the state — for it comes to this — were to transfer the right to them in their interest and for their purposes, and common sense did not prevent them from exercising it. But this has nothing to do with our case, viz. the case of granting credit and creating purchasing power for carrying out new combinations *which are remunerative at the existing level of prices* [1] — hence nothing to do with the meaning, nature, and origin of the creation of entrepreneurial purchasing power in general. I emphasise this expressly because the thesis concerning the unlimited power of the banks to create circulating media, after being repeatedly quoted, not only without the necessary qualifications, but also without the context in which it stands,[2] has become a point of attack and a ground for rejecting the new theory of credit.

CAPITAL

It is now time to give expression to a thought which has long been awaiting formulation and which is familiar to every business-

---

[1] Our theory has been interpreted to mean that credit creation facilitates the carrying out of new things by raising prices and thereby making remunerative what would not otherwise be so. This is *not* what it means.

[2] Cf. the otherwise excellent article by Hahn in the Handwörterbuch der Staatswissenschaften on "Kredit." Against his formulation it appears to me correct to say: although not by existing goods, the quantity of new purchasing power that it is possible to create is supported and limited by future goods, and, to repeat, by *future* goods at *present* prices.

man. That form of economic organisation in which the goods necessary for new production are withdrawn from their settled place in the circular flow by the intervention of purchasing power created *ad hoc* is the capitalist economy, while those forms of economy in which this happens through any kind of power of command or through agreement of all concerned represent non-capitalistic production. *Capital is nothing but the lever by which the entrepreneur subjects to his control the concrete goods which he needs, nothing but a means of diverting the factors of production to new uses, or of dictating a new direction to production.* This is the only function of capital, and by it the place of capital in the economic organism is completely characterised.

Now what is this lever, this means of control? It certainly does not consist of any definite category of goods, of any definable part of the existing supply of goods. It is generally recognised that we meet with capital in production and that it is useful in some way or other in the productive process. Hence we must also see it somewhere in operation in our case of carrying out new combinations. Now all the goods which the entrepreneur needs are on the same level from his standpoint. He wants the services of natural agents, of labor, of machinery, of raw material, all of them equally and in just the same sense, and nothing distinguishes one of these wants from the others. Of course this is not to say that there is no relevant difference at all between these categories of goods. On the contrary there are certainly differences, even though their significance was and still is overestimated by many theorists. But it is clear that the entrepreneur's behavior is the same towards all these categories: he buys all of them for money, for which he calculates or pays interest, without distinction, whether they are tools or land or labor. They all play the same part, are equally necessary for him. In particular it is quite immaterial whether he begins his production as it were *ab ovo*, that is merely buys land and labor, or whether he also acquires already existing intermediate products instead of producing them himself. Finally, if he should acquire consumption goods this would make no fundamental difference either. Nevertheless, it would look as if consumption goods had the first claim to be emphasised, especially if one accepted the theory that the entrepreneur "advances" consumption goods to the possessors of productive means, in the narrower sense of the word. In this case these goods would be characteristically different from other goods; they would play a special rôle, and indeed precisely the one which we assign to capital. From this it would follow that the entrepreneur would exchange productive services for consumption goods. Then we should have to say that capital consists of consumption goods. However, this possibility is already settled.

Setting aside this last interpretation, then, there is no reason for making any kind of distinction between all the goods which the entrepreneur buys, consequently no reason for including any group of them under the name capital. That capital defined so as to consist of goods belongs to every economic organisation and hence is not suitable for characterising the capitalistic one, requires no argument. Furthermore, it is not true that if the businessman were asked wherein consists his capital, he would point to any of these categories of goods. If he mentions his factory he includes the ground on which it stands, and if he wishes to be complete he will not forget his working capital in which directly or indirectly purchases of labor services are included.

The capital of an enterprise, however, is also not the aggregate of *all* the goods serving its purposes. For capital *confronts* the world of goods. Goods are bought for capital — "capital is invested in goods" — but this very fact implies the recognition that its function is different from that of the goods acquired. The function of the goods consists in serving a productive purpose corresponding to their technical nature. The function of capital consists in procuring for the entrepreneur the means with which to produce. It stands as a third agent necessary to production in an exchange economy *between* the entrepreneur and the world of goods. It constitutes the bridge between them. It does not take part directly in production, it is not itself "worked up"; on the contrary it performs a task which must be done before technical production can begin.

The entrepreneur must have capital before he can think of providing himself with concrete goods. There is a time when he already has the necessary capital but not yet the production goods, and at this moment one can see more clearly than ever that capital is not something identical with concrete goods but is an independent agent. And its only purpose, the only reason why the entrepreneur needs capital — I appeal to obvious facts — is simply to serve as a fund out of which productive goods can be paid for. Furthermore, so long as this purchase is not completed, the capital has absolutely no relation to any definite goods at all. It exists of course — who could deny it? — but its characteristic quality is precisely that it does not come into consideration as a concrete category of goods, that it is not employed technically as a good, but as a means of providing those goods which are to be employed in production in the technical sense. But when this purchase is completed, does the entrepreneur's capital then consist of concrete goods—of all kinds of land bought as well as of tools bought, but still of goods? If one exclaims with Quesnay: "Parcourez les fermes et les ateliers, et . . . vous trouverez des bâtiments, des bestiaux, des semences, des matières premières, des meubles et des instruments de toute espèce" — from our point of view one must add further: services of land and labor and also consumption goods as well — is not this justified after the purchase? The capital has now fulfilled the function ascribed to it by us. If the necessary productive means, and, as we shall assume, also the necessary labor services, are bought, then the entrepreneur no longer has the capital which was placed at his disposal. He has surrendered it for productive means. It has been dissolved into incomes. The traditional conception at present is that his capital now consists of the goods acquired. Indeed it is a presupposition of this interpretation that the function of capital in procuring goods is completely ignored, and replaced by the unreal hypothesis that the very goods which he needs are lent to the entrepreneur. If one does not do this and if, following reality, one distinguishes the fund out of which production goods are paid for from these productive means themselves, there cannot in my opinion be the slightest doubt that it is to this fund that everything that one is accustomed to say of capital and all that we designate as capitalistic phenomena refer. If this is correct then it is furthermore clear that the entrepreneur no longer possesses this fund, because he has just paid it out, and that the parts of it in the hands of the sellers of productive means can be no different in character from the sums received from the sale of bread in the hands of the baker. The everyday method of expression frequently met with, which describes the productive means when purchased as "capital," proves nothing, all the more when the other expression goes with it, namely that capital is "embodied in these goods." The latter method of expression can only be correct in the sense in which it can also be said that coal is "embodied" in a steel rail, that is in the sense that the use of coal has led to the creation of the steel rail. But for all that, does not the entrepreneur still have his capital? And can he not at least "draw out" his capital from this "investment" again, while the same coal cannot be obtained again? I believe that these questions can be satisfactorily answered. No, the entrepreneur has spent his capital. In return for it, he has acquired goods which he will not employ as capital, that is as a fund in paying for other goods, but in technical production. However, if he changes his mind and wishes to part with these goods, there will usually be other people ready to buy them — and then he can again obtain possession of a greater or smaller amount of capital. From this point of view, since his productive means can serve not only as productive means but also indirectly as capital — in so far as he can use them to obtain first purchasing power and then other productive means — he is right if he calls them elliptically his capital. Really they are the only source of purchasing power at his command if he should be in need of it before his production is completed. We shall come to still another reason for this interpretation. The second question is now also answered: the entrepreneur can obtain capital again by selling his production goods. He cannot of course get the identical capital again, in most cases not even the same amount. But since this does not matter, the plastic expression "to draw out his capital" has though only a figurative yet quite a sound meaning. It does not conflict with our interpretation.

What is capital then if it consists neither of a definite kind of goods nor of goods in general? By this time the answer is obvious enough: it is a fund of purchasing power. Only as such can it fulfil its essential function, the sole function for which capital is necessary in practice and for which alone the capital concept has a use in theory, which cannot be just as well replaced by enumerating categories of goods.

The question now arises as to what exactly constitutes this fund of purchasing power. This question seems to be very simple. Of what does my fund of purchasing power consist? Why, of money and of my other assets calculated in money. This answer would bring us practically to Menger's capital concept. Certainly I call this "my capital" innumerable times. Further, there are also no difficulties in distinguishing it as a "fund" from the "stream" of returns, so that here we take a step again in Irving Fisher's direction. Again, it might be said that I can embark upon an enterprise with this very sum or lend it to an entrepreneur.

However, this view, apparently so satisfactory at first sight, is unfortunately not completely adequate. It is not true that I can enter the ranks of entrepreneurs only with this sum. If I can draw a bill that will be taken in payment, then I can also buy production goods for its amount. One might now say that I simply contract a debt thereby, which is far from increasing my capital. One might say further that the goods "bought" with the bill are just lent to me. Yet let us look more closely. If I am successful I shall be able to redeem the bill with money or counter-claims, which do not come out of my capital but out of the proceeds of my product. Thus I have increased my capital, or if there is any reluctance in granting this, I have done something that renders me just the same service as an increase of my capital, without incurring debts which would later decrease my capital again. It might be objected that my capital would have grown if I had not had to repay debts. However, these debts were paid out of a gain, which we cannot even be certain would have been added to my capital if it had accrued to me unimpaired. For I might use it to acquire consumption goods, in which case it would be contrary to every kind of usage to describe it as a part of capital. If it is correct that the function of capital only consists in assuring the entrepreneur control over production goods, then we cannot evade the conclusion that my capital would be increased by creating the bill. If the reader keeps in mind what was said earlier in combination with what follows, our result will lose much of its paradoxical appearance. It is true, I have not become richer by creating the bill. But the term "wealth" (Vermögen) makes it possible to take account of this other aspect of the matter.

But it is also not true that expression in terms of money suffices to lend a capital character in our sense to property which is not itself held in the form of money. If one possesses some sort of goods it will not in general be possible to obtain by direct exchange the production goods which one needs. On the contrary one will always have to sell the goods one has and then employ the proceeds of the sale as capital, that is in obtaining the production goods required. Actually the conception under consideration recognises this also in that it stresses the money value of the goods which anyone possesses. It is easy to see that it is only an elliptical or figurative method of expression when one describes these goods themselves as capital. The same is also true of purchased means of production, as already mentioned, which this conception also treats as capital.

So far our definition is on the one hand wider and on the other hand narrower than Menger's and others related to it. Only means of payment are capital, not merely "money" but circulating media in general, of whatever kind they may be; not all means of payment, however, but only those which actually fulfil the characteristic function with which we are concerned.

This limitation lies in the nature of the thing. If means of payment do not serve to provide an entrepreneur with production goods and to withdraw the latter from their previous employment for this purpose, then they are not capital. In an economic system without development there is therefore no "capital"; or, otherwise expressed, capital does not fulfil its characteristic function, it is not an independent agent. Or, still differently expressed, the various forms of general purchasing power do not constitute capital there; they are simply exchange media, technical means for carrying out the customary exchanges. With this, their rôle in the circular flow is complete — they have none except this technical rôle, so that they can be neglected without overlooking anything very essential. In the carrying out of new combinations, however, money and its substitutes become an essential factor, and we express this by describing them as capital. Thus, according to our point of view, capital is a concept of development to which nothing in the circular flow corresponds. *This concept embodies an aspect of the economic process which only the facts of development suggest to us.* I should like to draw the reader's attention to this statement. It contributes much to the understanding of the point of view here developed. If one speaks of capital with the connotation which the word has in practical life, then one always thinks not so much of things as of processes or of a certain aspect of things, namely of the possibility of entrepreneurial activity, of the possibility of control over productive means in general. This aspect is something common to many concepts of capital, and the efforts to bring it out explain, in my opinion, the "protean" qualities of the concrete definition. According to it nothing is really in itself capital, absolutely and by virtue of immanent qualities, but that which is designated as capital is so only to the extent that it satisfies certain conditions, or only from a certain point of view.

We shall define capital, then, as that sum of means of payment which is available at any moment for transference to entrepreneurs. At the moment when development starts from a circular flow in equilibrium, only a very small part of that sum of capital could, according to our interpretation, consist of money; on the contrary, it would have to consist of other means of payment newly created for the purpose. If development is once in motion or if capitalist development joins a non-capitalist or a transitional form, it will start with a supply of accumulated liquid resources. But in strict theory it could not do this. And even in reality it is always impossible when something really significant is to be done for the first time.

Capital, then, is an agent in the exchange economy. A process of the exchange economy is given expression to in the capital aspect, namely the transfer of productive means to the entrepreneur. There is therefore in our sense really only private and no "social" capital. Means of payment can only perform their capital rôle in the hands of private individuals. Hence there would be little purpose in speaking of social capital with this meaning. Nevertheless, the sum of private capitals tells us something: it gives the magnitude of the fund that can be put at the disposal of entrepreneurs, the magnitude of the power of withdrawing means of production from their previous channels. Therefore the concept of social capital is not meaningless,[1] even though there would be no such capital in a communist economy. Yet one thinks for the most part of a nation's stock of goods when one speaks of social capital, and only the real capital concepts have led to that of social capital.

THE MONEY MARKET

One more step remains to be taken. Capital is neither the whole nor a part of the means of production — original or produced. Nor is capital a stock of consumption goods. It is a special agent. As such it must have a market in that theoretical sense in which there is a market for consumption goods and for production goods. And to this theoretical market something similar must correspond in reality as in the case of these other two. We saw in the first chapter that there are markets for the services of labor and land and for consumption goods in which everything essential to the circular flow is settled, while the produced means of production, transitory items, have no such independent market. In development, which introduces the new agent capital into the economic process, there must be still a third market in which something interesting happens, the capital market.

This does exist: reality shows it to us directly, much more directly than it shows us the markets for services and for consumption goods. It is much more concentrated, much better organised, much easier to observe than the other two. It is what the businessman calls the money market, that about which every

---

[1] This is especially true if one measures every unit of capital by the amounts of production goods obtainable for it at any time. If one does this then one may also speak of "real" capital — but only in a figurative sense.

newspaper reports daily under this title. From our standpoint the name is not wholly satisfactory: it is not simply money that is dealt in, and we might in part join the protest of economists against this conception of it. But we accept the name. In any case the capital market is the same as the phenomenon that practice describes as the money market. There is no other capital market.[1] It would be an attractive and a profitable task to outline a theory of the money market. As yet we have none.[2] It would be especially interesting and profitable to collect and test the theoretical meaning of the practical rules of experience which determine the practical man's decisions and his judgment of particular situations. They are indeed for the most part strictly formulated, and guide every writer of money-market articles. These practical rules for economic forecasting are at present quite detached from theory, although the study of them leads deep into the understanding of modern economic life. We cannot go into this here. We shall only say what is necessary for our purposes. This can be done in a few words.

In an economy without development there would be no such money market. If it were highly organised and its transactions were settled with credit means of payment it would have a central settlement bureau, a kind of clearing house or bookkeeping centre for the economic system. In the transactions of this institution everything that happens in the economic system would be mirrored, for example the periodical payments of wages and taxes, the requirements for moving the harvest and for holidays. But these would only be matters of accounting. Now these functions must also be performed if there is development. With development, moreover, there is always employment for purchasing power which is momentarily idle. And finally, with development, as already emphasised, bank-credit penetrates into the transactions of the circular flow. Thus it is, then, that these things become, in practice, elements of the function of the money market.

---

[1] At the most one may with Spiethoff (loc. cit.) distinguish the capital market as the market for long-term purchasing power from the money market as the market for short loans. But purchasing power is the commodity in each.

[2] Cf., however, A. Hahn, "Zur Theorie des Geldmarkts," Archiv für Sozialwissenschaft und Sozialpolitik (1923).

They become a part of the organism of the money market. And so the requirements of the circular flow are added to the entrepreneur's demand in the money market on the one hand, and money from the circular flow increases the supply of money in the money market on the other. Hence we feel in every money-market article the pulse of the circular flow, hence we see that the demand for purchasing power increases at harvest-time, when taxes are due and so forth, while after these times the supply increases. But this must not prevent us from distinguishing the transactions in the money market which belong to the circular flow from others. Only the latter are fundamental; the former are added onto them, and the fact that they appear in the money market at all is merely a consequence of development. All the reciprocal effects which obviously bind the two together do not alter the fact that, even practically, they may be distinguished in every case and that in the money market it is always possible to say what belongs to the circular flow and what belongs to development.

The kernel of the matter lies in the credit requirements of new enterprises. Of course we must remember that the influence of the international relations in which every economic system finds itself, and of non-economic intervention, to which every economic system is exposed, are neglected here, in order to shorten and simplify the exposition. Hence the phenomena of the national balance of payments, of the bullion trade, and so on drop out of sight. With this proviso, only one fundamental thing happens on the money market, to which everything else is accessory: on the demand side appear entrepreneurs and on the supply side producers of and dealers in purchasing power, viz. bankers, both with their staffs of agents and middlemen. What takes place is simply the exchange of present against future purchasing power. In the daily price struggle between the two parties the fate of new combinations is decided. In this price struggle the system of future values first appears in a practical, tangible form and in relation to the given conditions of the economic system. It would be wholly wrong to believe that the price of short-term credits is a matter of indifference for new undertakings since it is long-term credit that they want. On the contrary, the whole economic situation at every moment is nowhere so clearly expressed as in the price of short loans. The entrepreneur does not necessarily borrow for the whole period over which he needs credit, but as necessity arises and often almost from day to day. Moreover, speculators often hold shares, especially of new enterprises, with such short-term credit, which may be granted to-day and denied to-morrow. We may observe from day to day how the credit requirements of industry manifest themselves and how the banking world sometimes supports and encourages, sometimes curbs, the demand. While in other markets the demand as well as the supply exhibits a certain constancy, even in development, here surprisingly large fluctuations appear from day to day. We shall explain this by the special function of the money market. All plans and outlooks for the future in the economic system affect it, all conditions of the national life, all political, economic, and natural events. There is scarcely a piece of news that does not necessarily influence the decisions relative to the carrying out of new combinations or the money-market position and the opinions and intentions of entrepreneurs. The system of future values must be adapted to every new situation. This is of course not merely effected by variations in the price of purchasing power. Frequently, personal influence acts in addition to or in the place of the latter. But there is no need to go into these well known details.

The money market is always, as it were, the headquarters of the capitalist system, from which orders go out to its individual divisions, and that which is debated and decided there is always in essence the settlement of plans for further development. All kinds of credit requirements come to this market; all kinds of economic projects are first brought into relation with one another, and contend for their realisation in it; all kinds of purchasing power, balances of every sort, flow to it to be sold. This gives rise to a number of arbitrage operations and intermediate manoeuvres which may easily veil the fundamental thing. Nevertheless, I believe that at bottom our conception need hardly fear contradiction.

Thus the main function of the money or capital market is

trading in credit for the purpose of financing development. Development creates and nourishes this market. In the course of development it is assigned still another, that is a third, function: it becomes the market for sources of incomes themselves. We shall consider later the relation between the price of credit and the price of sources of permanent or temporary returns. Here so much is clear, that the sale of such sources of returns represents a method of acquiring capital, and their purchase a method of employing capital, consequently the dealing in sources of returns cannot be far removed from the money market. Traffic in land also belongs here, and only technical circumstances prevent it from appearing in practice as a part of money-market transactions; but there is no lack of causal connection between the two.

CHAPTER IV

ENTREPRENEURIAL PROFIT[1]

THE first three chapters laid the foundation upon which rests all that is to follow. As a first fruit we arrive at an explanation of entrepreneurial profit, and indeed so easily and naturally that in order to keep this chapter short and simple I prefer to put some more difficult discussions, which really belong here, in the next chapter, where all the knotty problems may be dealt with as a whole.

Entrepreneurial profit is a surplus over costs. From the standpoint of the entrepreneur, it is the difference between receipts and outlay in a business, as we have already been told by a long line of economists. Superficial as this definition is, it is sufficient as a starting point. By "outlay" we understand all the disbursements which the entrepreneur must make directly or indirectly in production. To this must be added an appropriate wage for labor performed by the entrepreneur, an appropriate rent for any land which may chance to belong to him, and finally a premium for risk. On the other hand I do not insist here that interest on capital should be excluded from these costs. In practice it is included in them, either visibly or, if the capital belongs to the entrepreneur himself, by the same accounting method as wages for his personal work or rent for his own land. This may suffice for the moment, all the more so since many theorists put interest on capital in the same category with wages and rent. I now leave it to the reader's discretion in this chapter either to neglect the existence of interest on capital, in the sense of our interpretation, or to recognise it, in the sense of any theory of interest whatsoever, as a third "static"

[1] The most important theories of profits may be characterised by the following terms: friction theory, wages theory, risk theory, differential rent theory. I refer to the discussion of them in Wesen, bk. III, and shall not here enter into a critique of them. For history of the doctrine see Pierstorff and Mataja. At the same time J. B. Clark, whose theory is nearest to mine, may be cited here; cf. his Essentials of Economic Theory.

branch of income and to include it in business costs. Its nature and its origin do not concern us here in any case.

Upon this definition of outlays it may appear doubtful whether there is any surplus at all as against costs. To prove that there is a surplus is therefore our first task. Our solution may be expressed briefly: in the circular flow the total receipts of a business — abstracting from monopoly — are just big enough to cover outlays. In it there are only producers who neither make profits nor suffer losses and whose income is sufficiently characterised by the phrase "wages of management." And since the new combinations which are carried out if there is "development" are necessarily more advantageous than the old, total receipts must in this case be greater than total costs.

In honor of Lauderdale,[1] who was the first to deal with our problem, I shall begin with the improvement of the productive process and indeed with the time-honored example of the power-loom, which is also commended by the fact that it has been subjected to a searching analysis by Böhm-Bawerk.[2] Very many if not most of the achievements of the leaders of modern economic life are of this kind; in particular the new era of the eighteenth and nineteenth centuries exhibits efforts in this direction. It is true that in this period we find the several functions which are to be distinguished in the process of introducing improvements in production even less separated than to-day. Men of the Arkwright type invented and at the same time put their inventions into practice. They had not our modern credit system at their disposal. However, I hope I have taken the reader so far that I may make use of our analytic tools in their purest form without further explanations and repetitions.

The matter then appears as follows. If anyone in an economic system in which the textile industry produces only with hand labor sees the possibility of founding a business which uses power-looms, feels equal to the task of overcoming all the innumerable difficulties, and has made the final decision, then he, first of all,

---

[1] Inquiry into the Nature and Origin of Public Wealth. It is true that he had an altogether different object in view, viz. the explanation of interest.

[2] In his Capital and Interest, VII, 3.

needs purchasing power. He borrows it from a bank and creates his business. It is absolutely immaterial whether he constructs the power-looms himself or has them constructed by another firm according to his directions in order to confine himself to employing them. If a worker with such a loom is now in a position to produce six times as much as a hand-worker in a day, it is obvious that given three conditions the business must yield a surplus over costs, a difference between receipts and outlay. First, the price of the product must not fall when the new supply [1] appears, or else not fall to such an extent that the greater product per worker brings no greater receipts now than the smaller product obtainable by hand labor did before. Secondly, the costs of the power-loom per day must either remain below the daily wages of the five workers dispensed with or else below the sum which remains after allowing for the possible fall in the price of the product and deducting the wage of the one worker required. The third condition supplements the other two. These two cover wages of the workers who attend to the looms, and wages and rent which go in payment for the looms. So far I have taken the case in which these wages and rents are simply those which ruled before the entrepreneur hit upon his plan. If his demand is relatively small we can rest content with this.[2] If not, however, then the prices of the services of labor and land rise because of the new demand. For the other textile businesses at first continue working and the necessary means of production need not be withdrawn directly from them, but from industry in general. This happens by means of an advance in prices. And therefore the businessman, who must anticipate and estimate the rise in prices in the market for production goods which follows his appearance, may not simply include the former wages and rents in his calculation, but must add an appropriate amount, so that yet a third item must be deducted. Only if the receipts exceed outlays after allowing for all three sets of changes is there a surplus over costs.

[1] Here we depart from Lauderdale's example in order to remain true to our whole conception of the process and at the same time to reality.

[2] This would be the case of completely free competition, to the concept of which it is necessary that no firm be strong enough perceptibly to influence prices by its own action on supply and demand.

These three conditions have been fulfilled innumerable times in practice. This proves the possibility of a surplus over costs.[1] However, they are obviously not always fulfilled, and when they are not, and the fact is foreseen, the new business is not organised; if this fact is not foreseen no surplus results but rather a loss. If the conditions are fulfilled, however, the surplus realised is *ipso facto* a net profit. For the looms produce a greater physical product than the services of labor and land contained in them could produce by the previous method, although in the case of constant prices of production goods and products this latter method would also enable production to be carried on without loss. Furthermore, the looms are obviously available at cost to our entrepreneur — we neglect the possibility of patenting as being intelligible without further consideration. Hence there arises a difference between receipts, which are determined according to the prices which were equilibrium, that is cost, prices when hand labor alone was being used, and outlays, which are now essentially smaller per unit of product than for other businesses. And this difference need not be annihilated by the price changes brought about by the appearance of the individual in question on the demand and the supply side. This is so clear that we may forego a more rigorous formulation at this point.

But now comes the second act of the drama. The spell is broken and new businesses are continually arising under the impulse of the alluring profit. A complete reorganisation of the industry occurs, with its increases in production, its competitive struggle, its supersession of obsolete businesses, its possible dismissal of workers, and so forth. We shall consider this process more closely later. Only one thing interests us here: the final result must be a new equilibrium position, in which, with new data, the law of cost again rules, so that now the prices of the products are again equal to the wages and rents of the services of labor and land which are embodied in the looms plus the wages and rents of the services of labor and land which must still cooperate with the looms in order

---

[1] It should be noticed that in this statement there is not an appeal to the reality of a phenomenon yet to be explained, of the kind found respecting the fact of interest in many representatives of the productivity theory. For the rest, further substantiation comes later.

that the product may come into existence. The incentive to produce more and more products will not cease before this condition is arrived at, nor before price falls as a result of the growing supply.

Consequently, the surplus of the entrepreneur in question and of his immediate followers disappears.[1] Not at once, it is true, but as a rule only after a longer or shorter period of progressive diminution.[2] Nevertheless, the surplus is realised, it constitutes under given conditions a definite amount of net returns even though only temporary. Now to whom does it fall? Obviously to the individuals who introduced the looms into the circular flow, not to the mere inventors, but also not to the mere producers or users of them. Those who produce them to order will only receive their cost price, those who employ them according to instructions will buy them so dearly at first that they will hardly receive any profit. The profit will fall to those individuals whose achievement it is to introduce the looms, whether they produce and use them, or whether they only produce or only use them. In our example the chief importance attaches to employment, but that is not essential. The introduction is achieved by founding new businesses, whether for production or for employment or for both. What have the individuals under consideration contributed to this? Only the will and the action: not concrete goods, for they bought these — either from others or from themselves; not the purchasing power with which they bought, for they borrowed this — from others or, if we also take account of acquisition in earlier periods, from themselves. And what have they done? They have not accumulated any kind of goods, they have created no original means of production, but have employed existing means of production differently, more appropriately, more advantageously. They have "carried out new combinations." They are entrepreneurs. And their profit, the surplus, to which no liability corresponds, is an entrepreneurial profit.

Just as the introduction of looms is a special case of the intro-

---

[1] Cf. Böhm-Bawerk, loc. cit., p. 174.

[2] However, for the sake of simplicity of exposition we confine the process in general to one economic period.

duction of machinery in general, so the introduction of machinery is a special case of all changes in the productive process in the widest sense, the aim of which is to produce a unit of product with less expense and thus to create a discrepancy between their existing price and their new costs. Many innovations in business organisation and all innovations in commercial combinations are included in this. For all such cases, what has been said may be repeated word for word. Representative of the first group is the introduction of large-scale manufacturing businesses into an economic system in which they were previously unknown. In a large-scale business a more suitable arrangement and better utilisation of the factors of production are possible than in smaller businesses; and furthermore the choice of a more favorable location is possible. But the introduction of large-scale businesses is difficult. Under our assumptions all the necessary conditions are wanting — workers, trained personnel, the necessary market conditions. Innumerable resistances of a social and political character work against it. And the organisation itself, still unknown, requires special aptitude to set it up. However, if anyone has in him all that pertains to success under these circumstances, and if he can obtain the necessary credit, then he can put a unit of product on the market more cheaply, and, if our three conditions are realised, make a profit which remains in his pocket. But he has also triumphed for others, blazed the trail and created a model for them which they can copy. They can and will follow him, first individuals and then whole crowds. Again that process of reorganisation occurs which must result in the annihilation of the surplus over costs, when the new business form has become part of the circular flow. But previously profits were made. To repeat: these individuals have done nothing but employ existing goods to greater effect, they have carried out new combinations and are entrepreneurs in our sense. Their gain is an entrepreneurial profit.

As an example of the cases of commercial combinations, the choice of a new and cheaper source of supply for a means of production, perhaps a raw material may be cited. This source of supply did not exist previously for the economic system. No direct and regular connection existed with its country of origin — if overseas, for example, neither a steamship line nor foreign correspondents. The innovation is hazardous, impossible for most producers. But if someone establishes a business having regard to this source of supply, and everything goes well, then he can produce a unit of product more cheaply, while at first the existing prices substantially continue to exist. He then makes a profit. Again he has contributed nothing but will and action, has done nothing but recombine existing factors. Again he is an entrepreneur, his profit entrepreneurial profit. And again the latter, and also the entrepreneurial function as such, perish in the vortex of the competition which streams after them. The case of the choice of new trade routes belongs here.

Analogous to the cases of simply improving the process of production is the case of replacing one production or consumption good by another, which serves the same or approximately the same purpose, but is cheaper. Concrete examples are offered by the partial replacement of wool by cotton in the last quarter of the eighteenth century, and by all production of substitutes. These cases are to be treated exactly as those just mentioned. The difference, that the new products here will certainly not bring the same price as those previously produced in the industry under consideration, is only one of degree, as may easily be seen. For the rest, exactly the same holds good. Again it is immaterial whether the individuals concerned produce the new production or consumption good themselves or only employ or dispose of it as the case may be, and draw it for this purpose from its possible existing uses. Here also these individuals contribute neither goods nor purchasing power. Here also they nevertheless make a profit which is connected with the carrying out of new combinations. We recognise them accordingly as entrepreneurs. Here too the profit will not last long.

The creation of a new good which more adequately satisfies existing and previously satisfied needs is a somewhat different case. The production of improved musical instruments is an example. In this case the possibility of profit rests upon the fact that the higher price received for the better commodity surpasses its costs, which are likewise higher in most cases. One can easily convince oneself of its existence. Furthermore, the adaptation of our three conditions to this case presents no difficulties and may be left to the reader. If a surplus exists and if, therefore, the introduction of better instruments occurs, then here also a tendency to reorganisation in the industry will set in, which will finally restore the rule of the law of cost. Hence, here also there is clearly a new combination of existing factors, an entrepreneurial act and an entrepreneurial profit, even though it is not permanent. A combination of the case of the better satisfaction of a need with the case of lower cost of the unit of product following the appearance of a very great increase in demand is presented by the example of railway and canal construction.

The search for new markets in which an article has not yet been made familiar and in which it is not produced is an extraordinarily rich, and in former times was a very lasting, source of entrepreneurial profit. Primitive trading profits belong here, and the sale of glass beads to a negro tribe may serve as an example. The principle of the matter is that a new commodity is valued by purchasers much as gifts of nature or pictures by old masters, that is its price is determined without regard to cost of production. Hence the possibility that it may sell above costs, including all the expenditure connected with overcoming the innumerable difficulties of the venture. At first only a few see the new enterprise and are able to carry it out. This also is an entrepreneurial act, the carrying out of a new combination; and it yields a profit, which remains in the entrepreneur's pocket. It is true, the source dries up sooner or later. To-day an appropriate organisation would soon come into existence and the trade in glass beads would very soon no longer yield a profit.

At the same time the above covers the case of the production of a completely new good. Such a good must first of all be forced on consumers, perhaps even given away gratis. A host of obstacles arise. But when these are overcome and the consumers take to the commodity, there follows a period of price determination solely on the basis of direct valuation and without much regard to costs, which here also consist fundamentally of the hitherto prevailing prices of the necessary services of labor and land. Hence a surplus can exist which remains in the hands of the successful producers. These again are entrepreneurs who have only contributed will and action and have only carried out the new combination of existing productive factors. Again there is an entrepreneurial profit. And this disappears again when the new commodity becomes part of the circular flow and its price is put in the normal relation to costs.

These examples show us the nature of profit as the result of carrying out new combinations. They show too how the process must be thought of — essentially as the new employment of existing production goods. The entrepreneur does not save in order to obtain the means which he needs, nor does he accumulate any goods before beginning to produce. Furthermore, when a business is not established all at once in its definitive form but slowly develops, the matter is not as different as one would believe. If the entrepreneur's strength is not exhausted on one project and yet he continues to carry on the same business, then he proceeds to new changes which are always new enterprises according to our terminology, often with means which he draws from his past profits. The process then appears to be different, but its nature is the same.

The same is true if a new enterprise is started by a producer in the same industry and is connected with his previous production. This is by no means the rule; new enterprises are mostly founded by new men and the old businesses sink into insignificance. But even if an individual who previously carried on his business by annually repeating his part in the circular flow becomes an entrepreneur, no change takes place in the nature of the proceeding. The fact that in this case the entrepreneur himself already has the necessary means of production, wholly or in part, or, as the case may be, can pay for them out of existing resources of his business, does not change his function as an entrepreneur. It is true our conception does not then fit the facts in every detail. The new enterprise still coexists with the other businesses, which at first continue to operate in the customary manner, but it does not increase the demand for means of production nor does it necessarily supply new products. Yet we only so arranged our picture because the practically more important case demands it and because it shows us the principle of the matter and especially the fact that the new business need not spring directly from the old. Appropriately interpreted, it also fits this case in essentials. Here also it is only a matter of carrying out new combinations and nothing else.

The entrepreneur is never the risk bearer.[1] In our example this is quite clear. The one who gives credit comes to grief if the undertaking fails. For although any property possessed by the entrepreneur may be liable, yet such possession of wealth is not essential, even though advantageous. But even if the entrepreneur finances himself out of former profits, or if he contributes the means of production belonging to his "static" business, the risk falls on him as capitalist or as possessor of goods, not as entrepreneur. Risk-taking is in no case an element of the entrepreneurial function. Even though he may risk his reputation, the direct economic responsibility of failure never falls on him.

It may now be briefly observed that profit as here conceived is the main element of the phenomenon which is described as promoter's profit. Whatever promoter's profit may be in addition, its basis is the temporary surplus of receipts over cost of production in a new enterprise. The promoter may indeed be, as we saw, the purest type of the entrepreneur genus. He is then the entrepreneur who confines himself most strictly to the characteristic entrepreneurial function, the carrying out of new combinations. If, during the founding of a business, everything were to proceed correctly and with ideal perfection and foresight on all sides, the profit would be what remained in the founder's hands. Of course, in practice it is quite different. But this still gives the principle of the matter. It is true, this applies only to the real promoter and not to the agent who sometimes performs the technical work of forming a company and frequently also goes by this name. The latter only receives a remuneration which is of the character of wages. Finally, everything new that is created in a company is not in most cases perfected with the promotion of it. On the con-

[1] Cf. Chapter II, p. 74 ff.

trary, its leading men often continually embark upon new enterprises, whereby they then continue the rôle of the original promoter and are entrepreneurs, whatever their official position in the
company may be. If we assume, however, that the company,
once founded, is simply carried on, then the promoter is the only
one who exercises entrepreneurial activity in relation to this business. Let us assume that the prices of the means of production [1]
are represented by bonds, that the capitalised higher return of the
lasting sources of gain associated with the enterprise are represented by shares, and that there are also promoter's shares which
were transferred to the promoter gratuitously. Then these promoter's shares will not yield a lasting income, but will only bring
to the promoter that temporary surplus which exists before the
enterprise is embodied in the economic system, and then they become worthless. In such a case profit would appear in its purest
form.

This picture of profit must now be worked out. And this is done
by our asking ourselves the question of what corresponds to this
phenomenon in other than the capitalist form of society. The
simple exchange economy, that is the kind of economic system in
which there is exchange of products but in which the "capitalistic
method" is unknown, gives us no new problem to solve. In the
units of such a society there must be a different kind of power of
disposal over means of production, in which respect the exchange
economy can be dealt with as in the case which we are about to
take up. For the rest, however, the same will hold true as for the
capitalistic system. Therefore in order to avoid repetitions I
shall turn to the simple non-exchange economy.

Here two types of organisation come into consideration. The
first is that of an isolated manorial estate in which most means of
production belong to the lord and all people are subject to him.
The second is that of an isolated communist society in which a
central organ disposes of all material goods and services of labor,
and expresses all value judgments. At first both forms may be

---

[1] That is, strictly speaking, those prices of the means of production constituting
the material investment, which correspond to their values in their hitherto prevailing
employments without regard to the contemplated new one, even though in practice
more would have to be paid in most cases.

treated in common. In both *some* individuals have absolute control over the means of production. They expect neither cooperation in production nor the offer of possibilities of profit-making from other economic units. The world of prices does not exist and only that of values remains. Thus, when we pass from the consideration of our examples to the treatment of the non-exchange economy we begin the investigation of value phenomena which are at the bottom of profit.

We know that here too there is a circular flow, in which the law of cost strictly rules, in the sense of equality between value of products and value of means of production, and that here too economic development in our sense is only accomplished in the form of carrying out new combinations of existing goods. One might think that the accumulation of stocks of goods would here be necessary and would form a special function. The first is in part correct; not always, it is true, but frequently the accumulation of stocks is a step towards the end of carrying out new combinations. But it never constitutes a special function to which special value phenomena may be attached. A different employment of goods is simply prescribed by the leader or leading organ of the system. Whether the desired result is reached directly or only indirectly through a preparatory stage of collecting stocks is completely immaterial. Whether all the participators individually agree with the new aims and are willing to undertake the collection of stocks is likewise immaterial. The leaders make no sacrifice and take no notice of a possible temporary sacrifice of those led — if and so long as the reins rest firmly in their hands. If the execution of far-reaching plans diminishes the present consumption of the people led — which is not necessary, but possible — the latter will oppose them, if they can.[1] Their opposition may make these plans impossible. But neglecting this, they have no direct and economic influence on what shall happen; in particular

---

[1] For they will have in view only the immediate loss, while the future gain may possibly have just as little reality as if it would never exist. This applies to all stages of civilisation of which we have any knowledge; throughout history the element of force has never been absent when it has been a question of development which presupposes the cooperation of great masses. In many cases, it is true, no sacrifice at all was exacted from the people.

a shrinkage of consumption and accumulation of stocks is not their voluntary service. Therefore this also involves no special function which should be inserted in our picture of the process of development. If the leader promises the people a premium it amounts to nothing more than when a general promises his soldiers some special remuneration; it is a gift intended to make the people more docile, but it is not part of the essence of the matter and forms no special, purely economic category. Hence the difference between the "lord" and the leader of a communist economy is only one of degree. The fact that according to the idea of a communist society the advantages accruing are to go to the whole community while the lord possibly has only his own interest in view, constitutes no fundamental difference.

From this it follows also that the element of time can have no independent influence here. It is true, leaders must compare the result of the contemplated combination not merely with the result that the same productive factors could produce in the same time in their previous method of employment, but also with the results of other new combinations which could alternatively be carried out with the same means. And if these latter require less time, the results of as many other combinations as could be carried out in the time saved must be allowed for in estimating the relative importance of the competing methods of employment. Therefore the time element will certainly appear in a non-exchange economy, while in the capitalist system its influence is expressed by the interest item, as we shall see later. This, however, is self-evident. Even here time plays no other rôle; none, for example, that would make the necessity of waiting or the smaller desire for future enjoyments special factors. One only waits unwillingly because, and as long as, one can do something else in the meantime. Future enjoyments only appear smaller because the further in the future their realisation lies, the greater become the deductions on account of "enjoyments realisable elsewhere."

Thus the leader of such a community, whatever his position may be, withdraws a certain quantity of means of production from their previous uses and with them carries out a new combination, for example the production of a new good or the production of a good already known by a better method. In the latter case it is quite immaterial whether he withdraws the necessary means of production from the branch of industry which hitherto manufactured the same commodity, or whether he allows existing firms to continue working in the habitual manner and begins to produce alongside of them with the new method and withdraws the necessary means of production from quite different branches of industry. The new products will be *ex hypothesi* of higher value than those produced previously by the same quantities of means of production — however valuations in such a society may be formed. How does the process of imputation proceed with respect to the new products? At the moment when the combination is completed and the products come into existence their value is determined. How will the values of the factors which have participated be formed? It is still better to choose the moment when the decision is made to carry out the new combination and to assume that everything happens exactly according to the decision.

First of all a valuation must be made by the producers: the value of the new products must be compared with the value of those products which the same means of production have been producing so far in the normal circular flow. Clearly this valuation is necessary in order to make any estimate of the advantage of the new combination, and without it no action would be possible. The central question for our problem is now, which of the two alternative values that may be produced by the means of production will be imputed to the latter. So much is clear: before the decision about carrying out the new combination is made, only that value which corresponds to the old employment. For there would be no sense in imputing beforehand the surplus value of the new combination to the means of production, since the carrying out of it would then no longer appear as an advantage and the basis for the necessary comparison of the values in the two uses would be lost. But how does the matter stand once the decision is made? Must not the whole gain in satisfaction be imputed in the Mengerian sense [1] to the means of production, just as in the circular flow, since they now realise the higher value; so

---

[1] Cf. Wieser, Natürlicher Wert, p. 70 f.

that if everything functions with ideal perfection the whole value of the new products will be reflected in the means of production used?

I answer no; and assert that even here the services of labor and land are to be estimated at their old values; and in fact for the following two reasons. First, the old values are customary values. Long experience has determined them, and they are established in the consciousness of individuals. They are only altered in the course of time and under the pressure of further long experience. Their values are stable to a high degree, all the more so since the services of labor and land themselves have not changed. The values of the new products on the contrary stand just as much outside the existing value system as the prices of new products in the capitalist system. They are not joined in continuity with the old values, but are separated discretely. Hence the justification of the method of interpretation [1] according to which any productive good is only assigned the value which it would realise in other than its actual employment. For only this value, that is in our case its hitherto prevailing value, is dependent upon the concrete means of production. If they ceased to exist they would be replaced by other units from these other employments. No unit of a commodity can be valued higher than another identical unit, if they exist simultaneously. Now the services of labor and land employed in the new combination are homogeneous with those simultaneously employed — if they were not there would indeed be a difference in value, but one easily explicable without affecting the principle — and therefore cannot have a different value from the latter. Even in the extreme case, if all productive powers in the economic system were put at the service of the new combination they would have to be invested at this stage with the values hitherto prevailing, which in case of failure they could realise again and upon which the magnitude of the losses would be based if they were completely annihilated. Therefore the successful carrying out of new combinations also results in a value surplus in the non-exchange economy, not only in the capitalistic; and in

---

[1] With which I do not agree in every respect; cf. Wesen, bk. II, and "Bemerkungen über das Zurechnungsproblem," Zeitschrift für Volksw., Sozialp. und Verw. (1909).

fact a value surplus in the sense of a quantity of value to which there is no corresponding claim of imputation by means of production, not merely a surplus of satisfaction as against the earlier position. As we may also put it, surplus value [1] in development is not only a private but also a social phenomenon, and so far is in every respect the same thing as the capitalistic entrepreneurial profit which we met before.

Secondly, the same result may be reached by another approach. The entrepreneurial activity of the leader, which is indeed a necessary condition of the realisation of the combination, may be conceived as a means of production. I do not so conceive it ordinarily, because more interest attaches to the contrast between entrepreneur and means of production. But here this method of consideration does good service. For the time being, therefore, let us constitute the leadership function a third original productive factor. Then it is clear that some part of the value of the new products must be imputed to it. But how much? Leader and means of production are equally necessary, and the whole surplus value of the new products depends upon the cooperation of both of them. This requires no further comment and does not contradict what was said in the preceding paragraph. The appropriate magnitudes of all value categories are only determined by the force of competition, whether of goods or of individuals. Since this second kind of competition does not exist in the non-exchange economy, and since in it the difference between what is and is not profit is also of much less significance than in an exchange economy (as we shall see immediately), its value would not always appear with the clearness that it does where this difference is very essential. But we can nevertheless specify for most cases how much is to be imputed to the entrepreneur's function. In most cases, as we have said, the means of production are replaceable, but not the leader.[2] Hence the former will have imputed to them

---

[1] Only this surplus, which appears from the private economic standpoint as profit *and* interest on capital, can be described as surplus value in the Marxian sense. No other surplus exists.

[2] Even if the activity of the leader competes with an irreplaceable means of production, a value surplus remains over in favor of the former. For, at the time of the introduction of the innovation, the latter is only to be assigned its hitherto prevailing value.

that value which will be lost in the event of replacement being necessary, and the leadership function will be assigned the remainder. To the leadership function is imputed the value of the new products minus the value which could be realised without it. Hence, the surplus here corresponds to a special claim to imputation, and can therefore in no case swell the claim which originates in the means of production.

In this it must not be forgotten, however, that it would not be quite right if we were always to speak of the imputation of the hitherto prevailing value to the means of production. The marginal value in the previous uses indeed rises in consequence of the withdrawal of means of production from them. We observed the same phenomenon in the capitalistic system. The rise of prices of means of production in consequence of new demand by entrepreneurs in the capitalistic system corresponds exactly to this valuation process. Our method of expression must be corrected accordingly. However, nothing is changed in fundamentals. This rise in value must not be confused, of course, with the imputation of the value due to development to the means of production.

No one can assert that the valuation process described above is not real and that profit as a special value magnitude has no meaning in a non-exchange economy. Even a non-exchange economy must know clearly what it is doing, what advantage its new combinations yield and also to what this advantage is to be attributed. One might assert, however, that profit has no significance as a distributive category in a non-exchange economy. In a certain sense this is true. In the feudal type of non-exchange economy the lord can indeed dispose freely of the quantity of product corresponding to his "service," but in it the lord can dispose freely of all returns — he can give the workers more but also less than corresponds to their marginal productivity. In the communist type the profit falls entirely to the people as a whole — at least in theory. This in itself does not concern us. But can one not infer from it, especially for the communist type, that profit is absorbed in wages, that reality pushes the theory of value aside and that wages embrace the whole product? No, one must distinguish the economic nature of a return from what happens to it. The economic nature of a return rests upon a productive service. In this sense we call wages that return which is to be imputed to a labor service. Under free competition in an exchange economy this return goes to the worker, but only because the principle of free competition is remuneration according to marginal significance. It is necessary only in the sense that in the capitalistic system precisely this wage calls forth the effort. If the effort were assured by another method — by the feeling of social duty or perhaps by compulsion — the worker might receive less; but his wages would nevertheless be determined by the marginal productivity of labor, and the amount by which his remuneration fell short of this should be classified as a deduction from his economic wage. This deduction would also be wages, quite on the same plane with the wage paid to the worker. In a communist society the leader would certainly not receive profit. And most decidedly it cannot be asserted that this would make development impossible. On the contrary, it is possible that the people in such an organisation would in time think so differently that they would no more lay claim to profit than a statesman or a general would wish to keep the spoils of victory wholly or partly for himself. But the profit would remain profit. That it will not do to characterise it as the wages of labor may be seen by adapting the argument which Böhm-Bawerk formulated classically with respect to interest.[1] It also applies to rent of land, in which likewise the nature and value of the productive contribution of land are to be distinguished from the revenue received by particular individuals.[2]

As the wage of which workers would the profit be designated? Two answers to this question are conceivable. In the first place it may be said: as part of the wage of the workers who worked on the new product. Now this cannot be. For then these workers would *ex hypothesi* get higher wages than their fellows. The latter, however, perform no less work of no inferior quality, so that if we accept this possibility we come into conflict with a fundamental economic principle, that excludes different values for different

[1] Positive Theorie, final chapter.
[2] Cf. Wesen, bk. III.

parts of homogeneous goods. Quite apart from the injustice that would lie in such a measure, privileged workers would plainly be created by it. The arrangement is possible, but the surplus received by these workers would not be wages.

The other conceivable answer is: the values which we call profit and the amounts of product corresponding to them simply constitute a part of the national dividend and are to be allotted equally to all labor services contributed in the relevant economic period — assuming homogeneity of the services or, as the case may be, taking account of disparities in any recognised way. In this case the laborers who have not worked on the new products get more than the product of their labor. Never yet has an economic meaning been associated with a wage that is higher than the total value product. Therefore it will easily be conceded that in this case the workers get their share not wholly as an economic wage but partially under a non-economic title. To be sure, this arrangement is also possible, and many others equally so. The community must indeed dispose somehow of its "profit" as of all other returns. It must dispose of it in favor of the workers since there are no others entitled to shares. In this it can proceed according to the most varied principles; it can for example distribute according to intensity of need or promote general ends without distributing it. But this alters nothing in the economic categories. In the normal circular flow it is not possible for the workers, any more than land, to receive directly or indirectly more than their economic product, for more does not exist. If this is possible in our case it is solely because some other agent does not receive its product. If we so define the ambiguous expression "exploitation" that exploitation occurs when a necessary agent of production, or the possessor of it as the case may be, receives less than its product in the economic sense, then we can say that this extra payment to the workers is only possible by exploiting the leaders. If we confine the expression to the case in which some personal service is deprived of its product — in order to exclude the concept of exploitation from being applied to land, where, considering the non-existence of landlords in the communist society, it would be out of place — then we can still say that exploitation of the leaders occurs, to be sure, without wishing to pass any moral judgment.

Therefore profit does not become wages in the economic sense even if it goes wholly to the workers. It is practically important for a communist system to recognise this clearly and always to separate profit from wages. For the general understanding of its life as well as decisions about concrete questions manifestly depend upon such recognition. This whole consideration teaches us the independence of the phenomenon from the concrete form of economic organisation. And then there is the general truth: profit as a special and independent value phenomenon is fundamentally connected with the rôle of leadership in the economic system. If development required no direction and no force then profit would indeed exist; it would be a part of wages and rents, but it would not be a phenomenon *sui generis*. As long as this is not the case, that is as long as the bulk of the people have the slightest resemblance to the masses of all nations of whom we have any knowledge, so long the whole return cannot be imputed to the services of labor and land, even in the ideally perfect case of frictionless and timeless economic process.[1]

But also in the non-exchange economy profit does not live eternally. Here too, necessary changes appear which put an end to it. The new combination is carried out; its results are at hand, all doubts are silenced; the advantages, and at the same time the manner of obtaining them, are henceforth evident. There is further need, at the most, of a manager or foreman, but not of the creative power of a leader. It is only necessary to repeat what has

---

[1] A word about the argument which is so often heard to-day: that the entrepreneur produces nothing, organisation everything; that no one's product is his own, but the product of the social whole. At the bottom of this is the truth that everyone is the product of his inherited and personal milieu and that no one can produce anything for which the conditions do not exist. But we can do nothing with this in the realm of theory, which is not concerned with the moulding of men but with men already formed. To the question whether individual initiative has a function, even the representatives of this interpretation would eagerly reply affirmatively. Further, it is precise and correct with respect to the secondary phenomena of development. For the rest, it is merely based upon the popular preconception that only physical work is really productive and upon the impression that all elements of development work harmoniously together and every phase of development is based upon preceding ones. This, however, is the result of development already set in motion and explains nothing. The principle of its mechanism is the main question.

been done before to acquire the equivalent advantages. And that can and will be done without a leader. Even if resistances from friction must still be overcome, the matter has become essentially different, and easier. The advantages have become realities to all members of the community, and the new products, uniformly distributed in time, are continually before their eyes; they free them, in the sense of what we said on this point in the first chapter, from every sacrifice or necessity of waiting for the completion of further products. The economic system is no longer expected to advance, but only to assure the continuity of the existing stream of goods. We can expect that of it.

Thus the new process of production will be repeated.[1] And for this entrepreneurial activity is no longer necessary. If we conceive it again as a third productive factor, then we can say that in the mere repetition of the familiarised new combinations one of the factors of production, which were necessary to carrying them out initially, disappears. At the same time the claim to imputation associated with it is abolished and the values of the others, that is of the services of labor and land, will be increased until they exhaust the value product. Only these are necessary now, they alone create the product. Imputation is to them alone; in the first place to the services of labor and land which are actually used in the given production, but subsequently, in accordance with well known principles, equally to all. *The values of the former services of labor and land will first increase and then will diffuse themselves over all others.*

Hence, the values of all services of labor and land will rise correspondingly. This rise, however, must be distinguished from that which appeared with the carrying out of the new combina-

---

[1] One might object that if the innovation is too far removed from the accustomed methods compulsion will still be necessary. We must differentiate as follows. First, in such a case it is not yet understood and has not become familiar. Then, the new combination is simply not yet carried out. We assume that this has happened, and it may last an indefinitely long time. After that, compulsion of the kind incident to organisation, especially in the ranking of workers in higher and lower classes, is certainly always necessary. But this is something different from the compulsion to carry out new things. Finally, in the feudal organisation a direct injury to the masses may be connected with the innovation. Compulsion is then also necessary if it is to be carried out. But this is again a different thing. In maintaining something already in existence our leader type is not necessary, but only a ruler.

tion, not only in degree but also in kind. It signifies no rise in their scale of values but only in their marginal utility in consequence of the fact that, because of the withdrawal of means of production from the hitherto prevailing uses, production cannot be carried as far as before, hence only needs of higher intensity than before can be satisfied. In the other case something quite different occurs, namely the entry of the value of the new products into the scale of values of means of production. This may also raise the marginal utility of the latter; but it raises their total value too, a difference which is of practical importance where the disposal of larger quantities of factors is concerned. Hence the values of the means of production now express the fact that the new increase in satisfaction depends upon them and them alone, that the product of labor and land has become greater. They will now no longer be assigned the values which they had in the former circular flow, but those which they realise in the new circular flow. At the time of the transformation there was no sense in imputing to them a value higher than their replacement value then. Now their replacement value already includes the value of the new employment. The rise in the value of the social product draws the values of the means of production after it and the new state of affairs will soon replace the old accustomed value by a new one, which will finally become the customary one, based upon the new marginal productivity. Thus the contact between value of product and value of means of production would be reestablished. There will be no more discrepancy between the two value categories in the new system than there was in the earlier. And if everything functions with ideal perfection then the communist society is now quite right if it considers all the resulting product as a permanent return to its labor and land and distributes it amongst its members for consumption.[1] The facts would not disavow it.

So far the elimination of profit in the non-exchange economy proceeds in a manner quite analogous to its elimination in the capitalistic system. But the other part of this process in the capitalist system, namely the forcing down of the price of the new

---

[1] As the capitalist system does too after its own fashion.

product in consequence of the appearance of competing firms, must be absent in the non-exchange economy. It is true that here too the new products have to be incorporated in the circular flow, that here too their values must be brought into relation with the values of all other products. Theoretically we can still distinguish the carrying out of the innovation and the process of its embodiment in the circular flow as two different things. But it is easily seen that it makes a considerable difference practically whether both actually take place *uno actu* or not. In a non-exchange economy the demonstration of a surplus attributable to entrepreneurial activity is quite enough to solve our problem. In a capitalist system these surpluses can only find their way to the entrepreneur with the help of the mechanism of the market and can be wrested from him again only by means of this mechanism. Thus there is besides the simple value problem the further one of how it happens that the profit actually accrues to the entrepreneur. And this mechanism creates many phenomena which must be absent in a non-exchange economy.

In spite of this, not only is the innermost economic nature of profit the same in all forms of organisation, but so is the innermost nature of the process that eliminates it. In all cases the matter turns upon the elimination of the obstructions which prevent the whole value product from being imputed to the services of labor and land, or, as the case may be, their prices from being put on a level with the price of the product. The ruling principles are always that the economic process, if unobstructed, first does not tolerate value surpluses in the case of individual products, and secondly always forces the values of the means of production up to those of the products. These principles are valid immediately in a non-exchange economy, and they are realised through free competition in a capitalist system. In the latter the prices of the means of production must under free competition be such that they exhaust the price of the product. In so far as this is not possible the price of the product must correspondingly fall. If under these circumstances profit exists at all, it is only because the transition from one position in which there are no surpluses to another new position in which there are again none cannot happen without the help of the entrepreneur, and unless the further condition necessary in a capitalist system is also fulfilled, namely that the profit cannot be immediately wrested from him by competition.

Profit clings to the means of production in no other sense than does the effort of a poet to his partly finished manuscript. No part of the profit is imputed to them, nor is the possession and the furnishing of them the content of the entrepreneurial function. And above all, as we saw, profit is not to be sought in the permanent increase in value which the original means of production experience in consequence of the new employment. Let us consider the case of a slave economy in which land and workers belong to the entrepreneur who has bought them for the purpose of carrying out new combinations. One could say in this case, if anywhere, that a price will be paid for land and workers corresponding to their hitherto prevailing employments, and that profit is the amount by which land and workers now permanently produce more. But this would be wrong for two reasons. First, the receipts for the new products will reach a height from which competition must pull them down again, so that this conception would not allow for an element of profit. Secondly, the lasting surplus amount — in so far as it is not quasi-rent — is economically simply an increase of the wages of labor, which, it is true, accrues to the "owner of labor" here, not to the worker, and of rent of land. Slaves and land certainly have a higher value now for their proprietor, but he has become permanently richer as their proprietor and not as an entrepreneur, if one neglects occasional or temporary profit. Even if a natural agent of production first comes into existence in the new combination, for example a brook as water-power, the matter is in no way different. It is not the water-power that yields the profit. What it permanently yields is rent in our sense.

Hence a part of what is in the first instance profit changes into rent. Thereby the economic nature of the quantity in question is changed. Let us assume that a planter who has previously cultivated sugar cane changes over to cotton-growing, which until recently was more lucrative than it is now.[1] This is a new com-

---

[1] Written in 1911.

bination; the man thereby becomes an entrepreneur and makes a profit. For the time being rent of land appears in the list of costs only at the amount appropriate to sugar cane cultivation. As has actually happened, we shall assume that competition sooner or later forces down the receipts. If a surplus still remains, however, how is that to be explained and what is it economically? Neglecting friction, it can only result because the land either is differentially suited to cotton-growing or the rent of land has risen in general as a result of the new employments — in principle it is always a consequence of both elements. This at once characterises that part of the increase in total return which is permanent as rent of land. The entrepreneurial function of this man disappears if he continues to grow cotton, and the whole return is henceforth imputed to the original factors of production.

A word about the relation of profit to monopoly revenue. Since the entrepreneur has no competitors when the new products first appear, the determination of their price proceeds wholly, or within certain limits, according to the principles of monopoly price. Thus there is a monopoly element in profit in a capitalist economy. Let us now assume that the new combination consists in establishing a permanent monopoly, perhaps in forming a trust which need fear absolutely no competing outsiders. Then profit is obviously to be considered simply as permanent monopoly revenue and monopoly revenue simply as profit. And yet two quite different economic phenomena exist. The carrying out of the monopolistic organisation is an entrepreneurial act and its "product" is expressed in profit. Once it is running smoothly the concern in this case goes on earning a surplus, which henceforth, however, must be imputed to those natural or social forces upon which the monopoly position rests — it has become a monopoly revenue. Profit from founding a business and permanent return are distinguished in practice; the former is the value of the monopoly, the latter is just the return from the monopoly condition.

These discussions cannot be continued further within the scope of this work. Perhaps they are too long already. But if I must reproach myself with having wearied the reader too much with these things, I still cannot spare myself the reproach that not all points are exhaustively explained and not all possible misunderstandings excluded. The fundamental aspects of the matter ought to be elucidated. A few more observations before we leave the subject.

Entrepreneurial profit is not a rent like the return to differential advantages in the permanent elements of a business; nor is it a return to capital, however one may define capital. So that there is no reason for speaking about a tendency towards equalisation of profits which does not exist at all in reality: for only the jumbling together of interest and profit explains why many authors contend for such a tendency,[1] although we can observe such extraordinarily different profits in one and the same place, at the same time and in the same industry. We want finally to emphasise that profit is also not wages, although the analogy is tempting. It is certainly not a simple residuum; it is the expression of the value of what the entrepreneur contributes to production in exactly the same sense that wages are the value expression of what the worker "produces." It is not a profit of exploitation any more than are wages. However, while wages are determined according to the marginal productivity of labor, profit is a striking exception to this law: the problem of profit lies precisely in the fact that the laws of cost and of marginal productivity seem to exclude it. And what the "marginal entrepreneur" receives is wholly a matter of indifference for the success of the others. Every rise in wages is diffused over all wages; one who has success as an entrepreneur has it alone at first. Wages are an element in price, profit is not in the same sense. The payment of wages is one of the brakes to production, profit is not. One might say of the latter, but with more right, what the classical economists asserted of rent of land, namely that it does not enter into the price of the products. Wages are a permanent branch of income, profit is no branch of income at all if one counts the regular recurrence of a return as one of the characteristic features of income. It slips from the entrepreneur's grasp as soon as the entre-

---

[1] Others, as Lexis for example, dispute also the uniformity of the rate of interest. The problem, which made so many difficulties for Marx, disappears if our conclusion is accepted.

preneurial function is performed. It attaches to the creation of new things, to the realisation of the future value system. It is at the same time the child and the victim of development.[1]

Without development there is no profit, without profit no development. For the capitalist system it must be added further that without profit there would be no accumulation of wealth. At least there would not be the great social phenomenon which we have in view — *this* is certainly a consequence of development and indeed of profit. If we neglect the capitalisation of rents and saving in the narrow sense of the word — to which we ascribe no very big rôle — and finally the gifts which development in its repercussions and chance throw in the lap of many individuals, which it is true are in themselves temporary but which may lead to the accumulation of wealth if they are not consumed, then by far the most important source of the accumulation of wealth still remains, from which most fortunes spring. The non-consumption of profit is not saving in the proper sense, for it is not an encroachment upon the customary standard of life. And so we may say that it is the entrepreneur's action that creates most fortunes. It seems to me that reality convincingly substantiates this derivation of the accumulation of wealth from profit.

Although I left the reader free in this chapter to put interest on capital beside wages and rent as a productive outlay, I have yet conducted the investigation as if the whole surplus over wages and rent passed to the entrepreneur. Actually he must still pay interest on capital. That I may not be reproached with designating a sum first as profit and then as interest, let it be expressly remarked that this point will be fully elucidated later.

The size of profit is not as definitely determined as the magnitude of incomes in the circular flow. In particular it cannot be said of it, as of the elements of cost in the latter, that it just suffices to call forth precisely the "quantity of entrepreneurial services required." Such a quantity, theoretically determinable, does not exist. And the total amount of profit actually obtained

---

[1] How very closely this corresponds to reality and how clearly it represents an unprejudiced view is seen in Adam Smith's observation — which any practical man might have made and actually does make in ordinary life — that new branches of production are more profitable than old.

in a given time, as well as the profit realised by an individual entrepreneur, may be much greater than that necessary to call forth the entrepreneurial services which were actually operative. It is true that this total amount is frequently overestimated.[1] It is true that it must be borne in mind that even obviously disproportionate individual success has its function, because the possibility of attaining it works as a stronger incentive than is rationally justified by its magnitude multiplied by the coefficient of probability. Such prospects also belong, as it were, to the "remuneration" of those entrepreneurs for whom they are not realised. Nevertheless it is quite clear that in very many cases smaller amounts and especially smaller total amounts would have the same result, as it is also clear that the connection between quality of service and private success is here much weaker than for example in the market for professional labor. This is not only important for the theory of taxation — even though the importance of this element in practice is limited by the need of taking account of "capital accumulation" in the sense of increasing the supply of produced means of production — but it also explains why the entrepreneur can be relatively so easily deprived of his profit and why the "salaried" entrepreneur, for example the industrial manager who frequently plays the entrepreneurial rôle, can generally be adequately remunerated with much less than the full amount of the profit. The more life becomes rationalised, levelled, democratised, and the more transient become the relations of the individual to concrete people (especially in the family circle) and to concrete things (to a concrete factory or to an ancestral home), the more many of the motives enumerated in the second chapter lose their importance and the more the entrepreneur's grip on profit loses its power.[2] To this process the progressive "automatisation" of development runs parallel, and it also tends to weaken the significance of the entrepreneurial function.

To-day, as well as in the epoch in which the beginnings of this social process were not yet known, the entrepreneurial function is

---

[1] Cf. on this Stamp, Wealth and Taxable Capacity, p. 103 f.

[2] Cf. on this my article, "Sozialistische Möglichkeiten von heute" in the Archiv für Sozialwissenschaft (1921).

not only the vehicle of continual reorganisation of the economic system but also the vehicle of continual changes in the elements which comprise the upper strata of society. The successful entrepreneur rises socially, and with him his family, who acquire from the fruits of his success a position not immediately dependent upon personal conduct. This represents the most important factor of rise in the social scale in the capitalist world. Because it proceeds by competitively destroying old businesses and hence the existences dependent upon them, there always corresponds to it a process of decline, of loss of caste, of elimination. This fate also threatens the entrepreneur whose powers are declining, or his heirs who have inherited his wealth without his ability. This is not only because all individual profits dry up, the competitive mechanism tolerating no permanent surplus values, but rather annihilating them by means of just this stimulus of the striving for profit which is the mechanism's driving force; but also because in the normal case things so happen that entrepreneurial success embodies itself in the ownership of a business; and this business is usually carried on further by the heirs on what soon become traditional lines until new entrepreneurs supplant it. An American adage expresses it: three generations from overalls to overalls. And so it may be.[1] Exceptions are rare, and are more than compensated for by cases in which the descent is still faster. Because there are always entrepreneurs and relatives and heirs of entrepreneurs, public opinion and also the phraseology of the social struggle readily overlook these facts. They constitute "the rich" a class of inheritors who are removed from life's battle. In fact, the upper strata of society are like hotels which are indeed always full of people, but people who are forever changing. They consist of persons who are recruited from below to a much greater extent than many of us are willing to admit. Whereupon a further host of problems is opened up, the solution of which alone will show us the true nature of the capitalist competitive system and of the structure of its society.

[1] We have only a few investigations into this fundamental phenomenon. Cf., however, for example, Chapman and Marquis: "The Recruiting of the Employing Classes from the Ranks of the Wage Earners," Journal of the Royal Statistical Society (1912).

CHAPTER V

INTEREST ON CAPITAL

Preliminary Remarks

After mature consideration I submit for the second time the theory of interest which I originally published in the first edition of this book, unaltered apart from quite unimportant verbal changes. To all objections which have come to my attention my only answer is to refer to the original text. They have merely induced me not to shorten it further. Otherwise I should have been glad to have done so. But since the things which seem to me most prolix and labored, and which impair the simplicity and cogency of the argument, anticipated correctly the most important objections, they have acquired a right to existence which they perhaps did not have originally.

In particular the previous exposition made it so clear that I do not deny that interest is a normal element of the modern economy — which would indeed be absurd — but on the contrary try to explain it, that I can hardly understand the assertion that I denied it. Interest is a premium on present over future purchasing power. This premium has several causes. Many of them constitute no problem. Interest on consumptive loans is a case in point. That anyone in unexpected distress (for example, if fire destroys a business) or in expectation of a future increase in income (for example, if a student is heir to a well disposed aunt of tender health) values a hundred present more highly than a hundred future marks requires no explanation, and it is self-evident that interest may exist in such cases. All categories of government credit requirements belong here. There have always been such cases of interest, and obviously they could also exist in the circular flow in which there is no development. But they do not constitute the great social phenomenon that needs explaining. This consists of interest on productive loans (Produktivzins). It is to be found *everywhere* in the capitalist system and not only where it originates, that is in new enterprises. I merely want to show that productive interest has its source in profits, that it is by nature an offshoot of the latter, and that it, like that which I call the "interest aspect" of returns, spreads from the profits incident to the successful carrying out of new combinations over the whole economic system and even forces its way into the sphere of old businesses, in whose life it would not be a necessary element if there were no development. This is all I mean by the statement: "the 'static' economy knows no productive interest" — which is certainly fundamental to our insight into the structure and workings of capitalism. And is it not almost self-evident in the last analysis? No one can deny that just as the business situation decides the movement of the rate of interest — and business situation means normally, that is to say, neglecting the effects of non-economic forces, simply the existing tempo of development — so the money required for innovations constitutes the chief factor in the industrial demand on the money market. Is it such a great step from this to the recognition that the chief real factor is also the fundamental theoretical factor, by which alone the other source of demand is brought into play, while the latter — that is the demand of the old businesses in the tested, continually repeated round — would normally not have to come into the money market at all, because old businesses are adequately financed by the current return from production? From this the rest follows — especially the theorem that interest attaches to money and not to goods.

I am concerned with the truth and not with the originality of my theory. In particular I willingly base it upon that of Böhm-Bawerk as much as possible — however decidedly the latter has declined all communion. From his point of view too it must be a question of purchasing power in the first place, even though he immediately passes to the premium on present *goods*. Actually, of the famous three reasons upon which he bases the value premium on present purchasing power, I reject only one: the "discounting" of future enjoyments, so far as Böhm-Bawerk asks us to accept it as a cause not itself requiring any explanation. On the other hand I could claim that reason which he calls the changing relation between wants and means of satisfaction, as a formula into which to fit my theory. And what of the third, the "roundabout methods of production"? If Böhm-Bawerk had kept strictly to his expression "*adoption* of roundabout methods of production" and if he had followed the indication which it contains, this would be an entrepreneurial act — one of the many subordinate cases of my concept of carrying out new combinations. He did not do this; and I believe it can be shown with the help of his own analysis that no net income would flow from the mere repetition of roundabout methods of production which have already been carried out and incorporated in the circular flow. A point soon comes at which our explanation enters upon a fundamentally different course. However, our analysis fulfils the requirements of Böhm-Bawerk's theory of value throughout, and at no point is it exposed to any of Böhm-Bawerk's objections so far advanced.[1]

§ 1. Interest on capital, so experience teaches us, is a permanent net income that flows to a definite category of individuals. From where, and why? First there is the question of the source of this stream of goods: in order that it may flow, a value, out of which it may come, must first of all exist.[2] Secondly there is the question of the reason why this value becomes the spoils of these particular individuals: the question of the cause of this current in the world of goods. Finally there is by far the most difficult question, which may be described as the central problem of interest on capital: how does it happen that this stream of goods flows permanently, that interest is a net income which one may consume without impairing one's economic position?

---

[1] This must be emphasised so much because outside of a narrow circle of specialists even the critical part of Böhm-Bawerk's contribution has not yet been fully absorbed. But I presuppose a knowledge of it. The following relates to it at all points, and whoever still maintains the self-evidence of interest and does not see the decisive problem must find the following unnecessarily tortuous, much of it incomprehensible, even false. In Böhm-Bawerk's work, however, the reader can find everything necessary and references to almost all the literature. General knowledge of it is necessary. Finally, I do not wish to repeat what I have already said: cf. Wesen, bk. III.

[2] Cf. Böhm-Bawerk, for example on Say, I, 142. Böhm-Bawerk's method of expression is, however, already influenced there by the fact that he has a definite theory of interest in mind.

The existence of interest constitutes a problem because we know that in the normal circular flow the whole value product must be imputed to the original productive factors, that is to the services of labor and land; hence the whole receipts from production must be divided between workers and landowners and there can be no permanent net income other than wages and rent. Competition on the one hand and imputation on the other must annihilate any surplus of receipts over outlays, any excess of the value of the product over the value of the services of labor and land embodied in it. The value of the original means of production must attach itself with the faithfulness of a shadow to the value of the product, and could not allow the slightest permanent gap between the two to exist.[1] But interest is a fact. What now?

This dilemma is difficult, much worse than the analogous one which was relatively easily overcome in the case of profits because there it was only a question of temporary, not of permanent, streams of goods, and consequently we did not come so sharply into conflict with the fundamental and undoubted facts of competition and imputation; on the contrary we could safely draw the conclusion that the services of labor and land are the only sources of income whose net return is not reduced to zero by those facts. In the face of this dilemma we may proceed in two different ways.

First, it may be accepted. It then appears that interest must be explained as a kind of wages or rent, and since the latter is not feasible, then as wages: as the spoliation of wage-earners (the theory of exploitation), as the wages of the labor of capitalists (labor theory in the literal meaning), or as the wages of the labor embodied in the instruments of production and raw materials (the conception for example of James Mill and McCulloch). All three efforts at explanation have been made. To Böhm-Bawerk's critique I have only to add that our analysis of the entrepreneur, especially his isolation from the means of production, also cuts part of the ground from under the feet of the first two variants.

Secondly, the theoretical conclusion which leads to the dilemma may be denied. Here again we may either extend the list of costs,

[1] Cf. Böhm-Bawerk, I, 230.

that is assert that with wages and rent all necessary means of production are not yet paid, or search in the mechanism of imputation and competition for a hidden brake which permanently prevents the values of the services of labor and land from reaching the height of the value of the product, so that a permanent value surplus is left over.[1] I turn to the cursory discussion of these two possibilities.

Extending the list of costs means in this sense not merely asserting that interest represents a regular expenditure in the accounts of a business. This would be self-evident and would have no explanatory force. It means much more, namely conceiving interest as an element of cost in the narrower and special sense which was formulated in the first chapter. This is equivalent to constituting a third original productive factor, which bears interest as labor receives wages. If this were satisfactorily achieved, our three questions, the question of the source, of the basis, and of the non-disappearance of interest, would obviously all be answered at once, and the dilemma would be escaped. Abstinence might be such a third factor. If it were an independent productive service all our requirements would be fulfilled in a manner free from objection, and the existence and source of a permanent net income as well as its assignment to definite individuals would be explained beyond doubt. Only it would still have to be proved that in reality interest does rest upon this element. But unfortunately this explanation is not satisfactory, because such an independent element does not exist, as has already been shown by Böhm-Bawerk, and need not be further discussed here.

Produced means of production might also be constituted a third productive factor independent of abstinence. With them it is the other way round. There can be no doubt about their productive effect. It is so clear, that the investigator's glance very soon fell upon it, and that to-day the fundamental proposition of the equality between the value of the product and of the services of labor and land still excites astonishment. It is so clear that even to-day it is still extremely difficult, as experience teaches, to divert even specialists from this wrong track. Yet it does not explain a

---

[1] Cf. the concluding considerations of Böhm-Bawerk, 1, 606 f.

permanent net income. To be sure, produced means of production have the capacity of serving in the production of goods. More goods may be produced with than without them. And these goods also have a higher value than those which could be produced without the produced means of production.[1] But this higher value must also lead to a higher value of these instruments of production, and this again to a higher value of the services of labor and land employed. No element of surplus value can remain permanently attached to these intermediate means of production. For, on the one hand, no discrepancy can exist permanently between the value of the products to be imputed to them and their own value. However many products a machine may help to produce, competition must always lower their price until equality is established. On the other hand, however much more than hand labor the machine may do, once introduced it does not continually save labor anew, so that it does not continually yield a new profit. The extra receipts due to it which are so conspicuous, the whole sum which the "user" is ready to pay for it, must be handed over to workers and landowners. In general it does not produce the value which it adds to the product, as is often naively [2] assumed, but the latter is only temporarily associated with it, as was argued in the previous chapter. A coat containing a bank-note has indeed, as long as this is the case, a correspondingly higher value for its owner, but it only received this higher value from outside and did not produce it. Similarly a machine has a value corresponding to its product, but has only received [3] it from the services of labor and land which existed before it was created, to which the value has already been imputed as a whole. It is true that a stream of goods flows to the machine, but it also flows through it. At this point it is not dammed to

---

[1] Cf. Böhm-Bawerk, I, 132, on the concept of physical and value productivity of produced means of production.

[2] Cf. Böhm-Bawerk's remarks, for example on Say and Roesler.

[3] To the machine, the value of its products is imputed; to the services of labor and land necessary to the production of the machine, the value of the latter is imputed. Consequently the services already have the value of the final product, and if they become a machine the latter simply takes their place. In this sense we say that the machine "receives" the value of the productive services. It is to be hoped that I am not misunderstood as deriving its value from its costs.

form a reservoir for consumption. The possessor of the machine does not permanently get more than he must pay out, either by value or by price accounting. The machine itself is a product, and therefore just like a consumption good its value is conducted on to a reservoir, from which no interest can flow any more.

Hence on the basis of the arguments in the first and fourth chapters and of the reference to Böhm-Bawerk we can state that the above opens up no way out of the dilemma and that no source of value at all exists here for the payment of interest. At the most a difficulty occurs in the case of goods which are said to increase "automatically" — for example seed-corn or cattle used in breeding. Do not the latter ensure to their owner more corn or more cattle in the future, and must not the more corn and the more cattle be more valuable than the original seed-corn and cattle? Everyone to whom these ideas are familiar knows how firmly most people are convinced that they are proof of the existence of an increase in value. But seed-corn and breeding cattle do not increase "automatically"; on the contrary, well known items of expenditure must be deducted from their "return." However, it is decisive that even the residue left over after this deduction represents no gain in value — for the crop and the herds are certainly dependent upon seed-corn and breeding cattle, and the latter must therefore be valued according to the values of the former. If seed-corn and breeding cattle were sold, then (assuming no substitution is possible) the value of crop and herd, after deducting costs still to be incurred and making allowance for risk, would be fully expressed in their price. Their price would be equal to the price of the product imputed to them. And corn and animals would be employed in reproduction until their employment no longer yielded a profit and their price only just covered the necessary expenditure in wages and rent. The marginal utility of "their" product, that is of the share of the product imputed to them, would consequently tend towards zero.

§ 2. Here I should like to observe that it is not correct, or rather not expedient — it means committing oneself to a definite view — to characterise the state of affairs represented in this stage of our argument as follows: "We cannot explain the gap between value of product and value of means of production in this way. But it actually exists. And we must try to explain it otherwise." On the contrary I deny the fundamental existence of such a permanent gap. We are faced only with an unanalysed fact, and it should rather be suspected — as I believe a glance at reality teaches us — that it is a consequence of interest on capital, which is to be explained quite differently, than that it is a primary fact independently explaining interest. Individuals may value means of production less than products because they must pay interest on the way from the former to the latter, but they do not perforce pay interest because they value the former less than the latter on other grounds. This is very important. Here I only wish to draw attention to the fact that the difficulty against which the whole of my exposition must fight is especially great in the case of interest — the difficulty, namely, that outside of certain fundamentals we have become accustomed to simply accepting a series of unanalysed facts, and instead of penetrating more deeply into the interior of things, to considering many things as elements which are complex combinations. Once this habit is acquired we proceed to further analysis only with reluctance; we are always inclined to point to such facts as to living objections. Abstinence is such a fact. The assertion that capital value is simply the capitalised value of the return is another. And because in making this assertion one always takes one's stand upon experience, the latter does not offer a sufficiently emphatic contradiction. For the time being, however, we must still retain this conception of the "gap."

A few remarks are now necessary to formulate precisely the process of computation (Einrechnungsvorgang). Hitherto we have always spoken of the process of imputation and have traced it back from its anchoring ground in the value of the product to the services of labor and land. It might now seem that the imputation could take still another step, that it might lead the value stream still further back, namely to the labor-power and to the land themselves. Since there is no reason in an exchange economy to become conscious of a value of labor-power as such, and since if there were the same would hold true of it as for land, we shall confine ourselves to the latter, and respecting labor-power merely emphasise again that it would only present a special problem if we regarded it (which we do not) as a product of the means of subsistence of the laborer and his family. Now, one might first of all conceive the services of land as the product of land and the latter itself as the true original means of production to which imputation must sweep the value of its product. This would be logically false.[1] For land is not an independent commodity, separate from its own services, but merely a bundle of these services. Therefore it is better not to speak of imputation at all in this case. For imputation involves the transference of value to goods of continually higher orders. It so operates that nowhere is a piece of value left hanging. In determining the value of land, however, something else is involved, namely the derivation of its value from the given values of the elements of which it "consists" economically, which were determined by imputation. Here it is better to speak of computation (Einrechnung).

In the case of every good, whether a consumption or a production good, these two processes are to be distinguished. Only its services have definite values, determined [2] directly by the scale of wants or indirectly by imputation, from which its value must be derived. But while the latter process is extremely simple in the case of produced goods, and through the necessity of their reproduction, which arises sooner or later, is reduced to fixed and known rules, in the case of land it is complicated by the fact that an unlimited series of uses inhere in land, which reproduce themselves automatically and in principle without cost.[3] Hence the

---

[1] Cf. Böhm-Bawerk, Rechte und Verhältnisse vom Standpunkte der Volkswirtschaftlichen Güterlehre. Also his observations on the "use" theories of interest, which are likewise applicable to our case. At the same time I may observe that I exclude the fundamental idea of the use theory of interest from my consideration because I have nothing to add to Böhm-Bawerk's arguments.

[2] Strictly speaking this method of expression is suited only to the case of a non-exchange economy. In an exchange economy the value of means of production is nowhere felt as indirect use value. Nevertheless, here also the conception of them as potential products gives the principle for the formation of their value. And a more correct method of expression only leads to the same result.

[3] The case of self-reproduction of the services of land is distinguishable from the case of the increase of a herd of cattle by the fact that one can allow the latter to in-

question arises, on account of which we have embarked upon this discussion: must not the value of land be infinitely great and so rent as a net income disappear through computation? I answer this question in a different way from Böhm-Bawerk.[1]

First, even if the value of land were infinitely great I should still describe rent as a net income. For the source of the return could not then be exhausted by consuming it and a continuous stream of goods to the landowner would be explained. The mere summation of net returns can never abrogate their character as net returns. Only imputation, never computation, annihilates a net return. Secondly, in real life, of course, the price of a piece of land is never infinitely great. However, my conception should not be reproached with leading to this infinite value, that is to an absurd result. It is not my conception that is false but the fundamental idea of the prevailing theory of capitalisation, namely that the value of income-yielding property is formed merely by the summation of appropriately discounted returns. On the contrary the determination of this value is a special, fairly complicated problem, which will be studied in this chapter. In this as in every case of valuation it is necessary to look at the concrete purpose in view. There is no rigid rule of addition here, since value quantities are mostly not simply additive. Within the normal course of the circular flow there is no reason at all to be aware of the value of land as such. It is different with a machine: every product must have a definite total value, since it is necessary in deciding the question of its reproduction. And the rule of addition applies here too. Competition enforces it. If a machine could be had for less than it produced, a profit would be made, which would necessarily raise the demand for and the price of machines; if it cost more than its employment yielded, a loss would result, which would lower the demand and the price. Land, on the other hand, is not sold in the normal circular flow, but only its uses. Therefore only their values and not the value of land as such are elements in eco-

crease in such a way that the value of a beast finally falls to its cost in labor and land. The services of land reproduce themselves automatically only by the same amount in every economic period. They are, it is true, not incapable of increase, but their increase involves costs.

[1] Cf. Kapital und Kapitalzins, vol. II.

nomic planning. And the processes of the normal circular flow can teach us nothing about the determination of the value of land. Only development creates the value of land; it "capitalises" rent, "mobilises" land. In an economic system without development the value of land would not exist at all as a general economic phenomenon. A glance at reality confirms this. For the only occasion on which there is any sense in being aware of the value of land is upon the sale of it. And actually this hardly occurs at economic stages in which economic reality most nearly approaches the conception of the circular flow. The market for trading in land is a phenomenon of development, and can only be understood from the facts of development in which alone we can find a key to this problem. For the time being we still know nothing about it. Thus, so far, we can say that our conception does not lead to an infinite value but in general to no value, that the values of the services of land are not to be related to any other values and hence are net returns. In case it is objected that incentives to sale must nevertheless arise, it must be said that these incentives must necessarily be sporadic and that personal conditions, like distress, dissipation, non-economic aims, and the like, must be deciding. Nothing else can be stated at this juncture.

Wherever the rule of addition yields an infinite value we thus speak of a net income just as in the case of wages. For our sole concern here is that a permanent stream of goods flows to an individual and that he is not required to pass them on. And the computation which yields an infinite result, far from excluding the possibility of such a stream of goods, is a symptom of its existence. This is in fact an essential element in understanding the theory of interest which is to be expounded.

§ 3. There is still a second method of escaping the "dilemma of interest." The question of how a permanent surplus over the values of the services of labor and land is possible may also be answered by pointing to a brake on the latter. If there were such a brake then the possibility of a permanent value surplus would undoubtedly be proved, and to the circumstance which brings it about would have to be ascribed — at least from the "private" standpoint — value productivity in the fullest sense. It — or the commodity in which it is embodied — would yield a net income. A special and independent value surplus would occur in every economic process. Interest would then not be an element of cost in the real sense; it would owe its existence to a discrepancy between costs and the value or price of the product; it would be a real surplus over costs.

Such a case occurs in an exchange economy when a product is monopolised — monopolies of original productive factors do not interest us here because it is clear from the outset that interest cannot be based upon them. The monopoly position actually operates as a brake and brings the monopolist a permanent net income. We regard monopoly revenue as a net income with the same right and for the same reasons as we do rent. In this case too, the rule of addition would give an infinite result. And here also this would not deprive the revenue of the character of a net income. Why the value of the monopoly — say of a perpetual patent — is not infinite, however, does not interest us at this point; the answer will appear later. Finally, here too the determination of the value of the monopoly is a special problem, and in solving it we must not forget that in the normal circular flow no motive to form such a value exists, hence the gain is not to be related to any other magnitude. However all this may be, the monopolist can at any rate never say: "I make no profit because I ascribe an extremely high value to my monopoly." This is sufficiently certain.

In discussing Lauderdale's theory of interest Böhm-Bawerk also comments upon the case in which a labor-saving and hence profit-yielding machine is monopolised. He emphasises rightly that this machine will be so dear that no profit, or only the minimum which will just induce people to purchase or hire it, will be connected with its employment. So much is certain. Yet a profit is undoubtedly connected with its production, which is as permanent as the patent. It might be said that the monopoly position is for the monopolist something analogous to a productive factor. Imputation takes place with reference to the "services" of this quasi-factor of production just as with reference to other factors. The machine as such is not a source of surplus value, nor are its means of production, but the monopoly makes it possible to obtain a surplus value with the machine or its means of production. Obviously nothing is changed if we allow producer and user to coincide in one person.

Hence we have a net income *sui generis*. If what is called interest were the same as this, all would be well. Our three questions would be satisfactorily answered. There would be a source of surplus value the existence of which would be explained by the theory of monopoly; there would also be a reason for the assignment of a return to monopolists; and finally the fact that neither imputation nor competition annihilates the return would be explained. However, such monopoly positions do not occur regularly and numerously enough for this explanation to be accepted, and moreover interest exists without them.[1]

Another case in which one might speak of a permanent and regular lagging of the value of the services of labor and land behind the value of the product would exist if future goods were systematically and in principle valued less than present goods. The reader knows already that this is not accepted here, but it is necessary to mention the case once more. While in all the cases treated so far a permanent source of income resulted simply from a permanent and — at least from the "private" standpoint — productive service, this case would involve something different, namely a movement in values themselves. While previously the explanation lay in the determination of the value of some productive service *sui generis*, here it would lie in the determination of the value of the services of labor and land on the one hand and of consumption goods on the other hand. Here there would be a surplus of the value of the product above the value of the means of production, in a narrower and truer sense than in the case of monopoly. And "surplus over costs" would *ipso facto* signify a net return and surplus above the "capital value" of the produced means of production. Hence it would be proved *ipso facto* that

---

[1] Yet a very elaborate attempt has been made in this direction: cf. Otto Conrad, Lohn und Rente. All other suggestions of this kind of explanation of interest are not of the rank of an elaborated theory.

the return would neither disappear nor be absorbed by the process of computation. For the full value of a future product cannot be imputed and computed if, at the moment when the imputation and the determination of the value of the means of production are to be undertaken, it appears not at its real magnitude but smaller. The possibility of a permanent stream of goods would thus undoubtedly be proved, whether or not it was the interest which we observe in real life. Our first question would be answered: a source of value from which interest can flow would exist. The second question, namely why the stream of goods flows to those particular individuals, would obviously not be difficult to answer. And the third, why the return does not disappear, by far the thorniest part of the interest problem, would be superfluous. Since the value surplus would have been explained by reason of non-imputation, there would be no sense in asking why it is not imputed.

Hence if the mere passing of time had a primary effect upon valuation, and if what reality shows us to be its influence were not merely an unanalysed fact which fundamentally rests in turn upon the existence of interest, which is again to be explained on other grounds, this line of argument would be in itself quite satisfactory, even though in my opinion it brings us into many a conflict with the actual course of the economic process. Purely logically it would be free from objections. But the passing of time has not this independent primary effect. And even the growth in the value of many goods in the course of time proves nothing. Since this fact is especially prominent and has played a certain rôle in the literature of the subject, a few words may be devoted to it.

There are two kinds of such increase in value. First, the services — actual or potential — of a good may alter automatically in the course of time and the value of the good increase. A young forest and a stock of wine are examples frequently cited. What happens in such cases? Now both forest and wine certainly become more valuable goods by natural processes which demand time. However, they only grow into the higher value physically; economically this higher value already exists in the small trees of the young forest and in the wine newly cellared, because it depends upon them. These small trees and this wine must therefore so far — from the standpoint of the facts with which we are already acquainted — be exactly as valuable as the timber fit for felling and the matured wine. In so far as wood and wine may also be sold to consumers before they are quite ripe, their owners will ask themselves which of two alternatives will yield the greater return per economic period: allowing time for further ripening or selling now and producing anew. They will choose the alternative which yields the greater return, and they will value accordingly the trees and wine and the necessary services of labor and land from the very beginning. In reality this is not so. For the forest and wine continually increase in value *pari passu* as they approach maturity. This is due, however, fundamentally to material and personal risk, especially the risk of life, and to the fact that interest already exists, a fact which under certain conditions makes time an element of cost, as we shall soon see. If it were not for these factors there would be no such increase in value. If it is decided to let the forest and wine ripen longer than was originally intended, that can only be because it has been discovered that it is more advantageous to do so. There then occurs a new method of employing the forest and the wine, which must obviously result at the time of the decision in a rise in value. But there is in general no real, continuous growth of value with the passing of time as a primary and independent phenomenon.

Secondly, it often happens that the services of a good remain absolutely the same physically but yet in the course of time increase in value. This can only be attributable to the appearance of a new demand, and is a phenomenon of development. It is easy to see how this case is to be regarded. If the increase in demand is not foreseen, then there is a gain, but not one which constitutes a permanent increase in value. If on the contrary it is foreseen, then it must be imputed from the very beginning to the good concerned, so that again there is no increase in value. If in reality it nevertheless appears that there is, we shall explain it in the same way as in the case of the improvement of physical qualities.

§ 4. We have exhausted the most important lines of thought which might have led us out of the dilemma of interest, and with a negative result. Hence we find ourselves driven back again to those surplus values of which we have already spoken repeatedly and which we can consider as net surpluses with a clear conscience, namely surpluses of the value of products above the value of the quantities of production goods embodied in them. They owe their existence to some special circumstance which raises the value of products above the equilibrium value that the commodities in question would have in the circular flow. The character of such surpluses as a net return and as the source of a flow of goods is thereby *ipso facto* established just as much as it would be in the case of systematic undervaluation of future goods.

Circumstances which raise the value of a product above that of its means of production, so that with the help of the latter a profit can be made, also occur in an economy without development. Errors and windfalls, unintentional and unexpected deviations of results from expectations, conditions of distress and accidental superabundance — these and many other circumstances may produce surpluses, but this kind of deviation of actual values from normal values, and at the same time from the values of the means of production used, is of little importance. We turn to those surplus values which owe their existence to development, and which are much more interesting. We have already divided them into two main groups. The one embraces those surplus values which development carries with it of necessity, in the creation of which development consists in a sense, and which are explained by the choice of new, more advantageous, uses of producers' goods, whose values were previously determined according to other, less advantageous, uses. The second group embraces those surplus values which are based upon repercussions of development, that is upon increases, actual or anticipated, of the demand for certain goods which development brings about.

To repeat, all these surplus values are — as Böhm-Bawerk would also admit — true and real surpluses in every conceivable sense, and have nothing to fear either from the Scylla of computation or from the Charybdis of the list of costs. All streams of goods which flow to individuals under any other title than wages, rent, and monopoly revenue must directly or indirectly be due to them. Let us recall, however, the proposition already derived, that competition and the working of the general laws of valuation tend to eliminate all surpluses above costs.[1] For example, if a business suddenly and unexpectedly requires machines of a certain kind the value of the latter will rise and the possessor of such machines will be assured of the surplus value, in whole or in part. But if the new demand is foreseen then it must be assumed that more of such machines have already been produced and are now supplied by competing producers. Then either no special profit will be realised at all or, if production cannot be appropriately extended, the surplus will be imputed to the natural and original productive factors, and surrendered to their owners, in accordance with well known rules. Even if the new demand is not anticipated, the economic system will finally be adjusted to it, and no permanent surplus value will be associated with the machines.

§ 5. We can now formulate five propositions of our theory of interest which follow almost automatically from the first elementary conclusion that interest is a value phenomenon and an element in price — we have this much in common with every scientific theory of interest — and which will have to be completed later by a sixth proposition.

First, interest flows essentially from the surplus values just considered. It can flow from nothing else since there are no other surpluses in the normal course of economic life. Of course this is only true for what we have called productive interest in the narrowest sense, which does not include "consumptive-productive interest."[2] For in so far as interest is only a parasite in the body of wages and rent it has clearly nothing to do directly with these surplus values. But the large, regularly flowing stream of goods on which the capitalist class lives and which flows to it in every economic period from the proceeds of production — this can only

[1] Cf. the argument of Chapter IV.

[2] Cf. Wesen, bk. III, ch. iii; also Chapter III, Part I, in the present work. Example: if a factory is destroyed by accident and if it is rebuilt by means of a loan, then the interest on this loan is what we mean by "consumptive-productive."

come from our surplus values. These points will be examined more closely later. Moreover, there is one surplus value which is not of this kind, namely monopoly revenue. Our thesis therefore assumes that the typical source of interest is not in monopoly revenue. This, however, as I have already said, should be sufficiently clear. Thus without development, with the qualifications mentioned, there would be no interest; it is a part of the great waves which development causes in the sea of economic values. Our thesis rests first of all upon the negative proof that the determination of value in the circular flow excludes the phenomenon of interest; this proof in turn rests first upon direct knowledge of the process which determines values and secondly upon the untenableness of various attempts to establish decisive differences between the values of products and of means of production in an economy without development. Then we have added the positive proof that such a difference in value does occur in development. The thesis will lose much of its strangeness in the course of the following discussion. It may be emphasised here at once, however, that it is not nearly so far from an unprejudiced treatment of reality as it might seem, for industrial development is certainly at least the chief source of the interest form of income.[1]

Secondly, surplus values in development fall, as we have seen, into two groups — entrepreneurial profit and those values which represent the "repercussions of development." It is clear that interest cannot attach itself to the latter. We can assert this so easily because the process of creating this kind of surplus is quite clear, so that we can see immediately what is and is not there. Let us consider the example of a tradesman who, in consequence of the establishment of factories in his village, receives more than equilibrium income for a time. Thus he makes a definite profit. This profit cannot itself be interest, for it is not permanent and is soon wiped out by competition. But neither does interest *flow* from it — assuming that the tradesman has done nothing more in the acquisition of it than simply stand in his shop and charge higher prices to his customers — for absolutely nothing further

---

[1] Only the regularity of interest supports the preconception that it must be explained "statically"; but we do account for this regularity.

happens to it: the tradesman pockets it and uses it as he pleases. The whole process leaves no room for the phenomenon of interest. Therefore interest must flow from entrepreneurial profit. This is an indirect conclusion to which I attach, of course, only secondary importance as compared with the other facts which support this thesis. Development, then — in some way — sweeps a part of profit to the capitalist. Interest acts as a tax upon profit.

Thirdly, however, it is obvious that neither the whole profit nor even a part of it can be directly and immediately interest, because it is only temporary. And analogously we see at once that interest does not adhere to any class of concrete goods. All surplus values adhering to concrete goods must be by nature temporary, and even though such surpluses constantly arise in an economic system in full development — so much so that it requires deeper analysis to recognise the ephemerality of any one of them — yet they cannot immediately form a permanent income. Since interest is permanent it cannot be understood simply as a surplus value from concrete goods. Although it flows from a definite class of surplus values no surplus value *per se* is interest.

These three propositions, that interest as a great social phenomenon is a product of development,[1] that it flows from profit, and that it does not adhere to concrete goods, are the basis of our theory of interest. The admission of them puts an end to all the continually repeated attempts to find an element of value in concrete goods corresponding to interest,[2] and thereby concentrates work on the problem of interest within quite a small field.

§ 6. It is now time to get the significant question more firmly in our grasp. The main question, the solution of which settles by far the most important point in the interest problem, now runs: *how*

---

[1] Cf. Wesen, bk. III, ch. iii.

[2] From this two practical results follow at once. First, the so-called primitive trading interest is not interest. In so far as it is not monopoly revenue or wages it must be entrepreneurial profit — also only temporary. Secondly, rental is not interest. Rental is partial purchase and can include no element of interest in the circular flow. The net income from a house could only be ground rent — and wages of "superintendence." How an element of interest can, in development, enter into the rental will be seen automatically from our argument. The fact that already existing interest on capital makes time an element of costs is especially important.

is this permanent stream of interest, flowing always to the same capital, extracted from the transitory, ever-changing profits? This statement of the question embodies the results so far attained and is independent of the direction in which we continue. If it is answered satisfactorily, then the interest problem is solved in a way that satisfies all the demands which Böhm-Bawerk's analysis has proved to be indispensable and — whatever its defects may otherwise be — it is not exposed to the objections fatal to previous theories.

We proceed with our fourth thesis, which differs totally from the usual theories, with the exception of the exploitation theory, and which has the weight of the most competent authority against it: *in a communistic or non-exchange society in general there would be no interest as an independent value phenomenon.* Obviously no interest would be *paid.* Obviously there would still exist the value phenomena from which interest flows in an exchange economy. But as a special value phenomenon, as an economic quantity, even as a concept, interest would not exist there; it is dependent upon the organisation of an exchange economy. Let us formulate this still more precisely. Wages and rent also would not be paid in a purely communist organisation. But the services of labor and land would still exist there, they would be valued, and their values would be a fundamental element in the economic plan. Nothing of this holds good for interest. The agent for which interest is paid simply would not exist in a communist economy. Hence it could not be the object of a valuation. And consequently there could not be a net return corresponding to the interest form of income. Thus interest is indeed an economic category — not created directly by non-economic forces — but one which only arises in an exchange economy.

Why is there no interest in a communist society, although there is in an exchange economy? This question leads us to our fifth thesis. It opens to us a first view of the nature of the suction apparatus that draws a permanent stream of goods from profits. The capitalist certainly has something to do with production. And technically, production is always the same process under whatever organisation it may occur. Technically it always requires goods and nothing but goods. Hence no difference can exist here. But elsewhere there is a difference. The entrepreneur's relation to his production goods in an exchange economy is essentially different from that of the central organ in a non-exchange community. The latter has the disposal of them directly, the former must first of all procure them by hire or purchase.

If entrepreneurs were in a position to commandeer the producers' goods which they need to carry their new plans into effect, there would still be entrepreneurs' profit, *but no part of it would have to be paid out by them as interest. Nor would there be any motive for them to consider part of it as interest on the "capital" they expend.* On the contrary, the whole of what they make over and above costs would be "profits" to them and nothing else. It is only because other people have command of the necessary producers' goods that entrepreneurs must call in the capitalist to help them to remove the obstacle which private property in means of production or the right to dispose freely of one's personal services puts in their way. No such help is wanted in producing within the circular flow, for firms already running can be, and in principle are, currently financed by previous receipts, which stream to them without the intervention of any distinct capitalistic agency. Hence nothing essential is obscured in the picture of the circular flow, if it is assumed that the means with which production is carried on consist of the products of preceding periods; but in the case of new combinations, entrepreneurs have no such products with which to procure means of production. Here, then, the function of capital comes in, and it becomes evident that nothing corresponding to it can exist either in a communist or even in a non-communist but "stationary" society.

§ 7. I should like to direct the reader's attention to the fact that our conception of the interest problem involves something different from the usual conception. Although this is really obvious it will nevertheless not be superfluous to elucidate the point still more.

For this purpose I shall start from the usual distinction between interest on loans and "original" interest on capital. It reaches back to the beginning of investigations into the nature of interest, and has become one of the foundation stones of the theory. Speculation about the interest problem started as a matter of course with interest on consumptive loans. First of all, it is in the nature of things that it should start with interest on such loans because this stands out as an independent branch of income distinguished by many clear features. It is always easier to grasp conceptually a branch of income which is also externally distinguished than one which must first be cleared of an admixture of other elements — therefore rent was first clearly recognised in England where it not only existed but was also as a general rule paid separately. But interest on consumptive loans was also the starting point because it was the most important and best known form in ancient times and in the Middle Ages. Interest on productive loans was not wanting, it is true; but in classical antiquity it operated in a world which did not philosophise, while the world which did philosophise only observed economic things fleetingly and only paid attention to the interest which was to be observed in their sphere. And also later, the elements of a capitalist economy which existed were familiar only to a circle which was a world in itself and neither pondered nor wrote. The church father, the canonist, or the philosopher dependent upon the church and Aristotle — all of them only thought of interest on consumptive loans, which made itself noticeable within their horizon and indeed in a very unpleasant manner. From their contempt for the bleeding of the necessitous and the exploiting of the thoughtless or profligate, from their reaction against the pressure exerted by the usurer, arose their hostility to charging interest, and this explains the various prohibitions of interest.

Another conception grew up from observation of business life, as the capitalist economy gathered strength. It would be an exaggeration to say that interest on productive loans was positively a discovery of later authors. But in effect the emphasis upon this came to much the same as a discovery. It immediately made clear that the old conception simply ignored one part, and indeed what now was by far the most important part, of the phenomenon, and at the same time that the debtor by no means always becomes poorer by borrowing. This took the edge off the fundamental reason for the hostility to interest and led scientifically a step further. The whole English literature on interest up to Adam Smith's time is filled with the idea that a loan often leads the borrower to business profit. In the place of the weak debtor there appears in the mind of the theorist a strong debtor, in the place of the piteous crowds of distressed poor and thoughtless landowners there appears a figure of another breed, the entrepreneur — not quite clearly and boldly defined, it is true, but still plain enough. And this is the point which the theory here expounded takes up.

But productive interest is still interest on loans for this group of theorists. Entrepreneurial profit is recognised as its source. However, from this it no more follows that entrepreneurial profit is simply interest than it follows that the total receipts of production are wages because these total receipts are the source of wages. If anything definite at all can be said in view of the shortness of these writers' arguments about interest, it is that they did not confound interest and profit in the least or view them as identical in character. They perceived, on the contrary, as is seen from Hume,[1] the difference between the two, and were far from seeing in profit nothing more than interest on one's own capital. They explain profit in a manner which is not at all applicable to interest on loans as such, but only to another kind of profit which is the *source* of interest on loans.[2] All these authors traced interest back to business profit as its source, but did not say that the latter itself is again only a case and indeed the principal case of interest. Their "profit" may not be translated by interest even when it occurs in the phrase "profit of capital." They did not solve the interest problem. But it would not be correct to say that they merely traced back one derived form, interest on loans, to the original and real interest, without explaining the latter. They merely failed to prove why the creditor with his capital is in a position to exact this share of profit, why the capital market always decides in his favor. Furthermore, the central problem

---

[1] Petty, Locke, and Steuart might also be quoted.

[2] This explains the disharmony actually exhibited upon a first glance into Locke's theory, as Böhm-Bawerk emphasises. (Cf. Kapital und Kapitalzins, 2 ed., I, 52.)

upon the solution of which insight into the interest phenomenon depends, certainly lies in business profit; not, however, because business profit is itself true interest, but because its existence is a prerequisite of the payment of productive interest. Finally, the entrepreneur is certainly the most important person in the whole matter; not, however, because he is the true, original, typical interest receiver, but because he is the typical interest payer.

In the case of Adam Smith we may still perceive a trace of the view according to which profit and interest do not simply coincide. Only with Ricardo and his epigoni are the two plainly synonymous. Not till then did theory come to see in business profit in general the only problem, and in fact the interest problem; not till then did the question, why does the entrepreneur obtain a business profit, become the interest problem; and finally not till then is the meaning of the English authors correctly rendered if their "profit" is translated by "profit on capital" (Kapitalgewinn) or "primary interest" (ursprunglicher Zins). This constitutes by no means merely the harmless substitution of interest on one's own capital for contractual interest on borrowed capital, but a new assertion, namely that the entrepreneur's profit is essentially interest on capital. The following facts must have contributed to what from our standpoint clearly appears as a deviation from the right path.

First of all, this statement of the question is extraordinarily obvious. Contractual agricultural rent is certainly only a consequence of the "original" phenomenon, namely of that part of the product which is "imputable" to land. It is nothing more than the latter itself, the net return of agriculture from the landlord's point of view. Contractual wages are only the consequence of the economic productivity of labor; they are simply the net return of production from the worker's point of view. Why should it be otherwise in the case of interest? Without special reason it will not be taken to be so. The conclusion, that corresponding to contractual interest there is an original interest and that the latter is just as much the typical income of the entrepreneur as rent is the typical income of the landlord, appears to be perfectly natural, almost self-evident. In practice the entrepreneur allows for interest on his own capital — this appears as an incontestable sanction if such is necessary at all.

The surplus of the value of products over their costs, then, is really the fundamental phenomenon upon which interest is also dependent. And it arises in the hands of the entrepreneur. Is it to be wondered at that only this problem was seen and that it was hoped that everything was settled with the solution of it? Economists had just wrested themselves free of mercantilist superficialities and become accustomed to looking at the concrete goods which lay behind the money veil. It was emphasised that capital consists of concrete goods, and the tendency was to constitute this capital a special productive factor. This standpoint, once taken up, leads directly to considering interest as an element in the price of stocks of goods, and hence it has simply been identified with what the entrepreneur obtains by means of these stocks. Because interest undoubtedly came from profit, and thus represented a part of profit, the latter or at any rate the better part of it became interest unawares, quite automatically at the moment when interest was connected with the concrete goods which the entrepreneur makes use of in production. That wages do not similarly become interest, because interest may be paid out of them, is a reflection that is remoter than one would think.

The unsatisfactory analysis of the entrepreneurial function contributed powerfully to make this view general. It is perhaps not quite correct to say that entrepreneur and capitalist were simply lumped together. But in any case one started from the observation that the entrepreneur can only make his profit with the aid of capital in the sense of a stock of goods, and placed an emphasis upon this observation which it does not deserve. One saw — and this was quite natural — in the employment of capital the characteristic function of the entrepreneur and distinguished him by it from the worker. He was regarded in principle as the employer of capital, the user of production goods, just as the capitalist was regarded as the provider of some kind of goods. The above statement of the question then readily suggests itself; it must appear simply as a more precise and more profound statement of the question concerning interest on loans.

This must obviously have had grave consequences for the interest problem. There was interest on loans because there was original interest and the latter arose in the hands of entrepreneurs. Thereby the whole apparatus for the solution of the problem was focussed on the entrepreneur. Now this led to a great number of false scents. Many attempts at explanation like the exploitation theory and some labor theories — as explanations of interest — became possible for the first time. For only when interest is linked with the entrepreneur can the idea arise of explaining it by his labor service or by labor contained in production goods or by the price struggle between entrepreneur and workers. Other attempts, such for example as all productivity theories, even though not made possible were nevertheless made essentially more obvious by this way of formulating the interest problem. It made a sound theory of entrepreneurs and capitalists impossible; it made the recognition of a special entrepreneurial profit difficult, and ruined the explanation of it from the outset. But by far the worst consequence of this interpretation was the creation of a problem that became a kind of economic *perpetuum mobile*.

Interest is, as experience teaches, a permanent income. It originates in the hands of the entrepreneur. Consequently a permanent income *sui generis* originates in the hands of the entrepreneur. And the question confronting the traditional theory of interest is: from where does it come? For more than a century theorists have been attacking this impossible, indeed meaningless, question.

Our position is entirely different. If traditional theory links up contractual interest with entrepreneurs' profits, it only traces the problem to what it believes to be its fundamental case, and has, after having done so, still to perform the main part of the task. If we succeed in linking up interest with entrepreneurs' profits, we shall have solved the whole problem, because entrepreneurs' profits themselves are not another case of interest, but something different from it which has been explained already. The statement that "there is interest on loans because there is a business profit" is only valuable as a more precise statement of the question for the prevailing theory; while for us it already has explanatory value. The question, but whence comes the business profit? which contains for the prevailing theory a summons to do its chief work, is for us settled. For us there remains only the question: *how* does interest arise from entrepreneurial profit?

It was necessary to draw the reader's attention especially to this different and narrower statement of the question in our interest problem because the objection that nothing more is done here than the reduction of interest to business profits, which theory accomplished long ago, would be particularly annoying. Thus the repeated emphasis upon things which the reader might easily have said himself is well justified. Now we shall proceed to the sixth and last proposition in our theory of interest.

§ 8. The surplus which forms the basis of interest, being a value surplus, can only emerge in a value expression. Therefore in an exchange economy it can only be expressed in the comparison of two money sums. This is self-evident, and *prima facie* completely uncontroversial. In particular, no comparison of quantities of goods can in itself assert anything about the existence of a value surplus. Wherever quantities of goods are spoken of in such a connection, they appear only as symbols of values. In practice the value expression is used and interest is represented in the money form alone. In any case we must accept this fact, but we can interpret it very variously. We might come to the conclusion that this appearance of interest in the form of money is merely dependent upon the necessity of a standard of value, and has nothing to do with the nature of interest. This is the prevailing view. According to it, money serves as the form of expression and nothing else, while interest on the contrary arises in goods of some kind as a surplus of the goods themselves. We take this view too in the case of entrepreneurial profit. A measure of value is also necessary to express it, and the money representation is therefore made use of as a matter of expediency. But in spite of this the nature of entrepreneurial profit has nothing at all to do with money.

Unquestionably it is extraordinarily tempting in the case of interest also to try to turn away from the element of money as quickly as possible and to carry the explanation of interest into the region where values and returns arise, namely in the realm of the production of goods. However, we cannot turn aside. It is true that in every case, corresponding to money interest, that is to the premium on purchasing power, there is a premium on goods of some kind. It is true that goods and not "money" are needed to produce in the technical sense. But if we conclude from this that money is only an intermediate link, merely of technical importance, and set about substituting for it the goods which are obtained with it and for which therefore in the last analysis interest is paid, we at once lose the ground from under our feet. Or more correctly expressed: we can indeed take a step or even a few steps away from the money basis into the world of commodities. But the road suddenly ends because these premiums on commodities are not permanent — and then we see at once that this road was wrong, for an essential characteristic of interest is that it is permanent. Therefore it is impossible to pierce the money veil in order to get to the premiums on concrete goods. If one penetrates through it one penetrates into a void.[1]

Thus we cannot move away from the money basis of interest. This constitutes an indirect proof that a second interpretation of the significance of the money form in which interest encounters us is to be preferred, namely the interpretation that this money form is not shell but kernel. Obviously such a proof alone would not justify far-reaching inferences. But it fits into our earlier arguments on the subject of credit and capital, by virtue of which we can understand the rôle played by purchasing power here. Hence as a result we can now state our sixth proposition: *interest is an element in the price of purchasing power regarded as a means of control over production goods.*

This proposition of course does not ascribe to purchasing power any productive rôle. Yet most people reject it *a limine* in spite of the fact that interest fluctuates in the money market with the supply of and demand for money, which undoubtedly points to our interpretation.[2] Another point may be added at once. That

---

[1] Here I shall not enter further into the expedients "stock of consumption goods" and "stock of accumulated services of labor and land."

[2] Cf. Marshall's remarks before the Commission on the Depression of Trade. In the discussion of the relation between the quantity of money and commodity

one gets wet when it rains is no more self-evident to the business-man than that interest falls when credit facilities increase, other things being equal. In reality, if a government were to print paper money and to lend it to entrepreneurs, would not interest fall? And would not the state be able to receive interest for it? Does not the connection of interest with rates of exchange and gold movements speak plainly enough? It is an extremely wide and significant range of everyday observations that supports us here.

Nevertheless, only a few significant theorists introduced these facts into the discussion of the interest phenomenon. Sidgwick represents an interpretation in which I perceive, with Böhm-Bawerk, essentially an abstinence theory. But before the *sedes materiae*, the chapter on interest, he treats of interest in the chapter on the value of money, and here he brings it into relation with money and recognises the influence of the creation of purchasing power upon interest in the statement: " . . . We have to consider, that the banker to a great extent produces the money he lends . . . and that he may easily afford to sell the use of this commodity at a price materially less than the rate of interest on capital gen-erally." [1] This statement contains several points over which we cannot rejoice. Furthermore, it provides no thoroughgoing foun-dation for the process. Finally, no further conclusions for the theory of interest are drawn. Yet it is a step in our direction, ob-viously made with reference to Macleod. Davenport applies him-self much more to the subject; but his analysis also comes to noth-ing. He rides quite nicely and willingly up to the fence but then refuses to take it. The prevailing theories completely neglect the element of money — they leave it to the financial writers as a technical matter without theoretical interest. This attitude is so general that it must rest upon an element of truth and in any case is in need of explanation.

prices he says, speaking of an increase in the quantity of money: "I should say it would act at once upon Lombard Street, and make people inclined to lend more; it would swell deposits and book credits and so enable people to increase their specula-tion. . . ." One who says this (and who could deny it?) cannot reject our interpre-tation lightly.

[1] Principles of Political Economy, 3 ed., p. 251.

Least may be said for the attempt to deny the statistical connection between the interest rate and the quantity of money. R. Georges Lévy [1] has compared the interest rate with the production of gold and, as was to be expected, found that no significant correlation exists. Neglecting the fact that the statistical method employed was defective, it does not justify the conclusion that the quantity of money and the interest rate have nothing to do with one another. In the first place, an exact time correlation is not to be expected. Then the supply of gold, even of the banks, is not simply proportional to the volume of credit granted — and only the granting of credit is significant for the rate of interest. Finally, the whole production of gold does not flow to the entrepreneur.

Nor does the inductive refutation attempted by Irving Fisher (Rate of Interest, p. 319 ff.) affect our argument. Yearly averages prove absolutely nothing as against the observations which may be made in the details of everyday dealings in money. Also, he compared the circulation of money per capita with the interest rate and thereby made the comparison completely irrelevant.

But of course economists of the eighteenth century had every reason to emphasise that interest is ultimately paid for goods. They had to fight not only mercantilistic but all sorts of other errors, both of businessmen and philosophers, and in so doing they did in fact establish valuable truths and expose a long list of popular fallacies. Law, Locke, Montesquieu, and others were undoubtedly quite wrong in making the rate of interest simply depend on the quantity of money, and Adam Smith was right in pointing out [2] that an increase in the quantity of money will *caeteris paribus* raise prices, and that, at a higher level, the same relation between return and capital which ruled before will tend to reestablish itself. Even the immediate effect of an increase of *money in circulation* would be to raise the rate of interest rather than to reduce it. For anticipation of such an increase must have that effect,[3] and in any case the demand for credit will be stimu-

---

[1] Journal des Economistes (1899).
[2] Cf. his short and pregnant argument in bk. II, ch. iv, of the Wealth of Nations.
[3] Cf. Fisher, Rate of Interest, p. 78.

lated by the rise in prices. But all this, while it explains and to some extent justifies the aversion which most of our highest authorities display against any "monetary" theory of interest, yet has nothing whatever to do with our proposition.

We can also discover other elements of truth in the point of view "hostile to monetary explanations."[1] Businessmen and financial writers often emphasise the importance of discount policy and the monetary system in a wrong way. The fact that the central banks can influence the interest rate no more proves that interest is the price of purchasing power than the fact that the state can fix prices proves that prices in general are explicable by governmental action. The interest rate can no doubt be influenced by the attention paid to the state of the currency, but the theoretical significance of this fact does not in itself go far. It is a case of influencing a price for motives which lie outside the market. The view that by the monetary system and by discount policy a country's interest rate can be kept lower than that of other countries, and that such a policy stimulates economic development, is nothing but a pre-scientific prejudice. The organisation of a money market is of course just as capable of improvement as that of a labor market, but nothing in the fundamental processes can be altered by this.

§ 9. Our problem now reduces to the simple question: what are the conditions for the emergence of a premium on present over future purchasing power? Why is it that if I lend a certain number of units of purchasing power, I can stipulate for the return of a greater number of such units at some future date?

This is obviously a market phenomenon. The market we have to study is the money market. And it is a price-determining process which we have to investigate. Every individual loan transaction is a real exchange. At first it seems strange, perhaps, that a

---

[1] For example its justifiable scorn of the causal connection between interest and the quantity of money in the following form: if more money exists then the value of money falls — and for this less valuable money less interest is paid. In this, of course, there is no redeeming feature. I have not discussed this interpretation at all in the text, but I believe that it has contributed largely to frightening off economists once for all from this nexus between money and interest.

commodity is as it were exchanged for itself. After Böhm-Bawerk's arguments on this point,[1] however, it is not necessary to go into it in detail: the exchange of present for future is no more an exchange of like for like, and therefore meaningless, than the exchange of something in one place for something in another place. Just as purchasing power in one place may be exchanged for that in another, so present can also be exchanged for future purchasing power. The analogy between loan transactions and exchange arbitrage is obvious, and may be recommended to the reader's attention.

If we succeed in proving that under certain circumstances — let us say at once in the case of development — present purchasing power must regularly be at a premium over future purchasing power in the money market, then the possibility of a permanent flow of goods to the possessors of purchasing power is theoretically explained. The capitalist can then obtain a permanent income which behaves in every respect as if it arose in the circular flow, although its sources are individually not permanent and although they are the results of development. And no imputation or computation can alter anything in the character of this stream of goods as a net return.

We can now state directly how high the total value of an interminable annuity must be. It must be the sum which, if lent at interest, will yield a return equal to the annuity, for if it were less, lenders would compete to buy the annuity, and if it were more, potential buyers would rather lend their money at interest than buy it. This is the real rule of "capitalisation" which already presupposes the existence of a rate of interest. From this it follows again that the valuation of permanent returns cannot take away the character of net incomes from them.

Therefore we answer all three questions of which the interest problem consists if we solve the problem of the premium on present purchasing power. The proof of a permanent flow of goods to capitalists, from which no deduction is to be made and which is not to be passed on to other individuals, completely settles the matter and explains *ipso facto* that this flow also represents a

[1] Cf. Kapital, vol. II.

gain, that it is a net return. We shall now proceed to produce this proof and enfold step by step our explanation of the many-sided problem of interest.

§ 10. It has been said already that even in the circular flow cases may and will arise in which people will be ready to borrow even on the condition of having to pay back a larger sum than they receive. Whatever the motive — temporary distress, expectation of a future increase in income, weakness of will, or foresight — such people will be able to express their valuation of present purchasing power in terms of future purchasing power, which determines their demand curve for the former in the ordinary way. On the other hand, there may be, and generally will be, people ready to meet this demand provided they get a premium which more than compensates them for the disturbance which the lending of sums held for definite purposes must entail. Therefore we can also construct supply curves, and it is hardly necessary to show in detail how a price — a determined premium — will emerge in this market.

But transactions of this kind could not normally be of any great importance and, above all, they *would not be necessary elements in the conduct of business*. Lending and borrowing can become part of the normal routine of industry and commerce, and interest can economically and socially acquire the importance that it actually has, only if the control of present purchasing power means more future purchasing power *to the borrower*. As the prospect of business profit is the pivot on which the valuation of sums of present purchasing power actually turns, we shall now put aside for the moment all other factors which may give rise to interest even where there is no development.

Now within the circular flow and in a market which is in equilibrium it is impossible with a given money sum to obtain a greater money sum. However I employ a hundred monetary units' worth of resources (including management) within the generally known and customary possibilities, I can obtain no greater receipts from them than exactly a hundred monetary units. To whichever of the existing possibilities of production I may apply any hundred monetary units I shall always receive for the product not more — possibly less, however — than a hundred monetary units. For that is precisely the characteristic of the equilibrium position, that it represents the "best" combination — under the given conditions in the widest sense — of the productive forces. The value of the monetary unit is in this sense necessarily at par, for *ex hypothesi* all arbitrage gains have already been made and are therefore excluded. If I buy the services of labor and land with the hundred monetary units, and with these carry out the most lucrative production, I shall find that I can market the product for exactly a hundred monetary units. It was precisely with regard to these most lucrative possibilities of employment that the values and prices of the means of production were established, and this most lucrative employment also determines the value of purchasing power in our sense.

Only in the course of development is the matter different. Only then can I obtain a higher return for my product, that is, if I carry out a new combination of the productive forces which I bought for a hundred monetary units and succeed in putting a new product of higher value on the market. For the prices of the means of production were not determined with regard to this employment, but only with regard to the previous uses. Here, then, the possession of a sum of money is the means of obtaining a bigger sum. On this account, and to this extent, a present sum will be normally valued more highly than a future sum. Therefore present sums of money — so to speak as potentially bigger sums — will have a value premium, which will also lead to a price premium. *And in this lies the explanation of interest.* In development the giving and taking of credit become an essential part of the economic process. There, the phenomena appear which have been described by the expressions "relative scarcity of capital" and "the lagging of the supply of capital behind the demand" and so forth. Only if and because the social stream of goods becomes broader and richer does interest stand out with such sharpness and bring us finally so very much under its influence that long analytical effort is required to perceive that it does not always appear where men act economically.

§ 11. Let us now look more closely into the process of the formation of interest. After what has been said this means that we shall examine more closely the method of determining the price of purchasing power. To this end let us confine ourselves first of all strictly to the case which we recognised as the fundamental one, and to which the argument of the earlier chapters was also directed, namely to the case of exchange between entrepreneurs and capitalists. Later we shall pursue the most important ramifications of the interest phenomenon.

Under our present assumptions, the only people who have a higher estimation for present as against future purchasing power are the entrepreneurs. Only they are the bearers of that market movement in favor of present money, of that demand which raises the price of money above par as we define it.

Capitalists on the supply side confront entrepreneurs on the demand side. Let us start with the assumption that the necessary means of payment for carrying out new combinations must be withdrawn from the circular flow and that there is no creation of credit means of payment. Furthermore, since we are considering an economy without results of previous development, there are no great reservoirs of idle purchasing power, for these are, as was shown above, only created by development. A capitalist would thus be one who is ready under certain conditions to transfer a definite sum to the entrepreneur by withdrawing it from its customary uses, that is by restricting his expenditure either in production or in consumption. We still assume that the quantity of money in the system does not increase in any other way, for example through gold discoveries.

Exchange will develop between entrepreneurs and possessors of money and will proceed just as in any other case. We have definite demand and supply curves for all the exchanging individuals. The entrepreneur's demand is determined by the profit which he can make with the help of a certain money sum by exploiting the possibilities hovering before him. We shall follow the practice of assuming these demand curves to be continuous just as we do in the case of other goods, although a very small loan, say of a few monetary units, will be of little use to the entrepreneur, and at certain points, namely where important innovations become possible, the individual demand curves will in fact be discontinuous. Beyond a certain point, namely beyond the sum which is necessary to the carrying out of all the plans which the entrepreneur has thought of at all, his demand will fall sharply, perhaps absolutely to zero. However, in considering the whole economic process, that is in considering very many entrepreneurs, these circumstances lose much of their importance. Therefore we shall imagine that the entrepreneur is able to attach determined quantities of entrepreneurial profit to the individual monetary units from zero to the limit for practical purposes, in the same way as every individual attaches certain values to the successive units of any good.

Any normal individual's valuation of his stock of money per economic period follows from the subjective exchange value of any unit, as was explained in the first chapter. The same rules are also valid for an increase in money beyond this accustomed stock. From this there results a definite utility curve for every individual, and from this again, according to well known principles, a definite curve of the potential supplies on the money market.[1] And now we have to describe the "price struggle" between entrepreneurs and potential suppliers of money.

Let us assume as a starting point that upon our money market, which might be regarded as similar to a stock exchange, someone offers a certain price for purchasing power by way of experiment. Under our present assumptions this price would have to be very high, since the lender would have to disturb severely all his private and business arrangements. Suppose then that this price of present purchasing power expressed in future purchasing power is 140 for one year. With a premium of 40 per cent only those entrepreneurs could exercise an effective demand who hoped to make an entrepreneurial profit of at least 40 per cent, or more correctly of over 40 per cent; all others would be excluded. Assume that a certain number of the former existed. According to the principle "better to exchange with small advantage than not to exchange at

[1] Cf. for details Wesen, bk. II. Here we are not concerned with an elaborate exposition of the theory of prices.

all," [1] these entrepreneurs will really be ready to pay this interest rate for a certain quantity of purchasing power. On the other side of the market there will likewise be lenders who will not exchange even at this rate. Assuming again that a number of people considered this compensation to be adequate, they would ponder the question of how much they should lend. The 40 per cent is only a sufficient compensation for a certain sum; for everyone there is a limit beyond which the magnitude of the sacrifice in the present economic period must exceed the magnitude of the increase in utility in the next. But the loan must also be actually so big that an increase would result in a surplus of disadvantage, for as long as it is smaller the lending of further monetary units at that rate would afford a surplus of advantage which, according to general principles, no individual can forego.

Supply and demand, therefore, are unequivocally determined in every such case of a "tentative" price. If they were by accident equally great, then the price would stand, in our case, a rate of interest of 40 per cent. If the entrepreneurs, however, can use more money at this rate than is supplied, they will outbid one another, whereupon some will drop out and new lenders will appear until equilibrium is attained. If the entrepreneurs cannot use as much money as is supplied at this rate, then the lenders will underbid one another, whereupon some of them will drop out and new entrepreneurs will appear until equilibrium is attained. Thus in the exchange struggle on the money market a definite price for purchasing power will be established just as on any other market. And since, as a rule, both parties value present more highly than future money — the entrepreneur because present money signifies more future money for him, the lender because under our assumptions present money makes possible the orderly course of his economic activity while future money is merely added to his income — the price will practically always be above par.

The result of our discussion up to this point may be expressed in terms of the marginal theory, just as in the case of any price-determining process. On the one hand interest will be equal to the profit of the "last entrepreneur," who is simply the one who an-

[1] Cf. Böhm-Bawerk, Kapital, vol. II.

ticipates from carrying out his project a profit which just makes the interest payment possible. If we rank entrepreneurs — with due regard to the element of variation in risk — in a row according to the size of the profits which they hope to make, so that the "borrowing capacity" of the entrepreneurs falls the further we advance in the row, and if we think of this array as continuous, then there must always be at least one entrepreneur whose profit exactly equals the interest and who stands between those who make bigger profits and those who are excluded from exchanging on the money market because their profit is smaller than the interest to be paid. In practice the "last" or "marginal" entrepreneur must also retain a small surplus, but there will be at times entrepreneurs for whom this surplus is so small that they can only exercise a demand for purchasing power at the actually ruling interest and not at a higher rate by however small an amount. These are in the position which corresponds to the theoretical marginal entrepreneur. We can say, then, that interest must in every case be equal to the smallest entrepreneurial profit that will be actually realised. With this statement we approach again the usual interpretation.

On the other hand interest must also be equal to the value estimate of a last or marginal capitalist for his money. The concept of such a marginal capitalist is attained *mutatis mutandis* in just the same way as that of the marginal entrepreneur. It can easily be seen that from this standpoint interest must be equal to the valuation of the last lender, and further, that the latter must also be equal to the valuation of the last entrepreneur. It is also obvious how this result could be developed further — it has already been done often in economic literature. Only one point must still be mentioned. The last lender's valuation rests upon the importance which he attaches to the habitual course of his economic life; and this may be expressed by saying that the loan involves a sacrifice, and indeed for the marginal capitalist a "marginal sacrifice," that corresponds to the valuation of the increase in income by the receipt of interest. Then interest is also equal to the greatest or marginal sacrifice that must be made in order to satisfy the existing demand for money at a given rate of interest.

And with this we approach the method of expression of the abstinence theory.

§ 12. Interest would have to be determined in this way if industrial development were actually financed with the resources of the circular flow. However, we observe that interest is also paid for purchasing power created *ad hoc*, namely for credit means of payment. This leads us back to the results which were developed in the second and third chapters of this book, and it is time to introduce them here. We saw there that in a capitalist society, industrial development could in principle be carried out solely with credit means of payment. We now adopt this conception. Let it be remembered once more that the great reservoirs of money which actually exist arise as a consequence of development and must therefore be left out of account at first.

By the introduction of this element our previous picture of reality is altered but is not made unusable in its main features. What we said about the demand side of the money market remains provisionally unaltered. Now as before, the demand comes from the entrepreneurs and indeed in the same way as in the case just considered. Only on the side of supply is there much alteration. Supply is now put upon another basis; a new source of purchasing power, of a different nature, appears, which does not exist in the circular flow. The supply also comes from different people now, from differently defined "capitalists," whom we call "bankers" in conformity with what was said earlier. The exchange, to which interest owes its origin in this case and which, according to our interpretation, is also typical of all other exchanges concerning money in modern society, takes place between entrepreneur and banker.

Hence we shall have grasped the fundamental case in the phenomenon of interest if we can give the conditions governing the supply of credit means of payment. We know already by what forces this supply is regulated: first with regard to possible failures by entrepreneurs, and secondly with regard to the possible depreciation of the credit means of payment. We can eliminate the first element from our consideration. For this purpose we only need to consider an addition for risk, which is known empirically, as included once for all in the "par price of the loan." This means that if it is known from experience that one per cent of loans is irrecoverable then we shall say that the banker receives the same sum that he lent if he actually receives an additional 1.01 per cent approximately from all debts which are not bad. And there is, of course, an element of wages for the professional activity of the banker, which we also neglect. The size of the supply will then only be determined by the second element, that is with regard to the necessity of avoiding a difference in value between the newly created and the existing purchasing power. We must show that the value- and price-determining process also creates a premium on the newly created purchasing power.

In the case previously treated it was not wholly impossible that negative interest should occur. It might possibly occur in that case if the demand for money for new enterprises were smaller than the offers by those people to whom a "favor would be done" in temporarily taking charge of their money. Here, however, this is excluded. The banker who received back less than he gave would suffer a loss; he would have to cover the deficiency, since he would not be able completely to meet the claims upon him. Therefore in this case interest cannot fall below zero.

But it will in general be above zero, because entrepreneurs' demand for purchasing power is distinguished in one important respect from the ordinary demand for goods. Demand in the circular flow must always be supported by an actual supply of goods or else it is not "effective." The entrepreneur's demand for purchasing power, however, in contrast to his demand for the concrete goods which he needs, is not subject to this condition.

On the contrary, it is only restricted by the much less stringent condition that the entrepreneur will be able later on to repay the loan with interest. Since, even if there were no interest, the entrepreneur would only demand credit in the event of his being able to make a profit with the help of the loan — for otherwise he would have no economic incentive to produce — we can also say that the entrepreneur's demand is subject to the condition or is effective upon the condition that he can make a profit with the loan. This leads to the relation between supply and demand. In any kind of economic situation whatever, the number of possible innovations is practically unlimited, as was explained in the second chapter. Even the richest economic system is not absolutely perfect and cannot be so. Improvements can always be made, and the striving after improvements is always limited by the given conditions and not by the perfection of what exists. Every step forward opens new prospects. Every improvement leads further away from the appearance of absolute perfection. The possibility of profit, therefore, and with it the "potential demand," have no definite limit. Consequently the demand with interest at zero would always be greater than the supply, which is always limited.

However, these possibilities of profit are powerless and unreal if they are not supported by the entrepreneur's personality. So far we only know that profit-yielding innovations are "possible" in economic life; we do not even know whether they will always be taken up by concrete individuals in such measure that the demand for purchasing power with interest at zero is always greater than the supply. We may go still further. The fact that economic systems without development may exist teaches us that individuals who are capable and inclined to carry out such innovations may even not exist at all. May it not be concluded from this that such individuals may also possibly exist in such a small number that the supply of purchasing power is not exhausted, instead of being insufficient for the satisfaction of all? There would be no creation of purchasing power at all and the total supply of credit means of payment would simply disappear [1] if no demand for purchasing power, or only an insignificant one, existed. But if *any* entrepreneurs' demand for credit exists at all, then it is impossible for it to be smaller than the supply with interest at zero. For the appearance of one entrepreneur facilitates the appearance of others. In the sixth chapter it will be shown that the obstacles with which innovations are confronted become smaller the more a community

---

[1] To avoid misunderstandings it may be remarked that it would be possible for exchanges in the circular flow to be effected with the help of credit means of payment. These would circulate without interest and at par. But in order that there may be an incentive to create more credit means of payment interest is certainly necessary.

gets accustomed to the appearance of such innovations, and that in particular the technical difficulties in founding new enterprises become smaller because connections with foreign markets, credit forms, and so on, when once created, benefit the epigoni of the pioneers. Therefore the greater the number of people who have already successfully founded new businesses, the less difficult it becomes to act as an entrepreneur. It is a matter of experience that successes in this sphere, as in all others, draw an ever-increasing number of people in their wake, hence that continually more people proceed to carry out new combinations. The demand for capital of itself continually engenders new demand. And therefore on the money market there is a limited effective supply, however big it may be, as against an effective demand which has no definite limit at all.

This must raise interest above zero. As soon as it comes into existence many entrepreneurs are eliminated, and as it rises more and more of them disappear. For although possibilities of profit are practically unlimited, they differ in size and most of them are of course only small. The appearance of interest again increases the supply which is not absolutely fixed, but interest must and will nevertheless continue to exist. A price struggle is started on the money market, which we shall not describe again, and under the influence of all elements of the economic system a definite price for purchasing power is established which must contain interest.

§ 13. We have now to connect the empirical facts, which we have so far excluded, with the fundamental principle relating to interest. First we must enumerate all those sources of existing, in contrast to newly created, purchasing power which actually feed the great money-market reservoir; and secondly we must show how interest spreads from its quite narrow basis over the whole exchange economy, permeates as it were the whole economic system, so that interest seems to occupy much more room than one would expect from our theory. Only if the whole area of the interest problem in these two directions can be exhaustively explored from our point of view can we consider our problem as solved.

The first task presents no difficulty. First of all, every concrete phase of development begins, as was said before, with a heritage from earlier phases. A reservoir of purchasing power may already be formed by the elements which the pre-capitalist exchange economy has created, and hence there will always be greater or lesser quantities of purchasing power in the economic system which are at the disposal of new enterprises either permanently or for a certain time. Moreover, when the capitalist development is in motion an ever-increasing stream of disposable purchasing power flows to the money market. We shall distinguish three branches of it. First, by far the largest part of entrepreneurial profit is employed in this way; the profit will be "invested." Here it is in principle quite immaterial whether an entrepreneur invests his profit in his own business or whether the sum in question comes on the market. Secondly, in the case of the retirement of entrepreneurs or perhaps of their heirs from active business life, if this leads to the liquidation of the enterprise, greater or lesser sums then become free without other sums always and necessarily at the same time becoming tied up. Thirdly and finally, those profits which development so to speak sweeps to other people than entrepreneurs, and which are based upon "repercussions of development," will to a greater or lesser extent come directly or indirectly into the money market. Let us notice here that this process is accessory in still another sense than in the sense that this sum only owes its existence to development: it is the fact that interest exists, the possibility of receiving interest for this sum of money, that draws disposable purchasing power to the money market. The acquisition of interest is the only motive that leads its possessor to offer it — if there were no interest the purchasing power would be hoarded or spent on goods.

It is similar in the case of another element. We saw that the significance of saving in an economic system without development [1] would be relatively very small, and that what is usually meant by the size of the savings of a modern nation is nothing but the sum of those profits from development which never become elements of income. Now the importance of saving in the real

[1] Cf. Chapter II.

sense might not be large enough, even in a system with development, to play a decisive part for industrial requirements, but for the fact that a new kind of saving — and indeed of "real" saving — appears which is absent in a system without development. The fact that one may be assured of a permanent income by lending a sum of money acts as a new motive to saving. It is conceivable that, just because a sum saved increases automatically and consequently its marginal utility sinks, less will sometimes be saved than if no interest were received. For the most part, however, the existence of interest, which opens up a new method of employing the money saved, leads clearly to a considerable increase in saving activity — which of course does not mean that every *rise* in interest must result in a proportional increase or any increase at all in saving. From this it follows that the saving which is actually observable is in part a consequence of the existing interest; and here also there is an "accessory stream of purchasing power" coming into the money market.

A third source which supplies the money market is money which is idle for a longer or shorter time and which is also lent if interest can be obtained for it. It consists of momentarily disposable business capital and so forth. The banks collect these sums and a highly developed technique enables every monetary unit, even if it is held ready for an impending expenditure, to contribute to increasing the supply of purchasing power. Still another fact belongs here. We saw that the nature of credit means of payment and the explanation of their existence must not be sought in the effort to economise metal money. Of course, credit means of payment cause less metal money to be used than would have to be used if the same transactions had to be carried out with metal money alone. But these transactions only arose with the help of credit means of payment, and as against the money requirement which would have developed in the same time if there had been no credit means of payment, no "economy" in money so far occurs. Yet we must now recognize that, apart from the credit means of payment which development brings into existence, further transactions which were perhaps carried out previously by means of metal money are settled with credit by the banks under the pressure of the desire to increase the quantity of interest-bearing purchasing power; that is, credit means of payment are likewise created by banking technique, consequently a still further increase in the disposable quantity of money results from this source.

All these elements increase the supply on the money market and lower interest far below the level at which it would be if they were not present. They would very soon reduce it to zero if development did not continually create new possibilities of employment. Whenever development stagnates, the banker hardly knows what to do with the disposable funds, and often it becomes doubtful whether the price of money contains more than the capital sum plus a premium for risk and compensation for labor. Then especially, and particularly on the money markets of very rich nations, the element of creation of purchasing power often recedes into the background, and the impression can easily be formed, so dear to economic theory as well as to banking practice, that the banker is nothing more than a middleman between borrowers and lenders. From this conception it is only a step simply to substitute for the lender's money the concrete goods which the entrepreneur needs, or even the concrete goods needed by those who transfer the necessary means of production to the entrepreneur.

It may be remarked further that there are cases, as Böhm-Bawerk has already emphasised, in which interest is only demanded and paid because it is possible to demand and pay it. Interest on bank balances is an example. No one transfers his purchasing power to the bank with the intention of investing his capital in this way. On the contrary, money is deposited only in so far as it is desirable to have a supply of purchasing power available for business or private reasons. This would happen even if something had to be paid for it. But actually the depositor receives, in most countries, a kind of share in the interest which the sums in question yield in the banker's hands. And when once this has become usual people will not be inclined to leave a balance at a bank which does not pay interest. Here interest accrues to the depositor without anything being done on his part. Now this phenomenon reaches very far into all economic life. The fact that every particle of purchasing power can obtain interest puts a premium on it, whatever purpose it may serve. Thus interest forces its way into the business of people who have not themselves anything to do with new combinations. Every unit of purchasing power has to fight as it were against the current that attempts to draw it into the money market. Furthermore, it is obvious that in all cases in which anyone needs credit for any reason at all, the loan transaction — state loans and so forth — will be linked with the fundamental phenomenon.

§ 14. In this way the interest phenomenon extends gradually over the whole economic system, and therefore it presents a much wider front to the observer than one would suspect from its innermost nature. Hence, time itself becomes in a certain sense an element of cost, as has already been indicated. This consequent phenomenon, which the prevailing doctrine accepts as the fundamental fact, explains — and at the same time justifies — the discrepancy between it and our interpretation. But we have still a further step to take, namely to explain the fact that interest finally becomes a form of expression for all returns with the exception of wages.

In practice we speak of land as yielding interest, likewise of a patent or of any other good which yields a monopoly revenue. We even speak of interest-bearing in the case of a non-permanent return; we say, for example, that a sum of money employed in speculation, even a commodity employed in speculation, has yielded interest. Does not this contradict our interpretation? Does it not show that interest is an income from the possession of goods, that it is in an altogether different category than it would be according to our interpretation?

This method of expressing returns has borne definite fruit in theory amongst American economists. The impetus came from Professor Clark. He called the return from concrete producers' goods rent; the same return conceived as a result of the enduring economic fund of productive power — which he calls "capital" — interest. Here, then, interest appears merely as a special aspect of the returns and no longer as an independent part of the national income stream. Professor Fetter [1] has developed the same idea still more strongly and in a somewhat different way. But here we are interested most of all in Professor Fisher's theory, expounded in his work The Rate of Interest. Professor Fisher explains the fact of interest simply by the underestimation of the future satisfaction of wants; most recently [2] he has expressed his theory in the statement: "Interest is impatience crystallised into a market rate." Accordingly he connects interest with all goods separated in time from final consumption. And since all returns to the latter can be "capitalised," consequently expressed in the form of interest, interest is not a part but the whole of the income stream: wages are interest on human capital, rent is interest on capital in the form of land, and every other return is interest on produced capital. Every income is value product discounted according to the rate of the undervaluation of future satisfactions. It is clear that we cannot accept this theory because we do not even recognise the existence of the fundamental element in it. It is just as clear that for Fisher this element becomes a central factor in economic life, which must be brought in to explain nearly every economic phenomenon.

The fundamental principle that comes into consideration here, and that should lead us to understand the universal practice of expressing returns in the form of interest, is the following. According to our interpretation concrete goods are never capital. Yet anyone who possesses concrete goods can, in a system which is conceived to be in full development, obtain capital by selling them. In this sense the concrete goods might be called "potential capital"; at least they are so from the standpoint of their possessor, who can exchange them for capital. In this connection, however, only land and monopoly positions [3] come into consideration, for two reasons. First, it is clear that one cannot sell one's labor-power as such, if we neglect the case of slavery. But there are no stocks of consumption goods and produced means of pro-

---

[1] Cf. my article "Die neuere Wirtschaftstheorie in den Vereinigten Staaten," Schmoller's Jahrbuch (1910).

[2] Scientia, Rivista di Scienza (1911).

[3] Though I use this method of expression I do not mean to cast doubt upon the fundamental fact that monopoly positions are not "goods," as will easily be seen.

duction in the sense asserted by the prevailing doctrine — so in principle we come back immediately to land and monopolies. And secondly, only land and monopoly positions are directly income-bearing. Since capital is also income-bearing, its owner would not exchange it for goods which yield no net income — or only if such a price reduction is conceded to him that he can realise a profit with the goods in the current economic period and then reinvest his capital uninjured; but in this case the seller would suffer a loss to which he would only make up his mind in abnormal conditions, especially in distress, as will be shown immediately.

The possessors of "natural agents" and monopolists thus have every reason, if there is development, to compare their income with the return on the capital which they could obtain by selling their natural agents or their monopoly, since such sale might possibly be advantageous. And capitalists have reason to compare their income from interest with the rent or permanent monopoly revenue which they can obtain with their capital. Now how high will be the price of such sources of income? No capitalist, in so far as he takes the acquisitive standpoint, can value a piece of land higher than the sum of money which yields as much interest as the former does rent. No capitalist can, with the same qualification, value a piece of land any lower. If the piece of land cost more it would — neglecting obvious secondary elements — be unmarketable: no capitalist would buy it. If it cost less, competition would arise among the capitalists which would raise its price to that level. No landowner who is not in distress will be inclined to give up his land for a lesser sum than that which yields him as much in interest as his piece of land yields in pure rent. But he will also not be able to get a bigger sum for it, because a large quantity of land would immediately be offered to the capitalist who was ready to give it. Thus the "capital value" of permanent sources of income is unequivocally determined. The well known circumstances which cause either more or less to be paid in most cases do not affect the principle.

In this solution of the problem of capitalisation the central and fundamental factor is interest on purchasing power. The return to every other permanent source of income is compared with this, and according to it — as a consequence of the existence of interest — its price is so fixed by the competitive mechanism that in conceiving the return of potential capital as real interest no practical error is made. In reality, therefore, every permanent return is connected with interest; but only externally, only in so far as the magnitude to which it is related is determined by the level of interest. It is not interest; the contrary method of expression in practice is merely brachylogy. And it is not directly dependent upon interest as would be the case if the nature of interest were correctly characterised by the expression "time discount."

Our result may also be extended to non-permanent net returns, for example to quasi-rents. It is not difficult to see that under free competition a temporary net return will be sold and bought for that sum of money which, if invested at interest at the moment of the conclusion of the business, would accumulate to the same sum by the time the net return ceased as all the net returns would if they were lent as they accrued. Here also in practice the buyer's capital will be spoken of as yielding interest — and with the same right as in the case of permanent returns — although the buyer no longer has his capital, and has changed from a capitalist into a rent receiver. And what sum will the owner of say a blast furnace be able to obtain for it if it is *not* the bearer of a permanent — perhaps monopolistic — or temporary net return, but is a business of the circular flow, that is — abstracting from rent, which we shall neglect here — profitless? Now no capitalist will "invest" his capital in such a business. The transaction, if it is to take place at all, must yield him not only the replacement of his capital after the plant is worn out, but also a net return during its lifetime corresponding to the interest which he could otherwise draw. Consequently, if the buyer has no other design for the furnace than simply to collect its returns in the circular flow, that is if it is not called upon to play a part in a new combination, it must be sold at a price lower than cost. The seller must make up his mind to a loss, for only so could the buyer obtain a profit equal to the interest which he could otherwise obtain with the purchase money.

In all these cases the businessman's interpretation and expression are not correct. But in all these cases the incorrectness has no practical consequences, and it is quite clear why the business-man makes use of this inadequate interpretation. In the modern economic system the rate of interest is such a ruling factor, in-terest is so much the barometer of the whole economic situation, that regard to it is necessary in the case of practically every eco-nomic action and it enters into every economic deliberation. It leads to the phenomenon observed by theory from time imme-morial, that all returns in the economic system, seen from a certain aspect, tend to equality.

§ 15. The elliptical expression of the practical man, which is always implied in speaking of interest on concrete goods, has cer-tainly led theory astray. But now I want to show that the theo-retical error which always lies in this extension of the idea of in-terest beyond its real basis may also bring practical errors in its train.

The "interest aspect" of returns is a harmless view to take in the case of permanent returns, that is rents and permanent monopoly revenues, but not in other cases. Let us consider first of all our example of the furnace in order to show this. Under our assumptions the buyer of the furnace receives enough during its lifetime to recover his purchase money and interest besides — which we shall assume he spends as income. Now if all economic conditions remain unchanged, when it is worn out he can build another furnace,[1] of exactly the same kind as the old and at the same costs as the old. But if these costs are higher than originally, the individual in question must add something to his amortisa-tion fund in order to cover them. And henceforth the furnace would accordingly no longer yield him a net return. Now if the buyer of the furnace perceived these conditions clearly he would not undertake the construction, but would invest the sum re-covered elsewhere. If he did not perceive them, if he allowed him-self to be deceived by the interest aspect, then he would be the loser, although the seller on his part might also have been the

[1] The reader will easily see that the argument is not changed if we assume that the buyer, who wishes to continue to work the furnace, does not let it perish and build it anew, but preserves it permanently by repairs.

loser and the buyer at the time rightly believed that he had made a good bargain. At first sight the case seems bewildering. But I shall not add another word of explanation because the matter must be clear to the reader who gives it the appropriate attention. Such cases are not rare in practice, and are consequences of the habit of attaching permanent net returns to goods which do not yield them. Of course other errors can also lead to such disappointments. On the other hand the disappointments may fail to materialise in consequence of particularly favorable circumstances. But I believe that everyone must find sufficient proofs in his experience for what has been said.

The case is similar if net returns really exist but are not permanent, if for example a business still yields a few instalments of entrepreneurial profit or temporary monopoly revenues or quasirents. If one nevertheless speaks of such things as interest-bearing it does no harm as long as one is aware of the temporary character of these returns. But at the moment when one explains them as interest the temptation is obvious to regard them as permanent; indeed, sometimes the expression is already a symptom of this error. And then of course one experiences the most unpleasant surprises. This interest has a way of diminishing obstinately, even of suddenly coming to an end. The businessman in this event complains of bad times, to be sure, and cries out for protective tariffs, government assistance, and so forth, or considers himself as the victim of a special misfortune or — with more reason — as the victim of new competition. Such occurrences are very frequent, and they substantiate our interpretation strikingly. Yet they obviously hark back to the fundamental error which leads in practice to false steps and bitter disappointments, in theory to those explanations of interest which we are criticising.

The statement is often heard that somebody's business "yields" say 30 per cent. Of course this is not simply interest. In most cases the result is arrived at by not counting the entrepreneur's activity as an outlay and consequently not including the payment for it under costs. If this is not the explanation then the return cannot be permanent. Business experience completely substantiates this conclusion of our interpretation. For what business "yields interest" permanently? It is true, the business-man often does not realise this temporary character of the return, and makes the most diverse hypotheses about its continual dwindling. And the buyer is very often lured by the expectation that such a return will be maintained — at the most he recognises that the experience of the previous owner may have something to do with its size. Then he automatically applies the interest formula instead of the correct method of calculation. If he does this strictly, that is if he "capitalises" the return at the current rate of interest, then failure will follow. The return of every business ceases after a time; every business, if it remains unchanged, soon falls into insignificance.

The individual industrial business is not a permanent source of any other income than wages and rent. The individual who is most inclined to overlook this in daily practice, and to suffer the unpleasant experience indicated above, is the typical shareholder. It might be thought that an objection against our theory of interest could be forged out of the "fact" that a shareholder may draw a permanent net income even without periodically changing his investment. According to our view the capitalist would first have to lend his capital to one entrepreneur and after a certain time to another, since the first cannot be permanently in the position to pay interest. Since we characterised the shareholders as mere contributors of money, and yet they draw a permanent income out of one and the same enterprise, the objection would seem to be very strong. But precisely the case of the shareholder — and of every creditor who throws in his lot permanently with an enterprise — shows how true our interpretation is to reality. For this "fact" is very doubtful. Do companies live eternally and do they pay dividends forever? Certainly there are such, but broadly only two groups of them. First there are branches of industry, some railways for example, which have, if not a perpetual, yet an assured monopoly for a long time. Here the shareholder simply receives monopoly revenue. Then there are kinds of enterprises which by nature and programme are continually doing new things and are really nothing but forms for continual new enterprises. Here the aims alter incessantly and the leading personalities also change, so that it is in the nature of the thing that people of considerable ability always appear in the leading positions. New profits are always arising, and if the shareholder loses his return this is not really necessary but just a misfortune to be explained by the individual case. But neglecting these two categories, that is if a company simply operates a definite business without a monopoly position, there is, at the most, rent of natural agents as a permanent income, and nothing more. Now experience confirms this strikingly, although in practice competition does not act promptly and hence enterprises remain in possession of surpluses for a considerable time. No industrial company of the type indicated gratifies its shareholders with a constant shower of gold; on the contrary it soon declines into a stage that has the most lamentable similarity with the drying up of a spring. Hence repayment of capital is frequently concealed in dividends, even though the wearing out of machines and so forth is ever so conscientiously taken care of by depreciation accounts. Quite rightly, therefore, much more than wear and tear is frequently written off and many companies strive to write off the whole capital as soon as possible. For the time comes for each when the business as such is really valueless, that is when its returns only just cover costs. So there is no such thing as a lasting income from interest out of one and the same business, as anyone who does not believe it and acts accordingly may learn to his cost. Hence the receipt of dividends by shareholders does not tell against our interpretation — quite the reverse!

§ 16. How far this theory will prove an efficient instrument in the analysis of statistical material and in the investigation of the questions which arise in relation to interest still remains to be seen. It certainly seems to bring the facts of money, credit, and banking into closer touch with pure theory than other interpretations do. The author hopes to be able to submit the results of some work on these lines in a book to be published in the near future, in which such problems as, for example, the relation between gold reserves and interest, the influence of the monetary system upon interest, the differences between interest rates of different countries, and the correlation between rates of exchange and interest will be discussed.

Our argument should also explain the movement in time of the rate of interest. It is from this class of facts that verification of the fundamental idea might primarily be expected. If the interest of business life — what it is usual to call "productive interest" — has its roots in entrepreneurial profit, both should move closely together. As a matter of fact, this is true of short period fluctuations. In longer periods we may still observe some relation between the prevalence of new combinations and interest, but there are so many elements to be taken account of, and "other things" remain so imperfectly equal as soon as we go beyond the span of say a decade, that verification becomes extremely complicated. It is then not only necessary to allow for government borrowing, migration of capital, and movements of the general level of prices, but there are also more delicate questions, which cannot be entered upon here.

There is nothing in our theory to support the old view — which with many people from the classical economists onwards has acquired the force of a dogma — that interest must of necessity display a secular tendency to fall. It may be shown, however, that the impression to that effect, which seems so strongly to suggest itself, is largely due to the element of risk, which accounts for medieval figures; and that the *real* rate of interest does not display any clear secular trend, that its history rather verifies our interpretation than disavows it.

These remarks must suffice. However incomplete our arguments may be, and however much more precise formulation and however much modification they may require, I believe the reader will nevertheless find in them some of the elements for understanding that part of economic phenomena which has hitherto presented most difficulties. I have only one thing to add: I wished to explain the interest phenomenon but not to justify it. Interest is not, like profit for example, a direct fruit of development in the sense of a prize for its achievements. It is on the contrary rather a brake — in an exchange economy a necessary brake — on development, a kind of "tax on entrepreneurial profit." Certainly this is not sufficient to condemn it, even if one includes condemnation or approbation of things in the tasks of our science. Against the condemnatory verdict we can assert the importance of the function of this "ephor of the economic system," and we may conclude that interest only takes away something from the entrepreneur which would otherwise accrue to him, and not from other classes — neglecting the cases of consumptive and of "productive-consumptive credit." Yet this fact, together with the fact that the interest phenomenon is not a necessary element in all economic organisations, will always result in the critic of social conditions finding more to object to in interest than in anything else. Therefore it is important to state that interest is only the consequence of a special method of carrying out new combinations, and that this method can be much more easily changed than the other fundamental institutions of the competitive system.

CHAPTER VI

THE BUSINESS CYCLE

Preliminary Remarks

THE following theory of crises, more correctly of recurrent business fluctuations, has still less claim to be considered a satisfactory representation of its subject-matter than the theories of the entrepreneurial function, of credit, capital, the money market, profit, and interest which have already been expounded. A satisfactory theory would require, to-day more than ever, a comprehensive treatment of the tremendously increased material, the working out of the numerous individual theories based upon different indices of business conditions and of their relation to one another. My work in this direction is a torso; the promise of exhaustive treatment has remained unfulfilled,[1] and according to my programme of work must long remain so. Nevertheless, I submit this chapter again without any alteration except in exposition, not only because it now has its place in the investigation of crises but also because I still hold it to be true; not only because I believe that it contains the contribution of the argument of this book to the topic but also because this contribution gives the essence of the matter. Hence I am ready to accept criticism on the basis of this chapter.

The study of the objections which have come to my notice has confirmed me in my conviction. I shall mention only two. First

---

[1] I have since published on the subject, apart from the article in the Zeitschrift für Volksw. Sozialpol. und Verw. (1910), the article "Die Wellenbewegung des Wirtschaftslebens," Archiv für Sozialwissenschaft und Sozialpolitik (1914). To this day my theory of crises is cited chiefly from this article. It was also expounded in 1914 in a lecture at Harvard University when in formulation and in the factual foundation — but without any essential change — a step beyond this chapter was taken. Furthermore, there is an article "Kreditkontrolle" (*ibidem*, 1925) which was primarily concerned with other things; and "Oude en nieuwe Bankpolitiek" in the Economisch-Statistischen Berichten (1925), which likewise barely touches the fundamental question. I expounded this in detail in a lecture at the Handelshochschule in Rotterdam in 1925. Finally, for a short exposition see "The Explanation of the Business Cycle," Economica (1928).

there is the criticism that my theory is merely a "psychology of crises." This objection has been made so urbanely by a most competent authority, and one most highly esteemed by me, that I myself must formulate its true content more sharply if the reader is to see what it really means. "Psychology of crises" means something quite definite, and is different from "psychology of value" for example: it means insisting on those tragi-comic aberrations of the frightened business world which we notice and specially *have* noticed in the past in every crisis. As a theory of crises, therefore, it would mean the basing of a scientific explanation either upon obvious accompanying and consequent phenomena (panic, pessimism, and so on) or, only a degree less bad, upon previous bullish tendencies, promotion fever, and so forth. Such a theory is barren; such an explanation explains nothing. But this is not my position. Not only do I always discuss external conduct, so that psychology can only be found in my argument in the sense in which it would be implied in every statement, even the most objective, about economic events, but I explain the phenomenon of business fluctuations — whether actually occurring now or not — solely by an objective chain of causation which runs its course automatically, that is by the effect of the appearance of new enterprises upon the conditions of the existing ones, a chain of causation which follows from the facts explained in the second chapter.

Then there is the objection formulated by Loewe: my theory does not explain the periodicity of crises.[1] I do not understand this. Two things may be meant by periodicity. First, the mere fact that every boom is followed by a depression, every depression by a boom. But this my theory explains. Or secondly, the actual length of the cycle may be meant. But this no theory can explain numerically because it obviously depends upon the concrete data of the individual case. Yet my theory gives a general answer: the boom ends and the depression begins after the passage of the time which must elapse before the products of the new enterprises can appear on the market. And a new boom succeeds the depression when the process of resorption of the innovations is ended.

[1] In the Festschrift for Brentano, II, 351.

But Loewe means something else, which has been formulated as follows by Emil Lederer.[1] My treatment is said to be "not satisfactory because it does not try at all to explain why the entrepreneurs appear periodically in swarms as it were, what the conditions are under which they can appear and whether they will always appear and why, if the conditions are favorable for them." Now one may assert that I have explained inconclusively the swarm-like appearance of entrepreneurs, which, with its consequential phenomena, constitutes the only cause of periods of boom. But that I have not tried at all to explain it — when my whole argument aimed at this — seems to me to be untenable. The conditions under which entrepreneurs may appear — neglecting the general economic and social conditions of the competitive economy — are shown in the second chapter and may be briefly and incompletely formulated as the existence of new possibilities more advantageous from the private economic standpoint — a condition which must always be fulfilled; the limited accessibility of these possibilities because of the personal qualifications and external circumstances which are necessary;[2] and an economic situation which allows tolerably reliable calculation. Why the entrepreneurs appear under these conditions is no more problematical if one adheres to the assumptions implied in our entrepreneurial concept than the fact that anyone seizes a gain when it is immediately before his eyes.

I should now like, without any critical design and solely in order to allow the ideas to stand out more clearly, to compare my theory with by far the most thorough effort in this field, that of Spiethoff[3] — little as it is capable of comparison with the latter in thoroughness and perfection. The point of view — deriving from Juglar — according to which the wave-like fluctuation in business and not the crisis itself appears to be the fundamental thing to

[1] Cf. his distinguished work, "Konjunktur und Krisen," in Grundriss der Sozialökonomik, vol. IV, pt. I, p. 368.

[2] The new formulation in Chapter II also clears up Loewe's objection, which he expresses with the concept of the "half-static" businessman.

[3] Cf. his more recent expositions, above all the article "Krisen" in the Handwörterbuch der Staatswissenschaften, but also the exposition in the Hamburger Wirtschaftsdienst (1926), Heft I, and his lecture, "Moderne Konjunkturforschung," before the "Freunde und Förderer der Universität Bonn."

be explained, is common to both. We agree in the conception —
which is established by me not in this chapter alone but also in
the second — that the alternating situations (Wechsellagen —
Spiethoff) are the form economic development takes in the era of
capitalism. Hence we also agree in the view that completely developed capitalism is to be dated historically only from the time
when such alternating situations first unmistakably occur (that is
in England, according to Spiethoff, only from 1821, in Germany
from the forties of the nineteenth century). Further, we agree
that the figure for the *consumption* of iron is the best index of business conditions; that is, this index which Spiethoff discovered and
worked out — I have no effort in this direction to exhibit — is
also recognised by me as the right one from the standpoint of my
theory. We agree that the causal nexus begins first of all with the
means of production which are bought with capital and that the
boom materialises first of all in the production of industrial plant
(factories, mines, ships, railways, and so forth). Finally, we agree
with the conception that the boom arises, as Spiethoff puts it, because "more capital is invested," is fixed in new businesses, and
that the impulse then spreads over the markets for raw materials,
labor, equipment, and so forth. We also understand the same by
capital in the sense which is here significant, with the exception
that the creation of purchasing power plays a fundamental part
in my argument which it does not in Spiethoff's. So far I should
only have to add one thing, that capital investment is not distributed evenly in time but appears *en masse* at intervals. This is
obviously a very fundamental fact, and for this I offer an explanation not offered by Spiethoff. I accept Spiethoff's conception of
the standard cycle (Musterkreislauf).

The difference between us lies in the explanation of the circumstance which cuts short the boom and brings about the depression.
For Spiethoff this circumstance is the overproduction of capital
goods relative on the one hand to the existing capital and on the
other hand to the effective demand. As a description of the actual
facts I could also accept this. But while Spiethoff's theory stops
at this element and tries to make us understand what circumstances induce the producers of factory equipment, of building

materials, and so forth periodically to produce more than their markets are capable of absorbing at the time, my theory tries to explain the state of affairs in the manner to be found in this chapter, which may be summarised as follows. The effect of the appearance of new enterprises *en masse* upon the old firms and upon the established economic situation, having regard to the fact established in the second chapter that as a rule the new does not grow out of the old but appears alongside of it and eliminates it competitively, is so to change all the conditions that a special process of adaptation becomes necessary. This difference between us would be still further reduced by more detailed discussion.

It was impossible to keep my old exposition short and yet to make it invulnerable. Nevertheless I have cut it down still further in order to let the fundamental idea stand out more clearly. For the same reason I shall number the steps of the argument.

§ 1. Our question is: does this whole development which we have been describing proceed in unbroken continuity, is it similar to the gradual organic growth of a tree? Experience answers in the negative. It is a fact that the economic system does not move along continually and smoothly. Counter-movements, setbacks, incidents of the most various kinds, occur which obstruct the path of development; there are breakdowns in the economic value system which interrupt it. Why is this? Here we meet with a new problem.

If these deviations of the economic system from a smooth line of development were rare, they would hardly constitute a problem with a special claim upon the theorist's attention. In an economy without development the individual may meet with misfortunes which are very serious for him without there being any reason for theory to go into such phenomena. Likewise, events which might perhaps destroy the economic development of a whole nation would require no general investigation if they were rare, if they could be conceived as isolated mishaps. But the counter-movements and setbacks of which we are speaking here are frequent, so frequent that upon first consideration something like a necessary periodicity seems to suggest itself. This makes it impossible, practically at all events if not logically, to abstract from this class of phenomena.

Further, if it were the case that after such a setback is overcome the earlier development begins again at the point reached before it was interrupted, then the significance of the setback would not in principle be very great. We might say that we had taken account of all the fundamental facts of development even if we could not explain these disturbing incidents themselves or had simply abstracted from them. However, this is not the case. The counter-movements do not merely obstruct development, they put an end to it. A great many values are annihilated; the fundamental conditions and presuppositions of the plans of the leading men in the economic system are changed. The economic system needs rallying before it can go forward again; its value system needs re-organising. And the development which then starts again is a new one, not simply the continuation of the old. It is true, experience teaches that it will move more or less in a similar direction to the earlier, but the continuity of the "plan" is interrupted.[1] The new development proceeds from different conditions and in part from the action of different people; many old hopes and values are buried forever, wholly new ones arise. Empirically it may happen that the main lines of all these partial developments, which lie between the setbacks, coincide with the broad outlines of the total development, but theoretically we cannot merely consider the contours of the total. Entrepreneurs cannot skip the setback phase and carry their plans over intact into the next phase of development, and scientific explanation cannot do so either without completely losing touch with the facts.

We have now to investigate this class of phenomena, which stand out so sharply against, apparently in a certain opposition to, other phenomena of development. At the outset the following possibilities exist. First, crises may or may not be a uniform phenomenon. The peculiar breakdowns of development which we know from experience and describe as crises always appear even to the naive mind as forms of one and the same phenomenon. However, this homogeneity of crises certainly does not go far.

---

[1] Always less, of course, the more trustification progresses.

On the contrary, it exists chiefly only in a similarity of the effects upon the economic system and upon individuals, and in the fact that certain events are in the habit of occurring in most crises. Such effects and such events, however, would appear with the most various external and internal disturbances of economic life and are not enough to prove that crises are always the same phenomenon. Actually, different kinds and causes of crises are distinguished. And nothing justifies us in assuming beforehand that crises have more in common with one another than the element from which we started, namely that they are all events which call a halt on the preceding economic development.

Secondly, whether homogeneous or heterogeneous phenomena, crises may or may not be capable of a purely economic explanation. Of course it cannot be doubted that crises belong essentially in the economic sphere. But it is by no means certain that they belong to the nature of the economic system or even to any one kind of system in the sense that they would necessarily result from the operation of economic factors left to themselves. On the contrary, it would be quite possible for the real causes of crises to exist outside the purely economic sphere, that is for them to be consequences of disturbances which act upon the latter from outside. The frequency and even the often asserted regularity of crises would be in itself no conclusive argument, since it can be readily conceived that such disturbances must often occur in practical life. A crisis would then simply be the process by which economic life adapts itself to new conditions.

As regards the first point we can at the outset say one thing. If we speak of crises wherever large disturbances are met with, then there is no general attribute beyond the fact of disturbance. For the moment, it is as well to conceive of crises in this broad sense. Economic processes are accordingly divisible into three different classes: into the processes of the circular flow, into those of development, and into those which impede the latter's undisturbed course. This arrangement is by no means remote from reality. We can clearly keep all three classes separate in real life. Only more detailed analysis will show whether one of them comes under one of the other two.

The absence of a general attribute in the disturbances is proved by the history of crises. Such disturbances have already broken out in every conceivable place in the economic body, and moreover in very different ways in different places. Sometimes they appear on the supply side, sometimes on the demand side: in the former case sometimes in technical production, sometimes in the market or in credit relations; in the latter case, sometimes through changes in the direction of demand (for example changes in fashion), sometimes through changes in the purchasing power of consumers. For the most part the various industrial groups do not suffer in the same way, but first one industry suffers more, then another. Sometimes the crisis is characterised by a breakdown of the credit system which especially affects capitalists, sometimes the workers or landowners suffer most. Entrepreneurs may also be involved in very different ways.

At first sight the attempt to seek the common element in crises in the form of their appearance seems to be more promising. Actually it is this element that has led to the popular and scientific conviction that crises are always one and the same phenomenon. However, it is easy to see that these external characteristics which may be seized upon superficially are neither common to nor essential for all crises in so far as they go beyond the one element of the disturbance of development. The element of panic, for example, is very obvious. It was a striking feature of earlier crises. But there are also panics without a crisis. And further there are crises without real panics. The intensity of the panic does not in any case bear a necessary relation to the importance of the crisis. Finally, panics are much more the consequences than the causes of the outbreak of crises. This is also true of catchwords like "speculative fever," "overproduction," [1] and so forth. Once a crisis has broken out and changed the whole economic situation, a great deal of speculation may appear senseless and almost every quantity of goods produced too large, although both were perfectly appropriate to the state of affairs before the outbreak of the crisis. Similarly, the breakdown of individual concerns, the lack of the

---

[1] By this we do not mean the elaborated overproduction theories but only the popular reference to this element.

proper relation between the individual branches of production, the incongruence of production with consumption, and other such elements are effects rather than causes. That there is no satisfactory criterion of crises in this sense is indicated by the fact that although in the descriptive literature of the subject a certain number of crises invariably recur, yet beyond this the individual enumerations of crises do not agree with one another.

We now come to the other question, whether all crises are not at least purely economic phenomena, that is whether they and all their causes and effects are capable of being understood by explanatory factors resulting from studying the economic system. It is clear that this is not always and not necessarily the case. It will be admitted at once that the outbreak of war, for example, may cause disturbances big enough for a crisis to be spoken of. To be sure, this is by no means the rule. The great wars of the nineteenth century, for example, did not for the most part lead immediately to crises. But the case is conceivable. Let us assume that an insular nation, which has an active trade with other nations and whose economic system may be conceived as in full development in our sense, is cut off from the outside world by an enemy fleet. Imports and exports alike are obstructed, the price and value system is shattered, obligations cannot be kept, the anchor chain of credit snaps — all this is conceivable, has actually occurred, and certainly represents a crisis. And this crisis is incapable of being explained purely economically since the cause, the war, is an element foreign to the economic system. By the operation of this foreign body in the economic sphere the crisis arose and is at the same time explained. Such external factors very frequently explain crises.[1] An important example is bad harvests, which may evidently evoke crises and, as is well known, have become even the basis of a general theory of crises.

But even circumstances which do not act from without on the economic system as strikingly as wars or meteorological conditions must be seen from the standpoint of pure theory as effects of exter-

[1] Not only do the crisis-like phenomena at the outbreak of the World War belong here, but also the post-war crises of all countries, the nature of which, moreover, is not exhaustively rendered by the catch-phrase "stabilisation crisis" or "deflation crisis" as the case may be.

nal causes of disturbance and hence in principle as accidental. To take an example, the sudden abolishment of protective tariffs may cause a crisis. Such a commercial measure is certainly an economic event. But we can assert nothing accurate about its appearance; we can only investigate its effects. From the standpoint of the laws of economic life it is simply an influence from without. Thus, there are crises which are not purely economic phenomena in our sense. And because they are not, we can say nothing in general, from the purely economic standpoint, about their causes. With us, they must pass for unfortunate accidents.

The question now arises: are there any purely economic crises in our sense, crises which would appear without the outside impulses of which we have just given examples? In fact the view is conceivable, and has been actually held, that crises are always effects of external circumstances. And it is undoubtedly very plausible. If it is correct, then there is no real economic theory of crises, and we can do nothing but simply establish these facts or at most try to classify those external causes of crises.

Before we answer our question we must get rid of a special kind of crisis. If the industry of a country is financed by another country and if a wave of prosperity sweeps over the latter, which offers capital more profitable employment than it has found hitherto in the former country, then there will exist a tendency to withdraw capital from its previous investments. If this happens quickly and inconsiderately it can clearly result in a crisis in the first country. This example should show that purely economic causes in one economic area may give rise to crises in another. The phenomenon is frequent and generally recognised. Obviously this can happen not only between two different countries but also between different parts of one country and finally, under certain circumstances, within one economic area between the different branches of industry. When a crisis has once broken out in one place it usually involves other places. Now the question is, are such phenomena purely economic, of the kind we are seeking? The answer is in the negative. The economic conditions of other regions are data for any given economic system and can only play the part of non-economic elements in explaining phenomena within it. For the economic system under consideration they are accidents, and it would be idle to try to find a general law for such crises.

Finally, after discarding all extraneous causes of crises, we find still others which are of a purely economic character in the sense that they arise from within the economic system, but which nevertheless do not present a new theoretic problem. Every new combination, to use our old expression, is exposed to an obvious danger of turning out a failure. Although cases in which whole branches of industry commit fatal mistakes will be rare, yet they happen, and if the industry in question is of sufficient importance, most of the symptoms of a crisis may be produced by them. But again, events of this class are merely mishaps, to be individually explained in each case and not inherent in the economic process in the sense of being the result of any element or factor *essential to it*.

If we consider this list of possible causes of disturbance, it may well become doubtful whether there will be anything left if we abstract from all its items, and whether, therefore, anything more can be said about the causation of crises than that they happen if, in consequence of outside or inside accidents, anything of sufficient importance goes wrong. History would not contradict this theory. For there are in almost every historical case so very many "accidents," which may without any glaring absurdity be held responsible for the crisis actually occurring, that the necessity of any search for more general and fundamental causes is less obvious than some of us seem to believe. It may be remarked in passing that, however we may decide this question, the individual setting of most of the great crises in history is more important for the explanation of the actual happenings observed in each case than anything which enters into a general theory — supposing such theory to be possible — which can therefore never be expected to yield more than a *contribution* to either diagnosis or remedial policy in any actual case. If businessmen nearly always try to account for any crisis by circumstances special to the case in hand, they are not entirely wrong. Nor is the "empiricist's" antagonism towards any attempt to construct a general theory without foundation — although it is not antagonism that is called for in this case but a clear distinction between two entirely different tasks.

The decisive discovery, which settled our question and at the same time shifted our problem onto somewhat different ground, consisted in establishing the fact that there is, at all events, one class of crises, which are *elements*, or at any rate regular if not necessary *incidents*, of a wave-like movement of alternating periods of prosperity and depression, which have pervaded economic life ever since the capitalist era began.[1] This phenomenon, then, emerges from the mass of multifarious and heterogeneous facts which may account for setbacks or breakdowns of all sorts. These great peripeteias of economic life are what we have primarily to explain. As soon as we seize upon this problem we are, for the purposes of theoretic analysis, not only justified but forced to assume the absence of all the other — external and internal — disturbances to which industrial life is exposed, in order to isolate the only question interesting from the point of view of theory. In so doing, we must never forget, however, that what we discard is not on that account of inferior importance, and that our theory, if kept within the narrow limits of our question, must become incommensurable with all analytic endeavors of wider scope which aim at providing an apparatus for the full understanding of the actual course of things.

That question may now be formulated as follows: why is it that economic development in our sense does not proceed evenly as a tree grows, but as it were jerkily; why does it display those characteristic ups and downs?

§ 2. The answer cannot be short and precise enough: exclusively *because the new combinations are not, as one would expect according to general principles of probability, evenly distributed through time* — in such a way that equal intervals of time could be chosen, in each of which the carrying out of one new combination would fall — but *appear, if at all, discontinuously in groups or swarms.*

---

[1] This discovery and the full perception of its consequences are due to Clément Juglar.

This answer is now (*a*) to be interpreted, this appearance in groups is then (*b*) to be explained, whereupon (*c*) the consequences of this fact and the course of the causal nexus called forth by them are to be analysed (in § 3 of this chapter). The third point contains a new problem without the solution of which the theory would be incomplete. Although we accept Juglar's statement that "the only cause of the depression is prosperity" — which means that depression is nothing more than the economic system's reaction to the boom, or the adaptation to the situation into which the boom brings the system, so that its explanation is also rooted in the explanation of the boom — yet the manner in which the boom leads to the depression remains a thing by itself, as the reader can see at once in the difference on this point existing between Spiethoff and me. It will also be seen immediately that this question is answered — without difficulty and without the aid of new facts or theoretical instruments — by our argument.

(*a*) If the new enterprises in our sense were to appear independently of one another, there would be no boom and no depression as special, distinguishable, striking, regularly recurring phenomena. For their appearance would then be, in general, continuous; they would be evenly distributed in time and the changes which would be effected by them in the circular flow would each of them be relatively small, hence the disturbances would be of only local importance and easily overcome for the economic system as a whole. There would be no considerable disturbances of the circular flow and therefore no disturbances of growth at all. It should be noticed that this is true for any theory of crises with respect to that element which it considers as the cause, in particular for all disproportionality theories; the phenomenon is never made intelligible if it is not explained why the cause, whatever it may be, cannot act in such a way as to allow the consequences to be continuously and currently absorbed.[1]

Even then there would be good and bad times. Gold or other inflation would still hasten economic growth, deflation would ob-

---

[1] By which I mean that this part of our argument must be simply taken for granted by every theory of crises. For even if otherwise free from objection, none explains precisely this circumstance.

struct it; political and social events and economic legislation would still exercise their influence. An event like the World War, for example, with the adjustment of the economic system to war requirements enforced by it, with the necessary liquidation after its conclusion, with its disturbance of all economic relations, its devastations and social upheavals, its destruction of important markets, its alteration of all data, would have taught men what crises and depressions are like even if they had not already known. But there would not be the kind of prosperity and depression which are here under consideration. Such events would not be regular, or necessary in the sense that they emerge from the working of the economic system itself, but would have to be explained by special external causes, as has already been sufficiently emphasised. One favorable circumstance, which always facilitates and partly explains a boom, must be particularly remembered, namely the state of affairs created by every period of depression. As is well known, there are generally masses of unemployed, accumulated stocks of raw materials, machines, buildings, and so forth offered below cost of production, and there is as a rule an abnormally low rate of interest. Indeed these facts play a part in nearly every investigation of the phenomenon, as for example with Spiethoff and Mitchell. But it is clear that we can never explain the phenomenon by these consequences of it if we wish to avoid first deriving the depression from the boom and then the latter from the depression. Therefore here, where it is only a question of the principle of the thing — and not of an exhaustive statement of the circumstances (bad harvests,[1] war rumors, and so forth) concretely operative in boom or crisis — we shall completely neglect these consequences.

Three circumstances increase the effect of the swarm-like appearance of new enterprises, yet without being real causes coordinate with it. First, our argument in the second chapter allows us to expect — and experience confirms it — that the vast ma-

---

[1] Good harvests, for example, facilitate and lengthen the boom, or alleviate and shorten the depression. They are often important in explaining an individual situation: so much H. L. Moore has certainly demonstrated. But they are never coordinate with our causal nexus; they only operate through it.

jority of new combinations will not grow out of the old firms or immediately take their place, but appear side by side, and compete, with them. From the standpoint of our theory this is neither a new nor an independent element; nor is it essential to the existence of booms and depressions, although it is clearly very important in explaining the amplitude of the wave-like movement.

Secondly, the fact that entrepreneurial demand appears *en masse* signifies a very substantial increase in purchasing power all over the business sphere. This starts a secondary boom, which spreads over the whole economic system and is the vehicle of the phenomenon of general prosperity — which can only be completely understood in this way and cannot be satisfactorily explained otherwise. Only because new purchasing power goes in bulk from the hands of entrepreneurs to the owners of material means of production, to all producers of goods for "reproductive consumption" (Spiethoff), and to the workers, and then oozes into every economic channel, are all existing consumption goods finally sold at ever-rising prices. Retailers thereupon place bigger orders, manufacturers extend operations, and for this purpose increasingly more unfavorable and often already abandoned means of production come into use again. And only on this account do production and trade *everywhere* temporarily yield a profit, just as in a period of inflation, for example when war expenditure is financed with paper money. Many things float on this "secondary wave," without any new or direct impulse from the real driving force, and speculative anticipation in the end acquires a causal significance. The symptoms of prosperity themselves finally become, in the well known manner, a factor of prosperity. For the theory of business indices and the understanding of the business situation as a whole, this is of course most important. For our purpose, however, only the division between primary and secondary waves is essential, and it is enough to note that the latter can simply be traced back to the former and that in a theory elaborated upon the basis of our principle everything that was ever observed in the cyclical movement would find its definite place. But in an exposition like the present, justice cannot be done to such things, hence an impression of remoteness from reality may arise which is actually not justified.[1]

Thirdly, it follows from our argument that errors must play a considerable rôle at the beginning of the boom and during the course of the depression. Most theories of crises in fact use this element in one way or another. Errors, however, do not normally occur to the excessive extent required; production is entered upon by sane men only on the basis of more or less careful investigation of the facts. Although miscalculations may occur on a scale that may well endanger an individual business, in exceptional cases perhaps a whole industry, this is not as a rule enough to endanger the economic system as a whole. How can such general mistakes be made, then, that the whole system is affected, *and indeed as an independent cause and not merely as a consequence of the depression which is to be explained*? Once it has set in for other reasons, depression certainly upsets many plans which were previously quite reasonable and makes mistakes dangerous which would otherwise have been easily rectified. The initial mistakes require a special explanation, without which nothing is explained. Our analysis supplies this explanation. If the characteristic feature of a period of boom is not merely increased business activity as such, but the carrying out of new and untried combinations, then it is immediately clear, as has already been mentioned in Chapter II, that error must play a special rôle there, qualitatively different from its rôle in the circular flow. Nevertheless, no "error theory" will be found here. On the contrary, in order to avoid any such impression we shall segregate this element. It is indeed a supporting and accentuating circumstance, but not a primary cause necessary to the understanding of the principle. There would still be cyclical movements — though in a milder form — even if no one ever did anything that could be described as "false" from his

[1] In particular, all the circumstances which in other theories of crises act in the capacity of causes find their place within the framework of our theory, as the reader can easily see if he is inclined to think the matter through. In this book, of course, our explanation of the cycle always remains exposed to an objection similar to the one made against the theory of development in Chapter II, namely, that it emphasises one-sidedly and exaggeratedly one element out of many. This objection confuses the problem of explaining the nature and mechanism of the cycle with the problem of a theory of the concrete factors of individual cycles.

point of view; even if there were no technical or commercial "error," or "speculative fever," or groundless optimism and pessimism; and even if everyone were gifted with wide foresight. The objective situation which the boom necessarily creates explains exclusively the nature of the thing,[1] as will be seen.

(b) Why do entrepreneurs appear, not continuously, that is singly in every appropriately chosen interval, but in clusters? *Exclusively because the appearance of one or a few entrepreneurs facilitates the appearance of others, and these the appearance of more, in ever-increasing numbers.*

This means, first, that for the reasons explained in Chapter II the carrying out of new combinations is difficult and only accessible to people with certain qualities, as is best seen by visualising an example from earlier times or the economic situation in the stage that most resembles an economy without development, viz. the stage of advanced stagnation. Only a few people have these qualities of leadership and only a few in such a situation, that is a situation which is not itself already a boom, can succeed in this direction. However, if one or a few have advanced with success many of the difficulties disappear. Others can then follow these pioneers, as they will clearly do under the stimulus of the success now attainable. Their success again makes it easier, through the increasingly complete removal of the obstacles analysed in the second chapter, for more people to follow suit, until finally the innovation becomes familiar and the acceptance of it a matter of free choice.

Secondly, since as we have seen the entrepreneurial qualification is something which, like many other qualities, is distributed in an ethnically homogeneous group according to the law of error, the number of individuals who satisfy progressively diminishing standards in this respect continually increases. Hence, neglecting exceptional cases — of which the existence of a few Europeans in a negro population would be an example — with the progressive

---

[1] Which of course does not mean that the practical importance of the element of error is denied, nor that of the elements which are usually designated by speculative fever, fraud, etc. — in which category overproduction also belongs. We assert only that all these things are in part consequential and that even in so far as this is not the case the nature of the phenomenon cannot be understood from them.

lightening of the task continually more people can and will become entrepreneurs, wherefore the successful appearance of an entrepreneur is followed by the appearance not simply of some others, but of ever greater numbers, though progressively less qualified. This is how it is in practice, the testimony of which we merely interpret. In industries in which there is still competition and a large number of independent people we see first of all the single appearance of an innovation — overwhelmingly in businesses created *ad hoc* — and then we see how the existing businesses grasp it with varying rapidity and completeness, first a few, then continually more. We have already come across this phenomenon in connection with the process of eliminating entrepreneurial profit. Here it comes into consideration again, though from another standpoint.[1]

Thirdly, this explains the appearance of entrepreneurs in clusters and indeed up to the point of eliminating entrepreneurial profit, first of all in the branch of industry in which the pioneers appear. Reality also discloses that every normal boom starts in one or a few branches of industry (railway building, electrical, and chemical industries, and so forth), and that it derives its character from the innovations in the industry where it begins. But the pioneers remove the obstacles for the others not only in the branch of production in which they first appear, but, owing to the nature of these obstacles, *ipso facto* in other branches too. Many things may be copied by the latter; the example as such also acts upon them; and many achievements directly serve other branches too, as for example the opening up of a foreign market, quite apart from the circumstances of secondary importance which soon appear — rising prices and so on. Hence the first leaders are effective beyond their immediate sphere of action and so the group of entrepreneurs increases still further and the economic system is drawn more rapidly and more completely than would otherwise be the case into the process of technological and commercial reorganisation which constitutes the meaning of periods of boom.

[1] For the elimination — mostly foreseen — of entrepreneurial profit is not "the" cause in our theory of crises. Cf. § 3, second paragraph.

Fourthly, the more the process of development becomes familiar and a mere matter of calculation to all concerned, and the weaker the obstacles become in the course of time, the less the "leadership" that will be needed to call forth innovations. Hence the less pronounced will become the swarm-like appearance of entrepreneurs and the milder the cyclical movement. And clearly this consequence of our interpretation is also strikingly confirmed by reality. The progressive trustification of economic life acts in the same direction, even though to-day a great combine with its sales and its financial requirements is still so dependent upon the market situation, which is to a considerable extent determined competitively, that the universally advantageous postponement of its innovations, and especially of construction, to periods of depression — as exemplified in the policy of American railways — is only possible sporadically. In so far as it operates, however, this element also confirms our interpretation.

Fifthly, the swarm-like appearance of new combinations easily and necessarily explains the fundamental features of periods of boom. It explains why increasing capital investment is the very first symptom of the coming boom, why industries producing means of production are the first to show supernormal stimulation, above all why the consumption of iron increases. It explains the appearance of new purchasing power in bulk,[1] thereby the characteristic rise in prices during booms, which obviously no reference to increased need or increased costs alone can explain. Further, it explains the decline of unemployment and the rise of wages,[2] the rise in the interest rate, the increase in freight, the increasing strain on bank balances and bank reserves, and so forth, and, as we have said, the release of secondary waves — the spread of prosperity over the whole economic system.

[1] Hence it hardly needs to be emphasised that our theory does not belong to those which seek the cause of the cycle in the money and credit system, however important the element of the creation of purchasing power is in our interpretation. Nevertheless, we do not deny that cyclical movements could be influenced and even prevented by credit policy — with them, indeed, also this kind of economic development in general.

[2] In principle rents must also rise. But where land is let on a long lease they cannot do so, and in addition many circumstances prevent the prompt rise of this branch of income.

§ 3. (*c*) The swarm-like appearance of entrepreneurs, which is the only cause of the boom, has a qualitatively different effect upon the economic system from that of a continuous appearance evenly distributed in time, in so far as it does not, like the latter, mean a continuous, and even imperceptible, disturbance of the equilibrium position but a jerky disturbance, a disturbance of a different order of magnitude. While the disturbances caused by a continuous appearance of entrepreneurs could be continuously absorbed, the swarm-like appearance necessitates a special and distinguishable process of absorption, of incorporating the new things and of adapting the economic system to them, a process of liquidation or, as I used to say, an approach to a new static state (Statisierung). This process is the essence of periodic depressions, which may therefore be defined from our standpoint as the economic system's struggling towards a new equilibrium position, its adaptation to the data as altered by the disturbance of the boom.

The essence of the matter does not lie in the fact that the individual entrepreneur, interested only in planning his own enterprise, takes no account of the swarm-like following of others, and so comes to grief. It is certainly true that conduct which is correct from the standpoint of the individual business may be mulcted of its fruits by the general effect of the similar conduct of many. We recognised the most important example of this when we explained how producers, in their very striving for the maximum profit, set the mechanism in motion which tends to eliminate surplus value in the system. Similarly, here also the general effect may render false what was correct for the individual, and this element will actually play a part in most crises, for although the swarming after the entrepreneur is known beforehand to the latter and cannot take him unawares, the magnitude and tempo may frequently be estimated wrongly. However, the essence of the disturbance caused by the boom does not lie in the fact that it often upsets entrepreneurs' calculations,[1] but in the following three circumstances.

---

[1] Nor in the fact that the consequent general extension of production proves to be wrong.

First, the new entrepreneur's demand for means of production, which is based upon new purchasing power — the well known "race for means of production" (Lederer) in a period of prosperity — drives up the prices of these. In reality this tendency is weakened by the fact that at least some of the new enterprises do not appear side by side with the old, but grow out of them, and that the old businesses do not simply work without profit, but may still earn some quasi-rent. We can best elucidate the nature of the operation, however, if we assume that all innovations are embodied in newly established businesses, are financed solely by newly created purchasing power, and take their place beside businesses which belong strictly to the circular flow and work without profit, and which, therefore, in consequence of the increase in their costs, begin to produce at a loss. Reality contradicts this construction less than one would imagine. Actually, only the atmosphere which hangs over the period of boom hides the fact that very soon after its beginning, and as long as it is expressed simply in the increased demand, the boom means distress for many producers, although it is diminished again when the rise in the prices of their products sets in. This distress is a form of the process by which means of production are withdrawn from the old businesses and made available for the new purposes, as explained in Chapter II.

Secondly, the new products come on the market after a few years or sooner and compete with the old; the commodity complement of the previously created purchasing power — theoretically more than counterbalancing the latter — enters into the circular flow. Again the consequences of this process are practically moderated by the causes mentioned in the preceding section, and further by the fact that because some investments are remote from finished products this complement appears only gradually. But this does not touch the nature of the process. At the beginning of the boom costs rise in the old businesses; later their receipts are reduced, first in those businesses with which the innovation competes, but then in all old businesses, in so far as consumers' demand changes in favor of the innovation. Apart from the possibility of profiting — secondarily — from the innovation, their working at a loss is only checked by the buffer quasi-rent, which is merely temporarily effective. And it is only because old businesses are mostly well established and appear as especially deserving of credit that this working at a loss does not lead at once to collapse. Their partial breakdown affects the success of the new undertakings. The breakdown is moderated by the fact, which fits so well into the framework of our interpretation, that the boom is never general at first, but centres in one branch or a few branches of industry, leaving the other areas undisturbed, and subsequently only affects the latter in a different, and secondary, manner. Just as entrepreneurs appear *en masse*, so do their products, because the former do not do different but very similar things, and hence their products appear on the market almost simultaneously. The average time [1] which must elapse before the new products appear — though of course actually dependent upon many other elements — fundamentally explains the length of the boom. This appearance of the new products causes the fall in prices,[2] which on its part terminates the boom, *may* lead to a crisis, *must* lead to a depression, and starts all the rest.

Thirdly, the appearance of the results of the new enterprises leads to a credit deflation, because entrepreneurs are now in the position — and have every incentive — to pay off their debts; and since no other borrowers step into their place this leads to a disappearance of the recently created purchasing power just when its complement in goods emerges, and which can henceforth be repeatedly produced in the manner of the circular flow. This thesis requires careful safeguarding. In the first place this deflation must be distinguished from two other kinds. The appearance of the new products must result in deflation, not only as against the price level of the boom period, but theoretically also as against that of the preceding period of depression, even if absolutely no means of payment disappeared in debt repayment by entre-

---

[1] This time is determined first technically, then by the tempo in which the multitude follow the leaders.

[2] This fall in prices is in practice generally postponed through many circumstances. Cf. *infra* on this. However, the underlying state of affairs is only accentuated, not eliminated, by the postponement of the fall in prices. The only thing eliminated by it is the serviceableness of price indices as symptoms of the cycle.

preneurs, for the sum of the prices of the new products must obviously be normally greater than the amount of these debts. This would have the same effect as the liquidation of debts, only to a smaller extent; but we are now thinking of the effect of debt reduction. Deflation also occurs in a depression which is already in being or is expected by the banking world, because the banks endeavor on their own initiative to restrict their credits. This factor is practically very important and frequently starts a real crisis; but it is accessory and not inherent in the process. Here we are not thinking of this factor either, though we deny neither its existence nor its importance, but only its primary causal rôle.[1] Then, further, our formulation contains two abstractions which will make the essentials stand out clearly, but which exclude moderating influences of great practical importance. First, it neglects the fact that the new products generally contain only small quotas for depreciation of the investments made in producing them, hence that only a part, mostly only a small part, of the total expenditure in the period of boom comes on the market in saleable form when the new enterprises are ready to produce; therefore the newly created purchasing power only gradually goes out of circulation, in part only when later periods of boom have brought more credit seekers into the money market. The resorption of the new purchasing power by savings alters nothing in this deflationary process — but the fact that many states, municipalities, and agricultural mortgage banks step into the place of the dwindling entrepreneurial demand does make a difference. Apart from this only gradual disappearance of entrepreneurs' debts, it must be borne in mind that, in the modern economic system in which interest has penetrated even into the circular flow, credit may even remain permanently in circulation, in so far as there are now goods produced year after year corresponding to it — which is the second factor moderating the process still further. But the deflationary tendency is operative, for all that, and liquidation of debts by successful enterprises takes place — so that deflation, even though in ever so mild a form, must always appear automat-

---

[1] Primary causal rôle, because the credit restriction initiated by the banks is certainly the "cause" of further occurrences which would not otherwise be expected.

ically out of the logic of the objective situation, when the boom has gone on far enough. A noteworthy verification of this theory, which leads to the conclusion that in the course of development the "secular" price level must fall, is in fact given by the history of prices in the nineteenth century. The two periods which were not disturbed by revolutionary monetary changes, that is the period from the Napoleonic Wars to the Californian gold discoveries, and the period 1873–1895, actually exhibit the feature which we should expect from our theory, namely that every periodic trough is deeper than the preceding and that a price curve eliminating cyclical fluctuations moves downwards.

Finally, it must still be explained why other entrepreneurs seeking credit do not always step into the place of those liquidating their indebtedness. There are two reasons, to which in practice others are added which can be described either as consequences of the elements which we call fundamental, or as accidental, or as influences operating from outside, and in this sense as secondary, unessential, or accessory. In the first place, if, under the stimulus of success in the industry in which the boom occurs, so many new enterprises spring up that they would produce, when in full swing, a quantity of product which, through the fall in prices and rise in costs — which occur of course even if the industry in question obeys the so-called law of increasing returns — would eliminate entrepreneurial profit, then the impulse to further advance in this direction is exhausted. In practice, even in a competitive society, the elimination of profit is only approximate and the process excludes neither the survival of some profit nor the immediate realisation of losses. The limit to which the appearance of entrepreneurs in other industries and the phenomena created by secondary waves of development can go is determined analogously. When it is reached, the impulse of this boom is exhausted. The second reason explains why a new boom does not simply follow on: because the action of the group of entrepreneurs has in the meanwhile altered the data of the system, upset its equilibrium, and thus started an apparently irregular movement in the economic system, which we conceive as a struggle towards a new equilibrium position. This makes accurate calculation impossible in general, but especially for the planning of new enterprises. In practice only the latter element — the characteristic uncertainty which results from the new creations of the boom — is always immediately observable; the first-named limit shows itself mostly only at individual points. Both of them, however, are obscured, first, by consequential phenomena which the foresight of many individuals anticipates. Some individuals begin to feel sooner than others either the strain, as is true of the banks, or the rise in costs and other elements, as in the case of many old businesses, and react accordingly — in most cases too late, it is true, but when they do, in panic-stricken fashion, especially the weaker ones. Secondly, they are obscured by fortuitous events, which always occur but which acquire an importance from the uncertainty created by the boom such as they did not have before. This explains why the practical man in almost every crisis thinks he can adduce fortuitous events, unfavorable political rumors for example, as causes, and why the impetus in fact frequently proceeds from these. Thirdly, they are obscured by acts of intervention from without, of which a conscious pull on the reins by the central bank is usually the most important.

§ 4. If the reader thinks through what has been said, and tests it on any factual material or on the arguments of any theory of crises and the business cycle, he must understand how the boom (which is now explained) creates out of itself an *objective situation*, which, even neglecting all accessory and fortuitous elements, makes an end of the boom, leads *easily* to a crisis, *necessarily* to a depression, and hence to a temporary position of relative steadiness and absence of development. The depression as such we may call the "normal" process of resorption and liquidation; the course of events characterised by the outbreak of a crisis — panic, breakdown of the credit system, epidemics of bankruptcies, and its further consequences — we may call the "abnormal process of liquidation." In completion and in repetition of some points we now have a few more things to say about this process, but only about the normal, since the abnormal presents no fundamental problems.

What has been said leads directly to the understanding of all primary and secondary features of the period of depression, which now appear as parts of a single causal nexus. The boom itself of necessity causes many businesses to run at a loss, causes a fall in prices apart from that due to deflation, and in addition causes deflation through credit contraction — phenomena which all increase secondarily in the course of events. Further, the diminution of capital investment[1] and entrepreneurial activity, and hence stagnation in the industries producing means of production, and the fall in the Spiethoff index (iron consumption) and similar barometers, such as the unfilled orders of the United States Steel Corporation, are all explained. With the fall in the demand for means of production, the rate of interest — if the coefficient of risk is removed — and the volume of employment also fall. With the fall in money incomes, which is causally traceable to the deflation, even though it is increased by bankruptcies and so forth, the demand for all other commodities finally falls, and the process has then penetrated the whole economic system. The picture of the depression is complete.

Two reasons, however, prevent these characteristics from appearing in the order in time which would correspond to their position in the causal nexus. First is the fact that they are not only anticipated by the conduct of individuals, but also anticipated in very unequal degrees. This happens especially in markets where professional speculation plays a great part. Thus the stock market sometimes exhibits speculative preliminary crises long before a real turning point arrives, which are then overcome and make room for a further upward movement, which still belongs to the same boom (thus 1873 and 1907). But something else is much more important. Just as in practice the rise in the price of a product often anticipates the increase in costs which is nevertheless its cause, so a similar phenomenon appears here. The decrease

---

[1] The phenomenon now under discussion is to be distinguished from the diminished investment involved in the contraction of credit by debt liquidation. The investment for additional new purposes is meant here. And the statistics of the issue of stocks and bonds, which are in practice such a good business index (Spiethoff), reflect mainly, though not only, a third element: the consolidating of bank credit by means of savings.

in capital investment in the sense just indicated, the parallel decrease in entrepreneurial activity, and the stagnation in the industries for producers' goods, for example, may occur, as far as the logic of the process is concerned, before the boom has attained its external culmination; but it is not necessary that they should. On the contrary, if these symptoms do regularly occur before the end of the boom, it is because they are under the influence of factors which anticipate relatively promptly what is coming. Secondly, however, various circumstances bring it about that in the actual course of events secondary elements often stand out more prominently than the primary. The anxiety of lenders, for example, expresses itself in a rise in the rate of interest, and only late in the depression does the effect appear which in the very nature of things would appear quite early in the normal course of events. The reduction in the demand for labor should be a very early symptom of the change, but just as wages do not rise immediately in prosperity because as a rule there are unemployed workers, so wages and the amount of employment do not usually fall as promptly as one would expect because a series of well known obstacles stands in the way. The business world tries to defend itself against a fall in prices, and where competition is not completely "free" — as is practically nowhere the case — and when the banks lend their support, it resists with temporary success, so that the maximum price level is often later than the turning point. It is a fundamental task of the investigation of crises to establish all these things. But here it is sufficient to state, without further substantiation, that all this no more alters the essence of the matter than the analogous phenomena in other fields, to which I referred above, support objections against the theory of prices.

The course of events in periods of depression presents a picture of uncertainty and irregularity which we interpret from the point of view of a search for a new equilibrium, or of adaptation to a general situation which has been changed relatively quickly and considerably. The uncertainty and irregularity are quite comprehensible. The customary data are altered for every business. The extent and nature of the change, however, can only be learned from experience. There are new competitors; old customers and dealers fail to appear; the right attitude towards new economic facts has to be found; incalculable events — unsuspected refusals of credit — may occur at any moment. The "mere businessman" faces problems which lie outside his routine, problems to which he is not accustomed and in the face of which he makes mistakes which then become an important secondary cause of further trouble. Speculation is a further cause, through the distress in which it involves speculators as well as through the fact that the latter anticipate a further fall in prices, so that all these well known elements mutually increase one another. Nowhere is the final result clearly in sight; weak points, which in themselves have nothing to do with the crisis, may come to light anywhere. Business contraction or business extension may finally prove to be the correct type of reaction without its being possible at the moment to advance trustworthy reasons for the one or the other. This complication and lack of clarity in the situation, of which theory in my opinion makes an unwarranted use in explaining the causes of depression, really becomes an important factor in the actual events.

The uncertainty of the data and values involved in the new adjustment, the losses which apparently occur irregularly and incalculably, create the characteristic atmosphere of periods of depression. Those speculative elements which make up stock exchange opinion and are commercially and socially so noticeable in prosperity suffer especially. To many people, particularly the speculative class and the producers of luxury goods who are partly dependent on its demand, conditions appear essentially worse than they are — to them the end of all things seems to have come. Subjectively, the turning point appears to producers, especially if they resist the unavoidable fall in prices, as an outbreak of hitherto latent overproduction, and the depression as its consequence. The unsaleableness of commodities already produced, still more of those producible, at prices which cover costs calls forth the well known further phenomenon of the tightness of money, possibly insolvency, which is so typical that every theory of the business cycle must be in a position to explain it. Ours does so, as the reader can see, but it does not employ this typical fact as a primary and independent cause.[1] The overproduction is accentuated by that skewness of the boom which we have already noticed and explained. This circumstance on the one hand, and the discrepancy between effective supply and effective demand which must occur in many industries during the depression on the other, make it possible to describe the external form of depressions in the language of the various disproportionality theories. The gist of every such theory lies in the manner in which it tries to explain the appearance of the disproportionality, and in the particular quantities between which disproportionality is held to exist. For us, the disproportionality between quantities and prices of goods, which results at many points because of the loss of equilibrium in the economic system, is an intermediate phenomenon just like overproduction and is not a primary cause. Connected with it there may be disproportionality between incomes in individual industries, but not between the incomes of different economic classes, for entrepreneurial profits bear no normal proportion to the incomes of other people which could be disturbed, and the other incomes, with the exception of those fixed in terms of money, have the tendency to move *pari passu* and to gain or lose ground at the cost or to the advantage of the fixed incomes, leaving the total consumers' demand undisturbed.

The skewness of the boom has the consequence, amongst others, that strain and danger in the situation are not equally great for

---

[1] Every theory of crises in which overproduction plays the part of one, or even the primary, cause seems to me to be exposed to the objection of reasoning in a circle (quite apart from the objection already formulated by Say), even if it does not assert "general overproduction." From this judgment I must exclude Spiethoff's theory. The very short arguments with which he tries to substantiate the periodical overproduction of goods for reproductive consumption allow no final judgment. Moreover, it is to be observed that Spiethoff's aim is a penetrating analysis of all the details of the subject. For such an analysis, the elements governing the external picture — the stagnation in industries producing means of production certainly belongs here — are really much more important in relation to the primary causes than for an exposition such as this. Finally, there is in the emphasis upon industries producing means of production a reference to the factors which in my opinion constitute the nature of the problem, so that it is by no means correct to describe Spiethoff's analysis as simply an overproduction theory; a more detailed exposition of his theory would perhaps show still more far-reaching agreement than I now suspect.

all branches of industry. Experience teaches also, as Aftalion [1] has already shown, that many branches are hardly disturbed at all, others only relatively little. Within every industry new enterprises are generally implicated considerably more than established businesses, which seems to contradict our interpretation. This is to be explained as follows: an old business has the buffer quasi-rent, and, what is more important, generally accumulated reserves. It is embedded in protecting relationships, often effectively supported by banking connections of many years' standing. It may be losing ground for years without its creditors becoming uneasy. Therefore it holds out much longer than a new enterprise, which is strictly and suspiciously scrutinised, which has no reserves but at best only overdraft facilities, and which only needs to give a sign of embarrassment to be considered as a bad debtor. Hence, the reaction of the change in all conditions upon new enterprises may become visible earlier and more strikingly than that upon old businesses. And therefore in the former it leads much more easily to the final consequence, bankruptcy, than in the latter, in which it rather initiates a slow decay. This distorts the picture of reality, and is also the reason why a selective process in crises may be spoken of only with an important qualification; for that firm which is well supported, and not the one that is most perfect in itself, has the best chance of surviving a crisis. But this does not affect the nature of the phenomenon.

§ 5. Although it stands to reason that the process of adjustment and resorption which makes up the period of depression causes discomfort to the most vigorous elements in the economic system, those which do most to create the *mood* of the business world, and although it necessarily annihilates many values and existences even if everything occurs with ideal perfection, yet its nature and effects would be inadequately grasped if it were seen only from the aspect of the cessation of the impulse to prosperity

---

[1] Les crises périodiques de surproduction, livre 1. To be sure, the other fact, different from the one we have in view here, that the cyclical movement is always particularly strongly marked in the industries producing new plant, stands out much more clearly. It is likewise intelligible from our standpoint. Of course this does not contradict the interpretation here presented, rather the contrary.

or described merely by negative characteristics. There are more cheerful sides to it which are much more characteristic of it than the things just indicated.

First, the depression leads, as stated already, to a new equilibrium position. To convince ourselves that all that happens in it is really to be understood from this point of view and is only apparently meaningless and unregulated, let us consider once more the behavior of individuals in a period of depression. They must adapt themselves to the disturbance caused by the boom, that is by the swarm-like appearance of new combinations and their products, by the appearance of them alongside of the old businesses and by the one-sidedness of their appearance. The old businesses — that is, theoretically, all existing ones with the exception of those formed in the boom, and with the further exception in practice of those removed from danger by a monopoly position, the possession of peculiar advantages, or lastingly superior technique — are faced by three possibilities: to decay if they are unadaptable for objective or personal reasons; to take in sail and try to survive in a more modest position; finally, with their own resources or with outside help either to change to another industry or to adopt other technical or commercial methods which amount to extending production at lower cost per unit. The new businesses have to undergo their first test, a much more difficult one than they would have to undergo if they appeared continuously and not in swarms. Once established, they must be properly incorporated in the circular flow, and, even if no mistake was made when they were founded, there must in many respects be much to revise. Even though from different, secondary, causes, problems and possibilities confront them similar to those confronting the old businesses; and, as mentioned above, they are in many respects less equal to cope with them than are the old. The characteristic conduct of businessmen in depression consists of measures, correction of measures, and further measures to solve this problem; all the phenomena, apart from panics unfounded in fact and the consequences of errors — which characterise the abnormal course of events in a crisis — may be included in this conception of the situation created by the boom and of businessmen's conduct enforced by it, of the disturbance in equilibrium and the reaction to it, of the change in data and the successful or abortive adaptation to it.

Just as the struggle towards a new equilibrium position, which will embody the innovations and give expression to their effects upon the old firms, is the real meaning of a period of depression as we know it from experience, so it may likewise be shown that this struggle must actually lead to a close approach to an equilibrium position: on the one hand, the driving impulse of the process of depression cannot theoretically stop until it has done its work, has really brought about the equilibrium position; on the other hand, no new disturbance in the form of a new boom can arise out of the economic system itself until then. Businessmen's conduct in the period of depression is clearly ruled by the element of actual or impending loss. But losses occur or are imminent — not necessarily in the whole economic system but in the parts exposed to danger — as long as all businesses, and hence the system as a whole, are not in stable equilibrium, which is as much as to say in practice until they again produce at prices approximately covering costs. Consequently there is, theoretically, depression as long as no such equilibrium is approximately attained. Nor will this process be interrupted by a new boom before it has done its work in this sense. For until then, there is necessarily uncertainty about what the new data will be, which makes the calculation of new combinations impossible and makes it difficult to obtain the cooperation of the requisite factors. Both conclusions fit the facts if the following qualifications are kept in view. A knowledge of the cyclical movement and its mechanism, which is peculiar to the modern business world, allows businessmen, whenever the worst is over, to anticipate the coming boom and especially its secondary phenomena; the adaptation of many individuals and hence of many values to the new equilibrium is frequently retarded or prevented by the expectation that if they can only hold out — which it is often in the interest of their creditors to facilitate — they will be able to liquidate on favorable terms in the next boom or will not find it necessary to liquidate at all — which is especially important in predominantly prosperous epochs and saves many firms really not fit to live as well as many that are, but in any case retards or prevents the attainment of a settled equilibrium position.

The progressive trustification of economic life facilitates the permanent continuance of maladjustments in the great combines themselves and hence outside of them, for practically there can only be complete equilibrium if there is free competition in all branches of production. Furthermore, in consequence of the financial strength of some firms, especially the older ones, the adjustment is not always very urgent, not an immediate question of life or death. There is also the practice of outside support being extended to firms or whole industries in difficulties, for example government subsidies, given upon the *bona* or *mala fide* assumption that the difficulty is only a temporary one, created by extraneous circumstances. In times of depression there is also frequently an outcry for protective duties. All this acts in the same way as the financial strength of old businesses. Furthermore, there is the element of chance — for example a good harvest occurring at the right moment. Finally, abnormalities in the course of the depression sometimes have the effect of producing over-compensations; if, for example, an unjustified panic has unduly depreciated the shares of a business and in consequence a corrective upward movement in them begins, this upward movement may in its turn overshoot the mark, maintain the shares at a quotation which is inappropriately high, and lead to a small pseudo-boom which may last under certain circumstances until a real one begins.

Of course the position reached in the end never completely corresponds to the theoretical picture of a system without development, in which there would no longer be income in the form of interest. The relatively short duration of depressions alone prevents this. Nevertheless, an approximation to a position without development always occurs, and this, being relatively steady, may again be a starting point for the carrying out of new combinations. In this sense, therefore, we come to the conclusion that according to our theory there must always be a process of absorption between two booms, ending in a position approaching equilibrium, the bringing about of which is its function. This is important for us, not only because such an intermediate position actually exists and the explanation of it is incumbent upon every theory of the cycle, but also because only the proof of the necessity of such a periodic quasi-equilibrium position completes our argument. For we started from such a position, out of which the wave of development first arises — without regard to whether or when this was the case historically. We might even merely assume an initial "static" state in order to let the nature of the wave stand out clearly. But for our theory to explain the essence of the phenomenon it is not enough that a trough *actually* follows every crest of the wave: it must do so *necessarily* — which cannot be simply assumed, nor may a proof be replaced by pointing to the fact. For this reason a certain amount of pedantry seemed to be required in this section.

Secondly, apart from the digestion of the innovations which has just occupied our attention, the period of depression does something else, which indeed comes less to the fore than those phenomena to which it owes its name: it fulfils what the boom promised. And this effect is lasting, while the phenomena felt to be unpleasant are temporary. The stream of goods is enriched, production is partly reorganised, costs of production are diminished,[1] and what at first appears as entrepreneurial profit finally increases the permanent real incomes of other classes.

This conclusion which emerges from our theory (cf. also the fourth chapter) is justified, in spite of the various obstacles which these effects meet with at first, by the fact that the economic pic-

---

[1] We have twice spoken of the boom's effects in increasing costs: first entrepreneurs' demand drives up the prices of production goods, then the following demand of all people who ride on the secondary waves of development do so still further. These increasing costs have nothing to do with the secular rise asserted by the classical economists on the basis of their assumption of the progressive outstripping of the possibilities of producing means of subsistence by the increase in population. Now the decreasing costs in question above are not the complement of these increasing costs in money. They are the consequence of the productive progress realised by the boom, and signify a fall in real costs per unit of product, first in the new enterprises as against the old, then also in the latter, since they must either adapt themselves — for example by reducing their output and confining themselves to the best possibilities — or disappear. After every boom the economic system as such produces the unit of product with less expenditure of labor or land.

ture of a *normal* period of depression [1] is throughout not so black as the mood pervading it would lead one to suspect. Apart from the fact that a great part of economic life remains almost untouched as a rule, the physical volume of total transactions in most cases falls only insignificantly. How exaggerated the popular conceptions of the ravages caused by a depression are, is shown by any official investigation of crises.[2] This is true not only of analysis in terms of goods but also of that in terms of money, in spite of the fact that the cyclical movement, with its inflation in prosperity and deflation in depression, must be especially strongly marked in the money expression. Total incomes rise in the boom and fall in the depression not more than 8 to 12 per cent as compared with the figures for average years, even in America (Mitchell), where the intensity of development presumably makes the fluctuations more strongly marked than in Europe. Aftalion has already shown that the fall in prices during depression only constitutes a low percentage on the average, and that really great fluctuations have their causes in the special conditions of the individual articles and have little to do with the cyclical movement. The same thing may be shown for all really large general movements, as for example the post-war period. When the phenomena of the abnormal course of events (panics, epidemics of bankruptcies, and so forth), which are continually becoming weaker, and with them anxiety about incalculable danger, disappear, public opinion will also judge of depressions differently.

We see the true character of a period of depression if we consider what it brings to and takes from different categories of

[1] Of course the post-war depression was not normal. In my opinion it is a mistake to try to read general results of the business cycle theory into the post-war material. But it is a mistake often made. Thus, many a judgment of the modern therapeutists of crises by means of credit policy is explicable by the fact that they assert of the normal cyclical movement what is only true for the post-war crisis.

[2] Cf., for example, those of the Verein für Sozialpolitik, or the English reports in the time of predominant depressions before 1895, say the famous Third Report on the Depression of Trade. Accurate investigations are only of more recent date, as for example in the Special Memorandum No. 8 of the London and Cambridge Economic Service (by J. W. F. Rowe), or, for America, the data and estimates in the Report of a Committee of the President's Conference on Unemployment. An interesting method, which leads to the same result for the year 1921, although this was not simply a year of depression (cf. the preceding note), is due to C. Snyder (in Administration, May, 1923).

individuals — always abstracting from the phenomena of the abnormal course of events, which is of no concern here. From entrepreneurs and all their followers, especially from those who fortuitously or speculatively enjoy the fruits of the rise in prices during the boom, it takes away the possibility of profit — which especially in the case of speculation is only very imperfectly replaced by bear possibilities which appear in the slump. The entrepreneur has in the normal case made his profit and embodied it in the now established and adjusted business; but he makes no further profits, on the contrary he is threatened with losses. In the general case his entrepreneurial profit would dry up, his other entrepreneurial income would be at a minimum, even in the ideal course of events. In the real course of events many adverse influences supervene, although mitigated by some factors already mentioned. The existences connected with the old businesses, which are now being competitively vanquished, of course suffer. People with fixed money incomes or incomes only alterable after a long time, such as pensioners, rentiers, officials, and landlords who have rented their land for a long term, are the typical beneficiaries of the depression. The commodity content of their money incomes, which is compressed in prosperity, now expands, and indeed in principle it must expand more than it was compressed before, as has already been shown (cf. above, § 3, "thirdly"). Capitalists with short-term investments gain from the increased purchasing power of the unit of income and capital, and lose by the lower interest rate; theoretically, they must lose more than they gain, but numerous secondary circumstances — on the one hand danger of loss, on the other hand high risk premiums and panic demand — deprive this theorem of its practical importance. Those landowners whose rents are not fixed in money by long-term contracts — hence above all the landowning farmer — are fundamentally in exactly the same position as workers, so that what is now to be argued of the workers is also true of them. The practically important, theoretically inconsiderable, differences are so generally familiar that we shall not go into them.[1]

---

[1] Likewise it is not necessary here to go into the different degrees in which the depression affects different industries — for example luxury industries more than those

In the boom wages must rise. For the new demand, first of entrepreneurs and then of all those who extend operations as the secondary wave rises, is, directly and indirectly, chiefly a demand for labor. Therefore employment must first increase and with it the sum total of wages of labor, then the rate of pay and with it the income of the individual worker. It is from this rise in wages that the increased demand for consumption goods proceeds which results in the rise in the general price level. And because part of the incomes of landowners, who are theoretically coordinate (Chapter I) with the workers, does not rise with wages for the reasons mentioned, and fixed incomes do not increase at all, the rise in total wages is not merely nominal, but is equivalent to a greater real income of labor, and this again to a greater share in the social product which has not as yet increased. This is a special case of a general truth: no inflation can be immediately prejudicial to the workers' interests if, and in so far as, the newly created purchasing power must first operate upon wages before it can affect the prices of consumption goods. Only in so far as this is not the case or as the rise in wages meets external obstacles (as for example in the World War) can wages lag behind [1] in the manner so frequently

producing foodstuffs. What there is of theoretical interest in this has already been touched upon in various places in this chapter.

[1] The statistical verification of this theory encounters various difficulties. First of all our data on the retail prices of the articles consumed by the workers do not go far enough back with the desirable completeness — and the mere movement of money wages of course means nothing; it would substantiate our thesis, it is true, if one were to be content with it. The measurement of the extent of employment is still less satisfactory, and yet we cannot do without it. As far as I know it was not possible to measure short-time work at all before the war, and complete unemployment only with the help of trade-union data and occasional censuses. To-day the attempt would be more successful, but for reasons already mentioned only pre-war figures come into consideration for our purposes. We now have a work which tries to find just what we need, namely that by G. H. Wood, "Real Wages and the Standard of Comfort since 1850," Journal of the Roy. Stat. Soc. (March, 1909). It extends to 1902 and confirms our expectation. However, at the turn of the century that non-cyclical and in this sense secular price movement appeared which distorts the picture, and also involves an aberration of the lines of the cyclical movement. According to Professor Bowley's continuation of Wood's work and also according to the work of Mrs. Wood in "The Course of Real Wages in London 1900–1912," J. Roy. Stat. Soc. (December, 1913), and to A. H. Hansen in "Factors Affecting the Trend of Real Wages," Amer. Econ. Review (March, 1925), which are not, it is true, concerned with the extent of employment, the theory does not fit the facts. But it is easy to see that our conclusion would be verified if the secular rise in prices were

depicted. If, indeed, the inflation is the vehicle of an excess in consumption, as for example if a war is financed by inflation, the consequent impoverishment [1] of the economic system must also react upon the workers' position, even though not so severely as upon the position of other groups of individuals. But in our case clearly the opposite happens.

In a depression the purchasing power of the unit of wages rises. On the other hand the money expression of the effective demand for labor falls in consequence of the automatic deflation which the boom starts. In so far as only this occurs, the effective real demand [2] for labor could remain undisturbed. The real income of labor would then still be higher, not only than in the previous approximate equilibrium position, but also than in the boom. For what was previously entrepreneurial profit flows — theoretically and according to our conception wholly, but practically only gradually and incompletely — to the services of labor and land, in so far as it is not absorbed by the fall in the price of the product (Chapter IV). But the following circumstances prevent this temporarily and cause the temporary fall in real income which is actually shown by statistics, while the rise finally to be expected in conformity with our theory is usually overshadowed in reality by the appearance of the next boom.

(*a*) First, the facts which we have called the uncertainty and apparent irregularity of the data and events in the period of depression, still more the panics and errors of the abnormal course of events, upset many firms and reduce others to idleness for a time. This must result amongst other things in unemployment,

eliminated. Upon the question of the connection between gold-production and wage level cf. Pigou in the Econ. Journal (June, 1923).

The argument which now follows in the text is adequately supported by the figures. Real wages regularly fall in depression, yet only by a part of the amount which they had gained in the boom. This is exactly what we should expect.

[1] Impoverishment and its consequences and hence also, in the case of an approximately constant quantity of means of payment, *relative* inflation would appear even without the employment of inflationary financial methods. The text refers to that intensification of the effects which paper money or credit inflation carries with it.

[2] This new concept means here simply demand expressed in units of an ideal standard which undergoes no cyclical changes of the kind due to changes in the quantity of circulating media; hence it only indicates real changes in the total demand for labor and not those which are merely nominal.

the essentially temporary character of which does not alter the fact that it is a great and under certain circumstances annihilating misfortune for those concerned, and that the fear of it — simply because of the incalculableness of its occurrence —contributes substantially to the atmosphere of depression. This unemployment is typical of periods of depression and the source of panic offers of labor, thus resulting in the loss of much ground previously gained by trade-union action and sometimes, though not necessarily, in a severe pressure on wages, the effect of which may be greater than might be thought from the number unemployed.

(b) From these things we must distinguish the fact that the new enterprises either completely eliminate the old businesses or else force them to restrict their operations. As against the unemployment so caused there is, to be sure, the new demand for the labor which is to carry on the new businesses. How much this demand often outweighs the unemployment created is shown by the example of the railway and the stage-coach. But this is not necessarily so, and even if it is so there may be difficulties and frictions which, with the incomplete functioning of the labor market, weigh disproportionately heavily in the balance.

(c) The new demand for labor mentioned above which springs up when prosperity is under way also loses in importance because of the fact that the entrepreneurs' demand for the labor which has created the new investments eventually ceases.

(d) As a rule the boom finally means a step in the direction of mechanising the productive process and hence necessarily a diminution of the labor required per unit of product; and often, though not necessarily, it also involves a diminution of the quantity of labor demanded in the industry in question in spite of the extension of production which occurs. Technological unemployment is thus shown to be a component part of cyclical unemployment, and should not be contrasted with it as if it had nothing to do with the cycle.

This element of practically every depression spells great and painful, but in the main only transitory, difficulties.[1] For the total

[1] Cf. on this my article "Das Grundprinzip der Verteilungslehre," Archiv für Sozialw. und Sozialp. (Bd. 42).

real demand for labor cannot in general permanently fall, because, neglecting all compensating and all secondary elements, the expenditure of that part of entrepreneurial profit which is not annihilated by the fall in prices necessarily more than prevents any lasting shrinkage. Even if it were expended solely on consumption it must be resolved into wages — and rents, for I repeat that everything said here holds good theoretically for them too. When, and to the extent that, it is invested, an increase in the real demand for labor takes place.

(*e*) The boom, directly or in its effects, can permanently lower the real demand for labor in only one way: if in the new combinations it shifts the relative marginal significance of labor and land which obtained in the old productive combinations sufficiently to the disadvantage of labor. Then not only the share of labor in the social product but also the absolute amount of its real income may permanently fall. Practically more important than this case — but again not necessarily of a permanent nature — is a shift in the demand in favor of produced means of production already in existence.

With this qualification, then, we return to our conclusion that the economic nature of depression lies in the diffusion of the achievements of the boom over the whole economic system through the mechanism of the struggle for equilibrium; and that only temporary reactions, which are only in part necessary to the system, overshadow this fundamental feature and produce the atmosphere expressed in the word depression as well as the repercussion which even those indices exhibit which do not (or not exclusively) appertain to the sphere of money, credit, and prices, and do not simply reflect the automatic deflation characteristic of periods of depression.

§ 6. The outbreak of a crisis initiates an abnormal course of events or that which is abnormal in the course of the events. As has been mentioned, it raises no new theoretical question. Our analysis shows us that panics, bankruptcies, breakdowns in the credit system, and so on *need* not but *may* easily appear at the point where prosperity turns into depression. The danger persists for some time, but it is smaller the more thoroughly the process of depression has done its work.[1] If panics occur, then errors, which are first made in such a situation or are merely thrown into relief by it, states of public opinion, and so forth become independent causes, which they could not have been in the normal course of events; they become causes of a depression which exhibits different features and leads to different final results from the normal. The equilibrium that is finally established here is not the same as that which would otherwise have been established. The blunders and destruction cannot in general be corrected and repaired again, and they create situations which in turn have further effects, which must work themselves out; they mean new disturbances, and enforce processes of adaptation which would otherwise be superfluous. This distinction between the normal and abnormal course of events is very important, not only for the understanding of the nature of the thing, but also for the theoretical and practical questions connected with it.

We have seen — in contrast to the doctrine which sees in the business cycle essentially a monetary phenomenon or one which has its root in bank credit, and which is to-day especially associated with the names of Keynes, Fisher, and Hawtrey and with the policy of the Federal Reserve Board — that neither profits in a boom nor losses in a depression are meaningless and function-

[1] As the depression continues, the danger of a collapse of the economic system and of its credit structure becomes continually slighter. This statement is compatible with the fact that most bankruptcies do not occur exactly at or near the turning point but only later, sometimes only when the danger to the economic system is past. For even the mortal wounding of a firm does not necessarily cause immediate flight to the bankruptcy court. On the contrary, everyone resists it as long as possible. And most firms can for a longer or shorter time. They themselves hope — and with them their creditors — for more favorable times. They deliberate, resort to shifts, seek new supports, sometimes with success, sometimes at least with such success that liquidation by consent is possible — more frequently, it is true, without success, but even then the death struggle results in postponing the bankruptcy or reorganisation, often into the next upward movement so that the drowning takes place in sight of dry land. This is not the result of new disasters, the danger of which actually falls progressively, but is the final consequence of those which happened long ago. Here, as elsewhere, we have to do with primary causes and the characteristic feature of the explanation, not with the question of when causes become visible. This creates an apparent discrepancy between our theory and observation. But every such discrepancy can only become an objection if it is shown that it is not satisfactorily explained.

less. On the contrary, where the private entrepreneur in competition with his equals still plays a part, they are essential elements of the mechanism of economic development and cannot be eliminated without crippling the latter. This economic system cannot do without the *ultima ratio* of the complete destruction of those existences which are irretrievably associated with the hopelessly unadapted. But the losses and destruction which accompany the abnormal course of events are *really* meaningless and functionless. Justification of the various proposals for a prophylaxis and therapy of crises chiefly rests with them. The other sound starting point for remedial policy is the fact that even the normal — still more the abnormal — depression implicates individuals who have nothing to do with the cause and the meaning of the cycle, above all the workers.

The most important remedy *à la longue,* and the only one which is exposed to no objections, is the improvement of business cycle prognosis. The ever-increasing familiarity of businessmen with the cycle is, together with progressive trustification, the chief reason why the real crisis phenomena — events like the World War and times like the post-war period do not belong here — are becoming weaker.[1] The postponement of new construction by government enterprises or by great combines to periods of depression appears from our standpoint as a moderation of the consequences of the swarm-like appearance of new combinations and as an attenuation of the inflation of the boom and the deflation of the depression, hence as an effective means of alleviating the cyclical movement and the danger of crises. An indiscriminate and gen-

---

[1] Increasing foresight also weakens the normal cyclical movement. It cannot prevent it, however, as will be recognised if our argument is scrutinised from this point of view. Therefore T. S. Adams goes too far when he states: "To anticipate the cycle is to neutralise it." It is different with the element mentioned earlier (§ 2, *b,* "fourthly") that in the course of time economic development becomes continually more a "matter of calculation" (Rechenstift). This element is something different from the familiarity and foresight of which we are now speaking. It also mitigates the cyclical movement, but for another reason: it tends to eliminate the fundamental cause of the boom and therefore acts much more slowly, but in tendency much more completely, than the mere anticipation of the course of the cyclical movement — which as long as the cause exists is nevertheless unavoidable. It is different again with trustification: this mitigates the normal and abnormal course of events for the same reasons.

eral increase in credit facilities means simply inflation, just as does a régime of government paper money. It may possibly obstruct completely the normal as well as the abnormal process. And it encounters not only the anti-inflationary argument in general, but also the argument that it destroys that measure of selection which can still be ascribed to the depression, and burdens the economic system with the unadapted and with those firms which are unfit to live. In contrast with this, credit restriction, which is usually undertaken by the banks unsystematically and without much foresight, appears in the light of a policy which is at least open to discussion, the policy of curing the evil by letting its acute consequences run their course. This procedure could be supplemented by other measures which would make it difficult for individual producers to resist the necessary fall in prices. But a credit policy is also conceivable — on the part of the individual banks as such, but still more on the part of central banks with their influence upon the private banking world — which would differentiate between the phenomena of the normal process of the depression, which have an economic function, and the phenomena of the abnormal process, which destroy without function. It is true, such a policy would lead far into a special variety of economic planning which would infinitely increase the influence of political factors upon the fate of individuals and groups. But this involves a political judgment which does not concern us here. The technical prerequisites for such a policy, a comprehensive insight into the facts and possibilities of economic and cultural life, although theoretically obtainable in time, are at present undoubtedly not available. But theoretically, it is of interest to establish that such a policy is not impossible and is not simply to be classed with chimeras or with measures which are by nature unsuited to attain their ends, or finally with measures the reactions to which necessarily more than compensate for their direct effects. The phenomena of the normal and of the abnormal course of events are not merely distinguishable conceptually. They are in reality different things; and with a sufficiently deep insight, concrete cases even to-day may generally be recognised immediately as belonging to the one or the other. Such a policy would have to distinguish, within the mass of businesses threatened by disaster in any given depression, those made technically or commercially obsolete by the boom from those which appeared to be endangered by secondary circumstances, reactions, and accidents; it would leave the former alone, and support the latter by granting credit. And it might be successful in the same sense as that in which a conscious policy of racial hygiene might lead to successes unobtainable as long as things are left to work out automatically. In any case, however, crises will disappear earlier than the capitalist system, whose children they are.

But no therapy can permanently obstruct the great economic and social process by which businesses, individual positions, forms of life, cultural values and ideals, sink in the social scale and finally disappear. In a society with private property and competition, this process is the necessary complement of the continual emergence of new economic and social forms and of continually rising real incomes of all social strata. The process would be milder if there were no cyclical fluctuations, but it is not wholly due to the latter and it is completed independently of them. These changes are theoretically and practically, economically and culturally, much more important than the economic stability upon which all analytical attention has been concentrated for so long. And in their special way both the rise and the fall of families and firms are much more characteristic of the capitalist economic system, of its culture and its results, than any of the things that can be observed in a society which is stationary in the sense that its processes reproduce themselves at a constant rate.